The Myth of Choice

The Myth *of* Choice

Personal Responsibility

in a World of Limits

Kent Greenfield

Yale

UNIVERSITY PRESS

New Haven and London

Published with assistance from the Louis Stern Memorial Fund.

Epigraph on p. vi: Isaac Bashevis Singer, as quoted in Stefan
Kanfer, "Isaac Singer's Promised City," *City Journal*, Summer
1997 (available at http://www.city-journal.org).

Yale University Press books may be purchased in quantity for
educational, business, or promotional use. For information,
please e-mail sales.press@yale.edu (U.S. office)
or sales@yaleup.co.uk (U.K. office).

Designed by Sonia Shannon
Set in Fournier type by Newgen North America.
Printed in the United States of America.

Library of Congress Cataloging-in-Publication Data

Greenfield, Kent.
The myth of choice : personal responsibility in a world of
limits / Kent Greenfield.
p. cm.
Includes bibliographical references and index.
ISBN 978-0-300-16950-8 (hb : perm paper)   1. Choice
(Psychology)   2. Decision making.   3. Responsibility.
I. Title.
BF448.G744 2011
153.8'3—dc22
2011013221

A catalogue record for this book is available from
the British Library.
This paper meets the requirements of ANSI/NISO Z39.48-1992
(Permanence of Paper).

10 9 8 7 6 5 4 3 2 1

For Dana

We have to believe in free will; we have no choice.
—Isaac Bashevis Singer

Contents

Introduction

MOST OF US, MOST OF the time, like to think we are in control of our lives. We are the masters of our own fate. We make our own decisions. In the words of the cheesy poster that hung on my bedroom wall during high school, we "follow our own star."

Whether politically liberal or conservative, we balk at government limitations on choice and fight those limits with legal arguments about rights and political rhetoric about freedom. Liberals demand access to abortions, want to be able to purchase "medical" marijuana, and don't appreciate being patted down to get on a plane. Conservatives don't like requirements to buy health insurance or pay taxes, bristle at limits on gun ownership and school prayer, and decry government regulation of everything from food to the environment. If you're on the left, you're called a civil libertarian; if you're on the right, you may call yourself a Tea Partier. Civil libertarians want the government out of their bedrooms; Tea Partiers want the government out of their wallets.

Liberals and conservatives may disagree about the specifics of what they want to be free to choose, but both sides believe that Choice is Good. And of course they are both correct that freedom and individual decision making need to be protected, applauded, and engendered.

But there are a couple of big problems with this fixation on choice.

The first is that we face a host of choices that we're unsure should "count" as choices. Examples abound. If your boss gives you a choice between losing your job and sleeping with him, that is not a choice that merits deference. In fact, he's not allowed to give you that choice at all. But it hasn't been this way for long. As we know from watching *Mad Men*, such understandings were long implicit in the workplace. What if you're on a bus trip and a policeman stands over you and gives you a choice between getting off and allowing him to search your luggage? Courts have said this is a choice that counts, even though it might not feel like much of a choice. The choice between serving your country in the armed services and being openly gay was seen as valid until recently; now it's not. A choice to engage in consensual sex gets respect—it counts—unless the choice is to have sex for money, in which case it does not count (at least in most parts of the United States). If a woman "chooses" to wear a burqa because of cultural expectations and religious beliefs, such a choice is usually respected (I saw a woman wearing one recently in my local mall), but not in France, where burqas are now banned in public.

All in all, we might think we like choice, but the question of which choices count and which do not is very, very tricky.

The second big problem with our fixation on choice is that both the civil libertarians and the Tea Partiers assume that if the government is not involved, what remains is a sphere of freedom, choice, and personal responsibility. But the reality is different. In fact, the most significant constraints on choice come not from government but from a host of other forces.

For example, we are constrained by our own biology. You can't open a newspaper or magazine these days without learning of some new study showing that our behavior is predictable and explainable as a matter of brain science. There is nothing hotter in the world of science, and no area of science that has captured more of the public's attention, than the study of how our behavior, beliefs, and decisions are profoundly influenced by what goes on in different areas of our brains. It is as if the brain is the new focus of science's age-long effort to explain seemingly random events in the world around us. The more we know about the brain, the easier it becomes to explain and anticipate the seemingly random behavior of any one of us.

Other constraints are just as profound. For example, the influence of culture is easy to ignore, but cultural norms about everything from gender roles to religious mores are pervasive and powerful. Most of us do not even recognize them, much less resist them. In all honesty, did you choose your gender role, or was it "chosen" for you by the culture you live in? Also consider the role of power and authority when it comes to choice. Most of us, most of the time, respect authority figures and do what they say. We follow orders, even when we shouldn't and even when they're not really orders. If a scientist told you to shock someone with an electronic pulse as a part of an experiment, would you do it even after it was clear you were causing pain? We'd like to think we wouldn't, but good evidence says we probably would, and we might even say that we "had no choice."

A final example of a pervasive influence is the market. Markets are wonderful in allocating goods and services to the highest bidder, and they might seem to embody the very notion of choice. (Coca-Cola recently ran an ad in my hometown newspaper crowing that it offers "over 650 ways to help you achieve a balanced diet and active lifestyle.") But depending on markets means that if you have few resources, you have little choice. Also, markets limit choice by making manipulation of our choices profitable. Markets also put price tags on things we don't want to commodify—left to their own devices, markets sweep up all kinds of things we'd otherwise choose to protect from markets, like babies or kidneys.

So we are faced with a tension. On the one hand, our political and legal rhetoric applauds and deifies choice, autonomy, and personal responsibility. On the other hand, we face profound questions about when choice is real, and about the reality of pervasive constraints on our choices. Once we take into account the influences of biology, culture, authority, and economics, the scope of our choices is much narrower than we have long assumed.

This book is about that tension. Can our legal system and our political debates become more sophisticated in their understanding of the nature of human choice? Can we craft public policy so that it takes into account these limits on choice? Can we use the insights we are gaining from neuroscience and psychology to create more opportunities for more of us to make more genuine choices more of the time? Can we find ways to build our individual capacity for choice, while creating the situations in which that capacity can be exercised? Can we use the understanding we are gaining about the real limits we face to help us determine when choices should count and to be more understanding when we or others screw up?

It's possible to be aware of the limits on choice and also believe in the importance of autonomy and personal responsibility. Possible, but not easy. This book is intended to help. I hope you choose to read on.

I

The Centrality *of* Choice

I

Choices, Choices, Choices

It is not our abilities that show what
we truly are. It is our choices.
—Albus Dumbledore in *Harry Potter and the
Chamber of Secrets* (Warner Bros. 2002)

I always believed that it's the things you don't
choose that make you who you are. Your city,
your neighborhood, your family.
—Patrick Kenzie in *Gone Baby
Gone* (Miramax 2007)

PEOPLE MAKE CHOICES ALL the time. We choose jitter-inducing coffee or waist-expanding frappuccino. Gluttonous SUV or holier-than-thou
hybrid. A ponderous grad school life or a nine-to-five rat race. We choose
our spouse; we decide whether and when to become a parent; we pick our
place of worship. We live the straight and narrow or a life of cheap whis-
key, meaningless sex, and bad disco. What we choose defines who we are,
and not only according to Dumbledore. Among the actually existing, Eleanor Roosevelt said, "We shape our lives and we shape ourselves . . . And
the choices we make are ultimately our own responsibility." Albert Camus

argued that "life is the sum of all your choices." William Jennings Bryan offered that "destiny is not a matter of chance, it is a matter of choice." W. H. Auden opined that "a man is responsible for his choice and must accept the consequences, whatever they may be."[1]

We're told early in life that we have choice and that we bear responsibility for our decisions. When I was in the third grade, my teacher—let's call her Mrs. Connor—had a rule that no one could utter a word while in line on the way to the lunch room, library, or restroom. We were required to walk quietly in our eight-year-old bodies from the time we left the classroom until we reached our destination. For someone like me, this was impossible. By the time we made it to the lunch tables, library, or little boy urinals I had invariably begun talking to whatever kid was in earshot about whatever synapse was then firing in my brain.

I was also pretty honest. When we got back to the classroom, Mrs. Connor would often ask who had talked in line that day. I would raise my hand. She would then impose her penalty of making me write sentences recalling the behavioral objective: "I will not talk in line on the way to the lunch room." I don't remember how many times she had me write the dreaded sentence—it felt like a thousand but was probably twenty-five or fifty. But whatever it was, the number increased each time I violated the rule. And I grew more righteously indignant, thinking the rule was inconsistent with the pedagogical goals of third grade and out of proportion to the offense. Okay, what I really thought was just that the rule was stupid.

So one day I refused to write the sentences.

This civil disobedience created quite a stir. I was called in for a chat with the school counselor, who reminded me of the importance of following rules. I told her the rule was stupid. The counselor was not impressed by my analysis and sent me back to Mrs. Connor, who wrote a letter to my parents, describing my intransigence.

My dad listened to my side of the story and wrote back to Mrs. Connor that he understood and supported my decision not to write the sentences.

But he included a line I did not know about: "Kent will also accept the consequences of his decision."

So after reading my dad's note the next morning, Mrs. Connor took me out to the hallway. In the wisdom of Nixon-era Kentucky public school education, she had decided to change the punishment and paddle me instead. Another teacher stood by to pay witness—if not homage—as Mrs. Connor told me to bend over. She then hit me on my rear five times with a wooden paddle. The paddle had little holes drilled in it to make it extra painful, a design innovation that at the time struck me as quite effective. My rear end bore the consequences of my decision.

I wish I could report that my civil disobedience led Mrs. Connor to see the error of her ways and adjust her rules for hallway conversations, but I have no memory of that. I do remember being more careful about my loose lips on the way to the lunch room. The next year, Mrs. Connor and the school principal recommended me for admission into a "special" educational program that, not coincidentally, was located at another school.

I had learned a lesson. Choices have consequences, some bad—a paddling on my behind—and some unexpectedly better—the special program, which turned out to be quite good. I also learned that I was supposed to accept the consequences of my decisions even if I had not anticipated them.

The notion that we're defined by, and responsible for, our choices is at the core of the American story. Even eight-year-olds are supposed to understand it. But it's not just something we teach our children. It is at the center of our political theory and our legal system, as well as our advertising. Our nation's founding documents base the legitimacy of government on the "consent of the governed." Our laws are based on the fundamental notion that people know what they're doing, whether in committing crimes or signing a contract. We idolize choice, using it to market everything from political causes (the right of access to an abortion, to its supporters, is the "right to choose") to fast food ("Have It Your Way").

But what if choice is fake?

What if we have much less ability to choose than we think we do? What if our choices—even the ones we *think* we are making—are so limited that we are less like wild horses on the plains and more like steers in a cattle chute? What if we are driven much more by the demands of economics, culture, power, and biology than we realize?

What if people "choose" outcomes in the same way I "chose" to be paddled when I stood up to my teacher? That is, hardly at all?

I.

Let's say you're a guy who works with his hands. Your job is in a small factory, painting hatchets. You paint them and then place them on a rack above you to dry. You've worked there for years. One day, your employer installs a new hatchet-drying rack and you quickly notice that the new rack is unstable. If it were to collapse, you'd probably get hurt by the falling newly painted hatchets. So you warn your boss that the new shelf is dangerous and needs to be replaced.

Your boss listens attentively but tells you he's not going to fix the shelf. It's your choice, he says. You can take the risk of working there, or quit. Since you need the job, you shut up and keep working under the rickety rack.

Would you think that you had made a real choice?

This really happened. The shelf really fell, and the hatchet painter, whose name was Henry Lamson, was really hurt. He also really sued.

The Massachusetts court deciding the case ruled for the employer. The opinion was written over a hundred years ago by Oliver Wendell

Oliver Wendell Holmes, Jr.

Holmes, Jr., who would later become one of the nation's most famous Supreme Court justices. He said that Lamson made his choice to accept the risk when he chose to go back to work knowing that the shelf might collapse. The fact that he needed his job to provide for himself and his family did not make his returning to work any less of a choice. "He stayed, and took the risk," said Holmes.[2] Lamson made his bed, so to speak, every day when he showed up to work.

To modern readers, this old case seems just that—old. We believe employers today have a responsibility to provide safe workplaces. This responsibility is both a legal and a moral obligation, and it's enforced with lawsuits and inspections. The market also helps: the lattes at Starbucks would be less popular if they included the occasional fingertip lost in the coffee grinder. An employer who makes money by risking his employees' lives and limbs is seen as a bad actor who cannot avoid responsibility by suggesting that the employees made their own choices when they came to work in a dangerous environment.

But there's nothing wrong with Holmes's *logic*. Henry Lamson knew and understood the risk he was taking when he stood under that rack every day. He had a way to avoid it, namely quitting. It wasn't a pleasant or easy choice, but it was a choice. And Holmes thought he should bear personal responsibility for his choice.

Do our modern sensibilities about that reasoning differ, and if so, why? Let's turn from the hatchet in the head and compare it to a baseball in the face.

In 1998, a woman named Jane Costa went with some friends to a Boston Red Sox game at Fenway Park. It was her first time attending a baseball game. Most people who go to Fenway remember it for great baseball—yes, I'm a Sox fan—and cramped, ancient seats that may or may not give you a view of the action and may or may not be covered by sticky substances with a nuclear half-life. Jane Costa will never forget her first game for a different reason. Arriving late, she had just taken her seat behind the home dugout when Red Sox batter Darren Lewis hit a foul ball directly at her. Since the ball was going more than ninety miles an hour when it left the bat, Costa had about a second to move out of the way. She didn't. The ball crushed her face, causing permanent and disfiguring injury. Costa spent many days in the hospital, running up nearly $500,000 in medical bills.

She sued the Red Sox in a Boston court. That's like suing the Pope in the Vatican, and she received about as much sympathy. The court denied her suit, saying that she should have known the risks of watching baseball, even if she had never been to a game before.[3] The court held that the Red Sox had no duty to protect her. She should have taken care of herself.

Here, too, our sense of the case depends on a notion of choice. Most people's reaction is: *Everybody knows you can get hit watching a baseball game. It even says so on the ticket.* Costa had made her choice, and she had to accept the consequences.

But there's something illogical in this. Compared to Henry Lamson's choice in going to work, Jane Costa's so-called choice was much less genuine. While Lamson had a pretty good idea of the risks he faced at work, Costa had very little understanding of the risks she faced when she entered the ballpark. Most people know that balls can go every which way, and that some will fly into the stands. But few understand how dangerous they can be, and even fewer know that about 300 people are seriously injured each year at American baseball games.[4] And as for the warning and waiver of liability on the back of the ticket, get real. I'm looking at an old ticket as I write this, and to call the warning "fine print" overstates the size quite a bit. I am reading it with a magnifying glass. Anyway, the last time you were at a baseball game, how many of the people sitting around you were in any condition to perform a sophisticated risk analysis? By the seventh inning, most of us at Fenway are lucky to find our way to the restrooms.

I am not saying that Costa should have won her suit. But the simple act of showing up at the game doesn't mean she understood the risk of getting hit in the face by a baseball. If she bears responsibility for her injuries, it's not because she chose to accept the risk in the same way as Henry Lamson chose to accept the risk of getting hit in the head by a hatchet.

I know of these two cases because I'm a law professor and have discussed them with students for many years. Most of them think Costa should have lost and Lamson should have won. In other words, the guy who actually knew, understood, and chose the risk of being injured should be able to recover for his injuries. The woman who knew nothing of the risk and did not choose to be subject to it should not be able to recover.

What explains these intuitions? There are a number of possibilities, including a belief that work is more important than baseball (I shudder to think), that the responsibility of an employer to one's employees is stronger than that of a baseball club to its fans, or that the costs of precautions in the hatchet factory were minimal and the costs of protecting fans in the ballpark would be too high.

What this means, then, is that even though both cases seem to depend on an examination of the nature of the choices Lamson and Costa made, the results we lean toward have little to do with choice. Or, maybe, what we mean by choice is elastic depending on the situation. If that's true, then our usual rhetoric about choice and personal responsibility is bound to be too simplistic. It's also bound to lead us to wrong conclusions.

2.

Why does all this matter? Why should anyone care so much about the meaning of choice?

The reason is that it is fundamental to the American sensibility to praise personal autonomy and require individuals to take responsibility for their decisions. We are the cowboy culture, prideful and self-assured.[5] We respect people's choices and hold them accountable for their decisions.

Except when we don't.

Here's the puzzle. While we laud choice and rail against those who want to avoid the effects of their decisions, we often seem to excuse people from the choices they make. Lamson is not an isolated example.

Take for example Hurricane Katrina, which devastated the Gulf Coast in August 2005. Some experts call it the worst natural disaster in the nation's history. Hardest hit were some 200,000 New Orleans residents who chose to stay in their homes in the face of a mandatory evacuation order issued the day before the storm landed. Most of those who stayed behind were poor and African American. Once the levees broke, their homes were flooded, they lost their possessions, and they were put in serious personal danger. Almost two thousand lost their lives. Those who lived sought refuge or waited for rescue in squalid conditions in the Superdome or elsewhere.

In the days following the disaster, some commentators placed blame for these horrors on the people themselves. Michael Brown, the head of the Federal Emergency Management Agency, said that the high death toll would be "attributable a lot to people who did not heed the advance warnings." Senator Rick Santorum suggested that people who had chosen to stay should be subject to criminal penalties. The conservative *Washington*

Times ran a harsh editorial, saying that "thousands of New Orleans residents . . . failed to show personal responsibility." Other commentators went further, saying that the victims had put themselves in harm's way through their poverty, which was their own fault. Talk radio personality Neal Boortz suggested that people around the country should be generous to the victims but not "ignore the behavior that put them in this position in the first place. Hurricane Katrina has shown all of us . . . that poverty is a behavioral disorder." He piled on: "What we saw in New Orleans was poor people demonstrating the very behavior that made them poor in the first place."[6]

In this view, the main blame for the horrors of Katrina should be borne by the victims themselves. They made themselves poor, and their decision not to evacuate was simply another example of the same kind of bad choices. In the days immediately following the disaster, this "blame the victim" view had some traction. According to a *Time* magazine poll in the week following the breach of the levees, 57 percent of Americans agreed that "people hit by the hurricane" bore some or a great deal of the responsibility for what went wrong with relief efforts.[7]

This narrative did not last long. The mantra of personal responsibility—mostly seized by conservatives—did not convince most people. Americans generally felt compassion and empathy for the victims in New Orleans, and the dominant story even at the time was more about the bumbling of government officials than about the choice of residents to ride out the storm.

Notice that our collective sympathy was not based on a notion that no choice had been made. Those who stayed behind were indeed making a choice, just as Henry Lamson chose to stay at his dangerous job. The Katrina victims were put in a tough position, and the alternatives were not good. But a choice it was.

Nevertheless, most Americans who watched their televisions in horror in the days after the hurricane seemed to understand the difference between choice and personal responsibility. Or maybe they realized that for a choice to be genuine and for personal responsibility to make sense, you have to have more information and more alternatives than most New Orleans residents in fact had.

There are lots of reasons why the personal responsibility mantra failed to carry the day. For example, the evacuation order came only twenty hours before the hurricane made landfall. Because of this, as many as one in four New Orleans residents did not hear about the order before the hurricane hit.[8] A majority of those who stayed had no way to leave, and only 20 percent had relatives or friends they could move in with if they did. Most had no financial wherewithal to rent hotel rooms—only 28 percent had usable credit cards, and only 31 percent had a bank account. A significant percentage of those who stayed behind were caring for a disabled person. And, of course, they had been assured of the integrity of the levee system for years. It's fair to say that many if not most of those who stayed to face Katrina were making a choice only in the most simplistic meaning of that term.

The interesting thing is that these facts did not have to be widely known for the victims to receive the benefit of the doubt. Most Americans seemed to recognize, in a simple but profound way, that the victims of the flood had had few real alternatives and should not be blamed for the "choices" they made. Polls taken a year after Katrina showed that Americans mostly blamed the government and government officials. Only 22 percent put primary blame on the residents.

Sometimes, we seem to excuse people from personal responsibility when they do make choices. About 16 months after Katrina, climbers on Oregon's Mount Hood were stranded by a winter storm that blew in as they tried to scale the summit. CNN streamed live video from the mountain to homes across the nation. State and federal agencies, including the military, picked up the tab for the search. Maybe the climbers had no warning of the storm, but maybe they did. They almost certainly had

Mt. Hood.

more warning of the storm than Jane Costa had of Darren Lewis's foul ball. And climbing such a mountain at any time of year, let alone in December, is a risky proposition. Nevertheless, the fact that they made a bad choice in deciding when and where to climb played no role in the media coverage. Understandably, we watched with dread instead of judgment, fearing the worst. In the end, one climber was found dead, and two others were still missing when the search was called off after two days, with another storm approaching. The news coverage was empathetic, mindful of the impacts of the tragedy on the climbers' families. The climbers themselves were adventurers, admired for their bravery and spirit.

So let me make a weird comparison. Among the most despised individuals in America are fat people. According to studies, young children are more likely to describe overweight playmates as stupid, mean, or ugly. Parents provide less financial support for overweight children pursuing education after high school than for their non-obese siblings. People say that if given a choice between marrying an obese spouse and someone else, they'd rather marry an embezzler, a drug addict, a shoplifter, or a blind person. More parents would abort a fetus if they knew it would be destined to be obese than if they knew it was mentally retarded. One recent study revealed that someone *standing next to* an obese person is considered less attractive than when standing close to a thin person.[9]

Here in America, where more of us are obese than ever before, we can't look at fat people without cringing. More important, we can't look at fat people without projecting character flaws onto them. Being fat is a failure of decision making, a sign of poor choices.

A few years ago, a couple of New York teenagers sued McDonald's for contributing to their obesity.[10] Their suit was quickly thrown out amid national ridicule. There was nothing more ridiculous, Americans agreed, than fat people suing McDonald's for their french-fry habit. It was as if people around the country said, *It's one thing for fat people to let themselves go. But it's another thing for the fatties to try to shift responsibility for their food addiction to a clown with red hair and yellow coveralls. People know what they are getting when they buy a Big Mac. They are getting cheap, fatty food that could give them a heart attack if they eat a lot of it. If they get fat, develop diabetes, or die of heart disease, they only have themselves to blame.*

But what if we learned that obesity is less a product of genuine choice than it seems? More and more studies show that people are "hard-wired" to eat by deep biological commands. Eating to excess is often a product of the kinds of foods available and how they are marketed, the cultural messages people receive about food, how much money they have, and the availability of safe places to exercise. In other words, what individuals choose to eat is very contextual. As a *New York Times* commentator said, "It's the environment, stupid."[11] Fast food companies are intensely aware of how contextual our food choices are, and they are brilliant at taking advantage of situations and environments—low-income neighborhoods, roadside rest stops, or airport concourses—that are conducive to selling unhealthy, fatty foods. (Why do you think there are so many Cinnabon stores in airports?)

I am not saying that people have no control over their muscles when they move a Whopper, chicken wing, or Cheez Whiz nacho from the plate to their mouths. But our decision to eat—even the decision to eat really bad food—is affected by what happens around us and inside us. Fast food companies, supermarkets, cigarette manufacturers, and beer makers know that choices can be affected, and they take advantage of it in decisions about what to put in products, how to advertise them, and where to sell them. People may have about the same level of choice about being obese as Henry Lamson did about getting hit in the head with a hatchet, as Jane Costa did about getting hit in the face with a baseball, and as New Orleans residents did about staying in their homes in the face of Katrina warnings. And fat people probably have *less* responsibility for their size than the climbers on Mount Hood had for being on the slopes of a mountain in December.

3.

So what is going on here? On the one hand, we revel in a culture of personal responsibility and choice. We hold people responsible for things that may or may not be their own doing, or that are due as much to the actions of others as to their own. On the other hand, we often let people off the hook for things that go horribly wrong because of something they did.

Maybe we need to be more consistent in applying notions of personal responsibility. Perhaps we are making a mistake when we excuse people from making bad choices—like to climb a dangerous mountain rather than stay home in the face of a coming storm. Or maybe the opposite is true—perhaps we should be more forgiving than we are, more understanding of the mistakes people make and of constraints that limit or compel their decisions.

This book is about our fixation on choice and our confused responses to it. The rhetoric of choice and personal responsibility is all around us, yet we have little real understanding of what makes choices valid and worth respecting. Sometimes we can be unforgiving. (*Jane Costa should have known that a hit baseball could ruin her life, even if she had never been to a baseball game. The obese should eat salad and go for a run, even if Mc-Donald's is the only place in their neighborhood they can afford to eat.*) Sometimes our judgments are much gentler. (*The people who stayed behind in New Orleans when the hurricane was coming maybe should've left. But it wasn't all their fault, and they have suffered enough. Give them a break.*)

Our ambivalent responses are not limited to these narrow situations. We face similar puzzles in all kinds of areas—from criminal law to business, from sexuality to religion. This might not be a big deal if the concept didn't mean so much. But it is a central concept—perhaps the *crucial* concept—in all of law, and also fundamental in economics, theology, political theory, marketing, literature, psychology, and philosophy.

Take business contracts, for example. Only contracts you freely enter into are considered valid. The notion of freedom of contract is seen as the chief embodiment in law of the respect for choice. But the law respects contracts only sometimes. Not only are there numerous ways to get out of contracts—such as bankruptcy or government bailouts—there are all kinds of contracts you can't enter into even if both parties want to: for instance, to take jobs that pay less than the minimum wage.

For another example, think about sex. Ever since the Supreme Court ruled in 2003 that laws criminalizing gay sex were unconstitutional, having sex with another consenting individual is a constitutional right—except when it's not. For example, that right does not exist when the other person is closely related to you, or when you're married and you choose to have sex with someone else, or when you choose to have sex with someone because they pay you. In those cases, not only is your choice not a constitutional right, it can be illegal. (Yes, adultery is still a crime in many states.)[12]

A person who has sex with someone who did not freely choose to have sex has committed rape, a heinous crime. But having sex with someone who does freely choose to have sex with you is not a crime, and it can be an extraordinary expression of love or simply a lot of fun. The law has wrestled for decades to try to define free choice in that situation, and the question of sexual consent is among the most serious in all of criminal law. A person's consent may not count if he or she is underage, unless their partner is underage as well. Consent may not count if a person is drunk, even if he or she got drunk in order to lose their inhibitions. In some jurisdictions, consent does not count if a person is under a mistaken impression of who they are with—there are cases where a twin has tricked his brother's wife into having sex with him. In other jurisdictions, shockingly, that isn't rape, presumably because it may be difficult to define how much deception it takes to vitiate consent.[13] (Would it be rape if a guy gets a woman to come home with him from a bar after telling her he's a movie director when in fact he works at a video store?)

The way the law considers choice varies across different areas of criminal law, creating some odd possibilities. For example, if you are drunk and have sex with someone who is just as drunk as you, their drunkenness may mean that their choice to have sex will not be valid, meaning that you have committed a sexual assault. But in most states you cannot use your own drunkenness as a defense, because the law assumes you intended to commit the crime even if you're inebriated. But then, your choice to have sex may not be valid either, since you were drunk. So it's possible that the other person committed a sexual assault on *you* while you were committing one on them.

In politics, consent and choice are central but disturbingly ephemeral. In democratic societies, the idea of "consent of the governed" has won adherents since Jean-Jacques Rousseau wrote about the "social contract" in the eighteenth century. He argued that "residence constitutes consent," meaning that anyone who chooses to live within a jurisdiction can be considered to have agreed to whatever laws that jurisdiction puts forth. That is the theory behind electoral politics: if your candidate doesn't win you still have to obey the laws. It was also the high theory behind the old bumper sticker "America: Love It or Leave It."

One of the nation's leading conservative constitutional law scholars, Steven Calabresi, has taken a similar view. He has written that the gay rights issue should be handled by having gays move to "secular" cities, while "Americans of faith" should "form and live in communities" where they can discriminate openly. Following Rousseau, he suggests that "those who choose to live in a part of the country where their views on homosexuality are in the minority should learn to gracefully put up with a prevalence of opposing views."[14]

That is not the correct answer. Mere presence in a jurisdiction cannot really mean that a person agrees with everything that goes on there, and probably does not even mean that every law is justly applied to her. Your presence in a community should not mean that you've waived your right to protest what you consider a violation of your rights. If simply being in a polity means that you consent to be governed by whatever laws then exist, then "consent" has little genuine meaning. We may want to *assume* that people have freely chosen their location, because it makes the theory of governance and state legitimacy work better, but it has little to do with what people actually have in their heads. It is often impossible to see from outside a person's head any difference between free choice—*I am here because I want to be here*—and coercion—*I am here because I have no other choice*. More profoundly, it may even be difficult to figure that out from *inside* a person's head.

Of course Rousseau and Calabresi are correct to say we need a theory of choice and consent to make democracy legitimate. But we don't really know what choice looks like.

The concept of political consent is so elastic that even Osama bin Laden tried to use it to excuse his attacks on American civilians. The 9/11 attacks were justified, he said, because "the American people are the ones who choose their government by their own free will," and they "have the ability and choice to refuse the policies of their government."[15]

Choice is an issue in religion as well. Tatian the Syrian explained in A.D. 170 that "the just man [is] deservedly praised for his virtuous deeds, since in the exercise of his free choice he refrained from transgressing the will of God." A couple of centuries later, St. Augustine wrote, "The commandments of God themselves would be of no avail to man unless he had the free choice of the will whereby by fulfilling them he could attain the promised reward." Twentieth-century Christian thinker C. S. Lewis said, "All that are in Hell, choose it. Without that self-choice there could be no Hell."[16]

In my family's Baptist faith, one is "saved" when one affirmatively chooses the spiritual path after the "age of accountability," which is when one can make choices for oneself. I was "born again" when I was eight. Looking back on it, I'm not sure I made that decision with any more thought or understanding than my choice of DC comics over Marvel. I certainly have different beliefs now about both religion and comics.

There are hundreds of other examples of the difficulties surrounding choice. Consent transforms an illegal police search into a legal one. A person injured in an accident can sue the person responsible, unless the victim had chosen to accept the risk. (Hence the waivers we all have to sign when we do anything from hiring a scuba instructor to joining a health club.) With "informed" consent, a doctor can perform life-saving surgery; without consent, the patient dies (unless he or she is somehow unable—rather than unwilling—to give consent, in which case consent is assumed).

So the notions of choice are everywhere, but what we mean by those words and the impact they have vary across situations. One purpose of this book is to examine the different ways we think of choice and try to make sense of them. In the end, we will discover that we are better than it appears in figuring out when choice should count and when it should not. We actually have a more nuanced view of choice than our rhetoric about choice and personal responsibility might suggest. We are well attuned to the fact that some choices are compelled, that alternatives are limited, and that people often do not have the information needed to make good decisions. We also know—at least at some level—that our choices are often manipulated by marketing and fraud, even if we don't always know how. As it turns out, our intuitions work pretty well, much of the time. We hold people accountable for "real" choices and give them a break when the choices aren't "real," or when their situation is more someone else's fault than their own. In the end, we are fundamentally decent and generous about choice.

This book will explore what most of us seem to understand intuitively, namely that choices are constrained, manipulated, and forced upon us. I will flesh out our intuitions and discuss the effects of biology, economics, power, and culture on people's choices. We will also discover areas where our intuition points us in the wrong direction. Obesity is one example, the Mount Hood climbers another.

This book will also look into why, if choice is so malleable and indistinct, we hear so much about it and its cousin personal responsibility. In fights about issues as diverse as health care reform, gay rights, educational policy, poverty, disaster relief, and abortion, why does so much of the debate turn on arguments about choice and personal responsibility? One answer is the rhetorical power of choice in a culture of individualism. We love to *think* we all have an abundance of choices and that we should take personal responsibility for the choices we make.

But there is a deeper reason choice is the preferred frame for so many political battles. In most cases, the rhetoric of choice gives the advantage to those in power. It is the rhetoric of the powerful. Saying that "people should bear responsibility for the choices they make" helps the powerful and hurts the powerless more often than not. Choice is a ready-made frame with which to oppose movements fighting for social justice, civil liberties, or economic rights, because opponents can point to people's existing behavior as representing a choice—whether to work at Walmart, to live on the street, or to live in a country where the government taps one's phone. In facing such assertions of choice, the person fighting injustice that occurs within the status quo must argue either that people are not really making the choices they seem to be making, that the choices made do not reflect the true preferences of the actors, or that the choices should not be respected. Those are hard arguments to make. This book will help make them, pointing out that people often have much less choice than we (and sometimes they) assume.

But this book will not take this state of affairs, this lack of choice, as unchangeable. I will also ask how we make choice more real. How can we give people the tools to take personal responsibility seriously? How should the law and public policy take into account the limitations on human decision making we know exist? How can individuals and law help build choice? Perhaps ironically, once we understand and take heed of our limitations as human beings, we can use this knowledge to become better decision makers and more confident and knowledgeable choosers.

2

In Love
with
Choice

Ultimately, everything about politics—
everything, everything—is about choice.
—Rahm Emanuel, 2010

For us to be able to choose, that's a blessing.
—Glenn Beck, 2011

IF ANY SLOGAN CAPTURES the American mindset, it's Burger King's "Have It Your Way." Originating in 1974, the slogan was linked to a catchy jingle that burrowed into your psyche like a Barry Manilow song.

Burger King revived the slogan a few years ago after ignoring it for a couple of decades because, according to a company spokesperson, "mass customization is what's in right now." The company wanted to emphasize the range of choices available to Whopper lovers, to mirror the choices consumers have "when buying everything from coffee and clothes to breakfast bars." The campaign makes sense, according to Burger King's ad agency, because "self-expression" is now a "critical element" of our culture.[1]

Not everyone will see their desire for extra tomatoes on a Whopper as self-expression. Some people might, though, and the campaign's point is worth emphasizing: Choice is in.

America's fixation on choice is apparent whenever you turn on the television. My cable provider gives me hundreds of channels, augmented by hundreds of additional viewing options on demand. DirecTV tells me that isn't enough, that its satellite service can give me even more channels—they call it their CHOICE ULTIMATE Package. If that doesn't satisfy me, I can use my Netflix subscription to order from more than one hundred thousand DVDs, several of which I can have at home at any one time. If I can't wait for the DVD to arrive in the mail, I can choose among thousands of Netflix films to watch instantly on my computer or Internet-enabled television. And if *that's* not enough, there is always Hulu, which offers thousands of TV shows, movies, and even commercials for free viewing on my computer. A popular advertisement for Hulu starred Alec Baldwin, who promised "more of those cerebral gelatinizing shows you want, anytime, anywhere, for free."

The grocery store where my wife and I sometimes shop, Whole Foods Market, offers perhaps twenty kinds of apples, some organic, some not so. There are hundreds of different kinds of cheese available. Milk, a relatively straightforward product, is offered in organic and non-organic; skim, 1 percent, 2 percent, and whole; lactose-free or not; soy or cow; chocolate or white. The variety of choice is remarkable. Once, as I stood befuddled in front of the pita chip section, scanning the shelf to locate my wife's preferred whole wheat, low-fat variety, I heard a man ask his wife: "Did you get the agave nectar?"

Not everyone, of course, lives near such a market or has the inclination and the coin to buy organic apples for their kid's lunch or agave nectar to sweeten their tea. But there is no doubt that the modern grocery shopper expects a wide range of choices, even if they never take advantage of them. Food Lion, though not as fancy as Whole Foods, also focuses its advertisements on the benefits of choice. A recent Food Lion television ad claimed that "Options are good. And when you shop for groceries you sure have plenty to choose from." Indeed, the notion that choice is good flourishes in grocery stores—the typical supermarket carries about forty-five thousand different items.[2]

It's easy to see the benefits. People can satisfy their desires, no matter how precise and idiosyncratic. Greater satisfaction of desires presumably leads to greater happiness. And happiness, by definition, is good. No wonder "Have It Your Way" is the slogan that won't die.

I.

The problems with choice are harder to see.

Providing choice is *costly*. I once dated a woman who was in charge of a line of men's clothing for Levi Strauss & Co. The difference between profit and loss for her line was often determined by whether she had developed just enough variety of pattern, color, and cut to appeal to most shoppers, but not so much variety that the production costs swamped the profits. Once you have the choices you need, producing more is a dead loss.

Often, choice is *unnecessary*. Of the hundreds of TV channels I receive, most merely pose obstacles to my switching between college basketball games and reruns of *House*. I pay hundreds of dollars a year for channels I never watch. (Research shows that most people regularly watch only about 16 channels.)[3] What's worse, some of the channels I do watch I only like because they are there—my life would be none the poorer if I lost access to the Syfy channel. Sometimes people want something only when it's there. Preference follows availability. That doesn't necessarily mean the choices should not be provided. But the argument that giving people what they want makes them happy sometimes goes the other way: making people want what they're given makes them happy.

Choice might be *meaningless*. A recent Wendy's commercial illustrates this. (Fast food companies are experts in choice.) The setting is an old west saloon, and bank robbers are getting away outside. When the sheriff runs out to give chase, the only horses tied outside are kids' hobby horses. The point of the commercial is that a choice among bad options is meaningless. At the end of the ad, the barkeep opines: "Choices don't mean a thing when there's nothing good to choose."[4]

Finally, choice is sometimes *overwhelming*, making it less likely that people will make decisions at all and increasing the risk of regret when they do. One notable experiment showed this effect by comparing two strategies for selling jam—by offering free sample tastes of a handful of choices or of many choices. When offered more choices, customers made fewer purchases, mostly because they had trouble deciding. Those who did buy from a bigger selection were less happy with their selection when asked about it later.[5] They worried that perhaps they had not made the best possible choice.

My wife and I experienced a real-life example of overwhelming choice when we went to our local Best Buy to shop for a vacuum cleaner. Our dog Murphy is a beloved member of the family, but he sheds his blond hair constantly. We needed a vacuum to deal with the omnipresent yellow fur clogging our life. We were even willing to consider two vacuums, one handheld and one regular-sized. As for the latter, we had done enough research—we had asked a friend's mother, who knows a surprising amount about vacuums—to have a vague preference for the type with the canister that rolls along behind you. As for the handheld, if we got one at all, we were totally at the mercy of whatever marketing pressure was brought to bear.

We were numbed by the choices. Vacuum cleaners lined both sides of one aisle and much of another. We tried to distinguish among brands, models, and capabilities, attempting to decipher the claims on the boxes and drawing on the "expertise" of the twentysomething clerk. We spent an hour trying to decide. Eventually my wife literally threw up her hands and declared that she was leaving. The choice was too hard.

I sprang into action, using my specialist-level knowledge of human choice. I am writing a book on the topic, I thought. I wasn't going to allow

Murphy.

us to be defeated by the plethora of vacuum choices. So I grabbed a small, expensive handheld model that resembled a futuristic ray-gun. I suppose you're to imagine fighting dust to the death. It looked cool, and I knew the brand name because of television advertising. I also quickly decided on a canister-type vacuum that a previous purchaser had returned to the store. It seemed like a good deal.

Less than a week passed before we came to our senses and returned the ray-gun to the store. It was just too expensive. The following week I was back again, this time to complain about some accessories missing from the canister vacuum box. So much for my expertise.

The point is that however much we modern humans are in love with choice, it is hardly an unabashed good. Yet notwithstanding the problems, it remains one of the most popular concepts around.

2.

Choice is not only used to sell hamburgers and ways to watch television. It is also a powerful notion in politics and law. People use choice rhetoric to animate political movements and to justify legal doctrines.

In politics, the entire concept of democracy is based on some form of social contract or democratic consent—another name for choice. In fact, choice is so engrained in our national mindset that it made it into the third sentence of the Declaration of Independence: "Governments are instituted among Men, deriving their just powers from the consent"—the choice—"of the governed." Without our consent, King George's rule was illegitimate, so "We the People" instituted a government of our own. (That "the People" omitted women and people of color was ignored in polite company for a century or more.) Consent as a basis for government legitimacy was derived from European thinkers like Jean-Jacques Rousseau and John Locke, who argued that governments derived power to infringe on individuals' liberty only if the subjects themselves consented either explicitly or implicitly to such authority. The American framers took this concept as the basis of their government.

Yet it is not just wig-wearing eighteenth-century types who think of consent and choice as a powerful political frame. Present-day political movements also use it with great regularity.

The biggest issue during Obama's first two years in office was the effort to reform health care, and much of the debate depended on rhetoric about choice, freedom, and personal responsibility. Obama and the Democrats initially advocated a "public option," which would give Americans an additional choice for health insurance, namely a government-run insurance company. The Republicans successfully opposed the public option by saying it was inconsistent with the free market. The Democrats were successful in winning protection for people with pre-existing conditions, giving them the freedom to buy health insurance and the right to protection from forced exclusion by insurance companies. But in order to make such coverage work as a financial matter, the bill had to include an individual "mandate"—a requirement that everyone buy insurance. This mandate is the target of a number of lawsuits around the country, with the principal argument being that the federal government does not have the constitutional authority to institute such a mandate. At the time of this writing, it is unclear how the constitutional debate will shake out. But it is clear how reform's opponents are attacking it. So-called "ObamaCare" is a "death of freedom" and a violation of "the growth of personal responsibility and self-reliance" as well as the "cultural movement to choice."[6]

Another contentious issue on Capitol Hill during the first years of the Obama presidency was the proposed bill to make it easier for unions to organize. The unions have framed the issue brilliantly, calling the bill the Employee Free Choice Act. Currently, employees must win a secret ballot election to authorize a union as their representative, and unions have long argued that such elections give employers too much power to intimidate employees and prevent them from voting to unionize. The act would allow workers to authorize a union as their collective bargaining representative by gathering a majority of employee signatures on cards designed for that purpose, rather than having to go through an election. In fighting for the bill, the Service Employees International Union organized protests around the country with labor union members chanting "Free Choice Now!" outside offices of the Chamber of Commerce.

Businesses, fighting against the unions' efforts to seize the "choice" frame, called the legislation the "card check bill," which sounds much less attractive. Business groups tried to recast the argument to reclaim the choice and freedom frames. The Workforce Fairness Institute, funded by business owners, argued that the bill should be called the "Employee *Forced* Choice Act," because it would "force employees and employers into unions whether they support them or not." The Facebook page for opponents of the bill said that "workers will be coerced and threatened into signing union cards, and their vote against unionization will no longer be private, leaving them open to further coercion, threats and harassment." The Chamber of Commerce named its efforts to oppose card check the Workforce Freedom Initiative.[7] It looks like both sides agree: coercion is bad, choice is good. Eventually, business groups captured enough of the rhetorical high ground and exerted enough political influence to stall the legislation.

Another example of the power of choice in political debate is so-called tort reform. For the past few years, Congress has been struggling over whether to limit the types of personal injury lawsuits that can be brought and the amounts that juries can award a successful plaintiff. The debate has focused on medical malpractice, with a leading argument in favor of tort reform being that patients should not be able to sue for injuries suffered in medical procedures that they choose to undergo while knowing their inherent risks. There have also been efforts to protect fast food companies and gun manufacturers, and Congress has considered bills barring suits by people claiming harm from these companies' products. The bill protecting fast food companies, called the Personal Responsibility in Food Consumption Act, was explicitly based on the notion that customers who choose to eat fast food should not be able to seek redress for harm that befalls them from that choice.[8]

Another prominent example of the political use of choice rhetoric is the area of gay rights. Questions from whether gay sex can be made criminal to whether same-sex couples can marry are discussed in terms of whether homosexuality is an "orientation"—something that is not a choice—or a "preference." Those opposing gay rights have claimed that some individuals have changed their preferences from gay to straight. Sarah Palin, in her ill-fated interview with Katie Couric during the 2008 presidential campaign, said that one of her best friends, who is gay, had made a "choice that isn't a choice that I have made."[9] Meanwhile, those supporting gay rights have cited scientific studies showing that orientation is hard-wired.

The assumption on both sides is that if sexuality is a choice it should be less protected; if it is not a choice then it should be more protected. If it is a choice, LGBT people are responsible for it and for whatever comes their way because of it. It is no wonder that millions of people care immensely about the outcomes of scientific studies into the biological basis

Is sexual orientation a choice?

(David McNew / Getty Images News / Getty Images)

of sexual orientation. It may be bizarre to think that civil rights should turn on whether one's sexuality is chosen (your religious beliefs are protected even though they are not hard-wired), but that is where the debate stands.

The most prominent example of choice rhetoric of politics is around the topic of abortion. Historian Rickie Solinger traces the use of the word "choice" in this context to a 1969 decision by the National Abortion Rights Action League to name its first national action Children by Choice.[10] "Choice" became the watchword of the abortion rights movement because it permitted advocates to talk about a difficult subject without alienating moderates. Solinger writes, "Many people believed that 'choice'—a term that evoked women shoppers selecting among options in the marketplace—would be an easier sell "

3.

In law, the notion of choice is also fundamental, driving legal decisions and underlying a host of legal doctrines. Choice goes by a number of names in the law: assent, consent, free will. It can also be defined as the absence of coercion or duress. There are gradations of meaning, but the concept, by whatever name, occupies a dominant role in virtually every area of United States law. The cases mentioned in the previous chapter— the falling axes and the baseball in the face—show the centrality of consent notions in tort law. Beyond that, the examples go on and on:

Contract law. A couple of years ago I got a home equity loan to pay off some credit card debt. It was the thing to do at the time. In my final meeting with the banker, he had me sign the last signature page and asked, as required by state law, "Do you sign this as your free act and deed?" He also informed me that if I had second thoughts, I had three days to back out of the contract. These requirements embody the legal notion that contracts depend on consent; the validity of a contract turns on whether it was entered into freely by both parties. The law validates those contracts because of the belief that a contract resulting from the assent of both parties must, by definition, make both sides better off. Otherwise, the theory goes, one or the other would not have agreed.

Contract law also has built-in exceptions that allow people to get out of contracts if they really had no choice. Contracts signed under duress—if Tony Soprano has a gun to your head—are not valid. The law can be quite nuanced in giving courts the authority to look behind appearances to see if the choices made by the parties were genuine. Courts do not enforce contracts that are the product of fraud or lying, which prevents the other party from understanding what they are buying. The doctrine of "unconscionability" is also related to choice. If a contract is so one-sided and unfair that it looks like the product of coercion, misunderstanding, or the misuse of power, it may be set aside.

One such case arose in California, in the bad old days when homosexuality was a crime.[ll] Donald Odorizzi, an elementary school teacher, was arrested for homosexual activity. After he was questioned, booked, and released on bail, the superintendent of his school district and the principal of his school showed up at his apartment with a letter of resignation they wanted Odorizzi to sign. The superintendent and principal told him that if he did not resign they would fire him and publicize the proceedings, humiliating him. Odorizzi had not slept in forty hours, and his bosses would not let him consult an attorney. He signed the letter. A month later, the criminal case against him was dropped and he sued to get his job back, saying that the resignation, which was a kind of contract, was a product of "undue influence." A lower court dismissed his complaint but an appeals court reversed, saying that a contract is not valid if it is a product of "persuasion which tends to be coercive . . . which overcomes the will without convincing the judgment."

This raises the question of how much persuasion is too much, or when a choice is not a choice. As the Odorizzi court said, in language only an appeals court could love: "The difficulty, of course, lies in determining when the forces of persuasion have overflowed their normal banks and become oppressive flood waters."

There is not a person alive who has not had second thoughts after a purchase or regretted listening to that salesperson who said, "Wow, that outfit looks great on you." Persuasion is not the same as coercion, and sometimes second thoughts are something we have to live with. Sometimes we can change our minds, sometimes not. In the Odorizzi case the court was correct to give Odorizzi a chance to recant, since sometimes people are under such pressure (for example, when they're essentially being blackmailed) that it is not fair to hold them accountable for their choices.

The difficulty is drawing the line between choice and coercion. As a descriptive matter, courts are increasingly stingy in giving people an out because they felt they were unduly pressured or mistaken. The law assumes assent in a wide range of so-called contracts even when no genuine choice existed. Think of this the next time you buy software only to find that you cannot use it unless you agree to a contract that appears onscreen only when you insert the disk or start the download. The contract is valid and limits your rights, even though you could not negotiate and had no way to review the terms before you purchased the software.

Criminal law. Within days of starting a law school criminal law course, students read famous cases in which someone committed a crime while sleepwalking, hypnotized, or suffering from mental illness. One early case from the 1800s concerns a sleepwalker who shot a porter in a small Kentucky hotel.[12] The accused, a man named Fain, was sleeping in the lobby and the porter was trying to wake him to get him to move along. Apparently without waking, Fain rose up, pulled a gun he was carrying, and shot the porter three times. The facts sound suspicious to me, but the court was told that Fain had a history of sleepwalking and was often violent and panicky in such condition. The court required the jury to be instructed that if Fain was not aware of what he was doing, then he could not be responsible for it. This is still a fundamental doctrine in criminal law. People who are not aware of what they are doing are not acting criminally: if you have not chosen your behavior, you are not responsible for it.[13] (By the way, sleepwalking is a problem outside criminal law as well. In 2004 a husband in Australia discovered that his wife had for months been sleepwalking at night and unconsciously having sex with strangers. Soiled condoms scattered around the house were apparently what tipped him off.)

Sometimes the law will excuse you from a crime even when you did make the choice, for example if you were under duress or faced such a horrible situation that you can claim what the law calls a necessity defense. But the law gives you only so much leeway. Some crimes are so serious that courts will not allow such an excuse. Even if Tony Soprano has kidnapped your family and requires you to murder Phil Leotardo in exchange for their release, murder is not a crime where duress gives you an "I had no choice" defense.

Search and seizure. Under the Constitution, police must generally have a warrant based on probable cause before they search your home, office, or private possessions. There are exceptions, and the biggest exception is that the police do not need a warrant if you consent to the search. Police increasingly depend on "consensual searches," since it allows them to bypass the warrant and probable cause requirements.

But how voluntary does the search need to be in order to be "consensual"? The answer, according to the Supreme Court, is not very. In one case, a bus was stopped in the middle of the night, far from its destination. Police boarded it and stood at the front and rear.[14] An armed officer walked up and down the aisle, approached two seated passengers and asked them to open their luggage. The officer stood over them, blocking their exit, and did not say they had a right to refuse. The passengers "agreed" to have the cops look in their bags, and as you might have guessed from the fact that we're talking about it, they were transporting cocaine. The Supreme Court held that this was a consensual search, since the passengers had a choice—they could have gotten off the bus. Your guess is as good as mine as to whether the police would have actually allowed the passengers to leave. But the Court assumed they had that choice.

It's hard to sympathize with guys who have several kilos of cocaine stashed in duffel bags in the overhead rack of a Greyhound bus. But it always strikes me as odd to claim that someone "consented" to a search that he knew would result in many years of jail time. Clearly the passengers felt intimidated and pressured. As Justice David Souter said in dissent, "The police not only carry legitimate authority but also exercise power free from immediate check, and when the attention of several officers is brought to bear on one civilian the balance of immediate power is unmistakable." He went on to say that such a "display of power" might "overbear a normal person's ability to act freely, even in the absence of explicit commands." Again, the question becomes how much choice counts as choice.

Free speech. One of the fundamental doctrines of free speech is that the government cannot force you to speak. During World War II, a number of states began requiring school children to begin their school day by saluting the flag and reciting the pledge of allegiance. In West Virginia, a child who was a Jehovah's Witness refused to say the pledge because it conflicted with his religious beliefs, and the school suspended him. Justice Robert Jackson's opinion for the Supreme Court striking down the compulsory pledge is among the most famous in free speech law: "If there is any fixed star in our constitutional constellation, it is that no official, high or petty, can prescribe what shall be orthodox in politics, nationalism, religion, or other matters of opinion or force citizens to confess by word or act their faith therein."[15]

Note that if the Court had had a different view of what choice meant, the case might have come out the other way. Justice Felix Frankfurter, one of the more scholarly justices of the last century, wrote in a dissent that no one was *forcing* the child to attend public school. If the school wanted to make the privilege of coming to school conditional on his saying the pledge, that should be permitted. The child could always go to a private school instead. In other words, Frankfurter was urging the Court to adopt the reasoning of Justice Holmes in the ax-in-the-head case: the kids were making their choice when they came to school, like Lamson was making his choice when he showed up to work.

The Court has been tempted by Frankfurter's view in some other cases. If the government gives you benefits, some cases seem to say, the government can condition those benefits on your giving up certain free

The Pledge of Allegiance, 1943.

speech rights, since no one is forcing you to accept the benefits. I was involved in a case a few years ago that raised this issue. Congress passed a law requiring universities, as a condition of receiving federal funds, to allow military recruiters on campus. A number of law schools around the country objected on the basis that the military refused to sign a pledge (which all other employers were required to sign) that they would not discriminate against students on the basis of race, sex, disability, religion, or sexual orientation. Because it discriminated against gays and lesbians under the "Don't ask, don't tell" policy (now repealed), the military refused to sign the pledge, and the law schools wanted to restrict their recruiting on campus. The schools sued, using an organization I helped create called the Forum for Academic and Institutional Rights (FAIR) as the plaintiff. We argued that the universities had a free speech right to exclude the discriminatory recruiters, even if they were part of the government. We also argued that it made no difference that the requirement to allow recruiters on campus came not as a direct command but as a condition of funding—a threat of a funding cutoff was coercive, too. Over several years, we fought the case all the way to the Supreme Court.

In the oral argument at the Supreme Court, the question of whether conditioning the funds amounted to compelled speech was front and center. Our attorney argued that cutting off millions of dollars to a university amounted to a punishment for exercising its speech rights. Chief Justice John Roberts was not convinced, saying that the statute "doesn't insist that you do anything. It says that, '*If you want our money*, you have to let our recruiters on campus.'"

The Supreme Court eventually decided against us, but it sidestepped the question of whether the threat of a funding cutoff amounted to compulsion. It decided the case on different grounds, saying that the statute requiring universities to allow recruiters on campus was not about speech but behavior. This was a dubious distinction, and the Court still lacks a clear rule about when the government can condition government benefits on the recipients' giving up speech rights. The question of choice is still alive.

The law of sex. Over the past few years, several female schoolteachers have been sentenced to jail for as long as thirty years for having sex with their underage male students. The definition of statutory rape varies across states, but in most states having sex with a child under a certain age (usually fourteen or sixteen) is always illegal, even if the other person is a teenager too. That's the age of consent. Most states also define the crime according to the age difference between the parties. If the definition is met, it's statutory rape even if both parties consented. The thought is that when a person is young or when there is enough of an age difference, the consent of the younger party does not count. That is why these teachers went to jail and are labeled sex offenders.

Nevertheless, many people think that statutory rape laws should not apply in such situations, in part because of the traditional but controversial notion that boys who have sex with adult women "got lucky." Some researchers are even proposing that the law relax its ban on adult/adolescent sex, claiming that such sexual interaction is not particularly harmful if consensual. That of course begs the question of what counts as consent. The power dynamic is real, and perhaps it is better to err on the side of caution. A case in point: a few years ago an Australian judge released nine young men who had gang-raped a ten-year old Aboriginal girl. The judge said that the girl was not forced and that she had probably agreed to have sex with the boys, igniting a firestorm about whether such a verdict could be justified by Aboriginal culture's supposedly lax attitude towards child sex. The next year, the same judge allowed a man accused of sexually assaulting an eleven-year-old boy to present evidence in his defense that sexual relations between older men and young boys was justifiable under Aboriginal culture.[16] Neither case sounds like consent to me.

In the law of sex, the question of consent is inescapable. The crime of rape is *defined* by reference to consent. The entire determination of whether rape has occurred turns on whether both parties agreed, explicitly or implicitly, to have intercourse. Traditionally, the rule was that it was impossible for a husband to rape his wife, since marriage constituted consent to sexual intercourse for all time. Also, rape victims were traditionally required to prove lack of consent by showing evidence that the assailant had used physical force and that they had fought back. In New York, the standard was that "rape is not committed unless the woman oppose the man to the utmost limit of her power." Evidence of resistance was seen as a solution to the "he said, she said" problem, an "outward manifestation of nonconsent, [a] device for determining whether a woman actually gave consent."[17] So the victim who was so terrified for her life that she failed to fight back was, by definition, not raped.

Courts eventually realized that the coercion inherent in rape might not only be by force. One New Jersey case concerned a fifteen-year-old girl who testified that a seventeen-year-old boy visiting in her home had penetrated her while she was asleep.[18] (It was not statutory rape because she was over the age of consent and they were both under eighteen.) The boy's testimony was that the girl was not asleep and had agreed to make out with him, and that he had not used physical force. The court called it acquaintance rape and announced that the victim would no longer have to show that physical force had been used in the course of the rape. The test instead was whether the alleged victim had given "affirmative and freely given permission" to engage in sex.

There is no doubt that this standard is better than the one requiring evidence of physical force. But we're back to trying to figure out what "freely given permission" means. This is so difficult to determine that some experts have suggested that the law require something akin to real contractual negotiation before sexual relations.[19]

Choice matters outside of rape cases, too. Are sex workers—prostitutes, porn stars, strippers—engaging in consensual sex acts (albeit for cash), which means that their choices should be respected? Or are sex workers so constrained by their situations and by the sexism of society in general that their choices are not really free? In November 2008, a group of sex workers placed a measure on the San Francisco city ballot to decriminalize prostitution. The measure received 41 percent of the vote, and the group promises on its web site to introduce the measure again. The site's headline reads "My Body, My $$$, My Choice! Consensual Sex Is Not a Crime!"[20]

In these examples and many others, free choice is often the key issue in the debate. What is choice, who has the right to choose, and what power does choice have? Usually, if a person agrees to something—if a person makes a choice—she is considered to have accepted the responsibilities and to bear the moral burden of that choice. Except when she is not. Sometimes we respect the choices of individuals, and sometimes we do not. The law frequently fixates on the question of consent as the only controlling legal issue. At other times it dismisses consent as beside the point.

Choice is the elephant in the room, whether we are discussing money, sex, politics, or crime. Yet we don't recognize it, much less understand it.

So let's start understanding choice where most of the action happens—in our brains.

II

Limits *and* Influences

3

Our Choices, Our Brains

My will is strong, but my won't is weak.
—Cole Porter, 1928

One never learns how the witch became wicked,
or whether that was the right choice for her—is
it ever the right choice? Does the devil ever
struggle to be good again, or if so is he
not a devil?
—Gregory Maguire, *Wicked: The Life and
Times of the Wicked Witch of the West*, 1995

CHOICES DEPEND, FIRST AND FOREMOST, on our brains. Ambrose Bierce once wrote that the brain is "an apparatus with which we think what we think,"[1] and for the non-neuroscientists among us that is about all we know. But we do have a sense that if our brains work well, we have a good chance of making a good decision. If our brains are not working well, then we might make bad decisions.

Here's a sad story. Raelyn Balfour, an auburn-haired thirty-six-year-old administrator for the U.S. military, left her office in Charlottesville, Virginia, on a cool day in March a couple of years ago after a day of work. She was tired. She had been up most of the previous night, babysitting for a friend and then caring for her nine-month-old son, Bryce, who was suffering from a cold.[2]

The moment she returned to her car, parked all day in the office lot, was to be the worst in her life. Bryce was in his car seat, dead. Balfour had forgotten to drop him off at day care that morning, and even though the temperature that day was only in the 60s, the interior of the car had risen to over 110 degrees. The heat had killed him.

The 911 recording of a passerby calling for an ambulance is heart-wrenching. You can hear Balfour wailing, "Oh my God, no! No, no, please, no!"[3]

Balfour's dreadful mistake is not as uncommon as you might think: it happens in the United States fifteen to twenty-five times a year. Usually a few circumstances conspire together—the parent is tired and distracted and stressed; there is a change in routine; and there is some kind of break-down in precaution or preventative stopgap. In Balfour's case, because Bryce had been sick the night before, he dozed off in the car, making no sound. Balfour herself was sleep-deprived and stressed, spending much of the drive to work talking on her cell phone, dealing with crises at work and with relatives. Bryce's usual car seat, positioned where she could see it behind the passenger seat, was empty. Balfour had planned to take the car seat to the local fire station to be professionally installed. So Bryce was sitting in another car seat, directly behind Balfour, where he was both quiet and out of sight. She simply forgot about dropping him off. Later, when she was at work, the babysitter called Balfour to ask why Bryce had not been dropped off, but she dialed Balfour's mobile phone and not her office. The cell phone went unanswered inside Balfour's purse.[4] It might have been too late even if she had picked up, since the car got hot enough to kill Bryce in as little as forty minutes.

Balfour's mistake was gut wrenching and perhaps inexcusable. But it is not incomprehensible. Stories like this give me a sick feeling in the pit of my stomach because I can empathize completely with Balfour's situation.

I have never forgotten my child in the back of the car, or at school, or at a friend's house. But I understand how it could happen, and I bet most parents can too. On the morning I was writing this chapter, I offered to walk my wife to the train, forgetting for a moment that by doing so I would leave our young son sleeping alone in the house for fifteen minutes. That's not the same as forgetting my child in a car, but a serious mistake nonetheless, especially if he woke to find no adult in the house. So as I think about Balfour's story, I think of what my own parents might say: "There but for the grace of God go I."

The day of Bryce's funeral, Balfour was charged with murder. The charge was eventually downgraded to involuntary manslaughter, and a jury acquitted her after a trial. She is now an activist for child car safety, making speeches to other parents around the country. She talks openly about her pain and gives parents tips about how to avoid her fate. One such tip: leave something you will need at work—your purse or briefcase—beside your child's car seat.[5]

Why do such horrors occur? How can someone become so distracted that they leave their child to swelter to death in a car? Part of the answer has to do with the way the brain works.

I.

Our brains comprise a number of different structures, some highly evolved, nimble, and sophisticated, others much more primitive. At the top of the evolutionary brain heap are the prefrontal cortex, which thinks and analyzes, and the hippocampus, which creates and stores new memories. More basic are the basal ganglia, which control actions that are voluntary but "barely conscious."[6] This portion of our brain is so primitive that it is not very different from what a reptile has.

Usually, these various components work like a finely tuned Ferrari. The prefrontal cortex takes care of the conversation you're having on your cell phone with your spouse or friend while the basal ganglia control the familiar, routine task of driving the car, guiding your feet down the sidewalk, or whisking the scrambled eggs. Your basal ganglia can put you on autopilot for the basic stuff, while the more highly evolved parts of your brain work on the hard or less familiar stuff. This is why you can arrive at work and remember the news story you heard but not what you saw while you drove. A brain that functions well at both the basic reflexive level and the more sophisticated, analytic level gives us humans an ability to perform at a cognitive echelon unmatched by any other species. We really can multi-task, as long as we're using different brain structures to do it.

The problem is that the analytic parts of our brains are easily overtaxed, and you cannot dependably ask them to do more than one thing at a time. That is why students who check their email on their laptops while listening to a class lecture are wasting their time and their (or their parents') money, and it's why I ban laptops in my classroom. It's also why having my email inbox open on the screen as I write this chapter is slowing the writing to a crawl.

What's more, one of the analytic parts—the prefrontal cortex—is also in charge of willpower. So you can exhaust it not only by thinking but also by trying to keep yourself from snacking on a brownie. In one revealing study, people were asked to remember a seven-digit number and then offered a snack. Other test subjects were asked to remember a one-digit number and offered the same snack. Those who were trying to remember the longer series of digits were much more likely to choose chocolate cake over fruit. Remembering the seven-digit number had made the prefrontal cortex less able to restrain itself from choosing the cake.[7]

One problem with how our brain works is that if the prefrontal cortex is tired or overtaxed or distracted, our basal ganglia take over. I was once driving to Middlebury College to participate in a debate on the First Amendment, and on the stretch of interstate between Boston and central

Vermont I tested various riffs I would use on my certainly doomed opponent. My driving brain went on autopilot as my prefrontal cortex devised sophisticated rhetorical punches and my hippocampus attempted to commit them to memory. Meanwhile, I drove thirty miles past my exit. When I realized what I had done, I could not even remember seeing the exit I was supposed to have taken. My damned basal ganglia had completely taken over the driving chore, and I could have easily maintained my trance until Canadian border police nudged me back to full awareness. As it was, I had gone too far to backtrack, so I navigated over a mountain pass on an icy, unpaved road and arrived minutes before the debate was to begin, with the organizer waiting at the front door with a worried look on her face. It would only have made matters worse to blame my basal ganglia.

According to David Diamond, a professor of molecular physiology at the University of South Florida, this "autopilot" feature of the basal ganglia is responsible for many of the forgotten baby cases. Think of the circumstances facing Raelyn Balfour—the lack of sleep, the stressful phone calls, the child sitting in a different car seat. These kinds of stresses can make the higher-functioning parts of your brain more susceptible to bullying by the basal ganglia. Unless something happens to reboot the hippocampus, the basal ganglia can take over and put you on autopilot. As psychology professor Gary Marcus explains, "When we are stressed, tired, or distracted, our deliberative system tends to be the first thing to go, leaving us at the mercy of our lower-tech reflexive system—just when we might need our deliberative system the most."[8]

If you have ever put your dry cleaning in your car on the way to work and forgotten to drop it off, or been asked to stop on your way home to buy a gallon of milk and not done it, then you have felt the power of the basal ganglia autopilot.

And, the experts say, if you can forget your dry cleaning or a gallon of milk, you can forget your child.

Balfour's choices that morning were flawed, but in hindsight we can understand what might have gone wrong. The analytic part of her brain was tired and distracted, and the reflexive part of her brain took over with horrific results. She was simply too overwhelmed to think straight, let alone actively decide what to do. Certainly what she did was not "intentional" in the way we generally use that word. To say she "chose" to leave Bryce in her car does not capture what really happened and does not do justice to her situation.

The jury that acquitted Balfour almost certainly had an intuitive understanding of this, even if they had no knowledge of neuroscience. The jurors did not necessarily believe that Balfour bore *no* fault for what happened that March day. But her level of responsibility was not so great that she deserved to be punished more than she was already punishing herself. She did not deserve to go to jail. If I had been on the jury, I would have voted to acquit, too.

The more difficult question is *how much* allowance we should give people who make these kinds of mistakes. One of the touchstones of criminal law for centuries has been that people who do not intend to commit an act should not be held responsible for it. The law establishes levels of intent required for various levels of crimes, and the differences among types of crime are sometimes defined solely by differences in levels of intent. Traditionally, a murder is any killing committed "with malice aforethought."[9] But usually the most serious punishment is reserved for first-degree, or premeditated, murder. A murder in the second degree can be the same killing but done "in the heat of passion." You meant to do it, even though in a calmer moment you would not have. Manslaughter can be voluntary—you intend to commit an act, but don't intend that it will result in the victim's death—or involuntary—you acted with "reckless disregard" to whether your action was going to result in someone's death. These formulations vary somewhat across jurisdictions, but you get the idea.[10] Whatever the standard, the case is often won or lost over the question of whether the defendant "really meant" it.[11]

Our collective sense, reflected in the law, is that the more intentional something is, the more responsibility the person should bear for it. The moral intuition of the common law therefore lines up with our new understanding about the brain. Defendants are more blameworthy when the more sophisticated parts of their brains become involved in making the criminal choice. "Malice aforethought" is another way of saying that the murderer's prefrontal cortex was involved. The basal ganglia are capable of no worse than manslaughter.

The reason Anthony Hopkins's Hannibal Lecter in *The Silence of the Lambs* is one of the most unnerving villains in the history of film is that he was so calculating. His murders were not haphazard, reflexive acts. They were artfully planned and executed down to the "fava beans and a nice Chianti" that accompanied his meal of a victim's liver.[12]

Our implicit understanding of how brains work explains why Hannibal Lecter strikes us as chillingly evil while it's easy to feel sympathy for Raelyn Balfour. A jury didn't hold her criminally responsible for her bad decision in part because the jurors felt that what she did was less than completely rational or intentional. This fits with our sense that responsibility follows intentionality.

3.

But there is more to good choices than making sure the more highly evolved portions of our brains, such as the prefrontal cortex, are doing the work. Hannibal Lecter is über-rational, and he is an excellent decision maker in a technical, amoral sense. But he does not have the "correct" emotion about what he does, so he seems inhuman and cold. Even excellent analysis alone isn't enough; our emotions have to be working well too in order for our decisions to count as well-made.

Brain scientists tell us that emotions are governed by a number of areas of the brain. One of these areas is called the ventromedial prefrontal cortex, a primitive part of the cortex that seems to have evolved to help humans navigate social interactions. The area has connections to deeper, reflexive regions like the brain stem, which transmits physical sensations of attraction or discomfort, and the amygdala, an almond-shaped bundle of neural tissue that helps process emotional reactions and create memories of emotions. Scientists hypothesize that the ventromedial area probably evolved to help early humans make moral decisions about others in small kin groups—to spare a group member's life after a fight, for example.[13] As human interactions became more complex, the brain's structures evolved to parse more complex ethical dilemmas. But the ventromedial area continues to insist on an ancient, emotional respect for the life of another human being.

This emotional insistence does not always make sense as a matter of costs and benefits, even though it may seem right to most of us in other ways. Take, for example, the famous "trolley car problem."[14] Imagine that you see a trolley hurdling down its track, out of control. It is about to run over five people who cannot be warned in time. (I know it's an unlikely scenario, but I didn't come up with it. Philosophers make their livings by inventing hypotheticals to isolate moral questions.) You can throw a switch to divert the train onto a spur, where it will kill only one person. Do you throw the switch? Most people would, since saving five people is worth the cost of one.

Now imagine that instead of waiting next to a switch you are standing on an overpass, and the only way to stop the trolley is to push a large person standing next to you off the bridge and onto the track. (The question assumes you're smaller than the pushee, so sacrificing yourself will not stop the train.) Do you push? The cost-benefit analysis is the same as in the first example, but most people see a difference and say no. The difference has to do with your emotional connection with what is being done. Pushing someone off a bridge is more viscerally disturbing than throwing a switch, even if the result is morally identical.

We cannot say with certainty that our decision not to push someone off the bridge to save five others is the best one. That evaluation turns on a host of philosophical, ethical, and religious considerations on which people can reasonably disagree. On the one hand, perhaps our refusal to push amounts to moral squeamishness, something to be overcome in order to save five people. On the other hand, perhaps our feelings guide us to a proper recognition that pushing someone off a bridge to a certain death is murder, and we cannot avoid responsibility for it just because our action saves others. On the third hand, maybe the dilemma cannot be resolved.

But I can say this about the trolley problem: there is a difference between what the final answer should be and *how* people should arrive at it. In other words, while I cannot know the ultimate right answer, I know how people should *feel* about the problem. Someone who saw the trolley coming and made the push-or-not-to-push decision in a cold, utilitarian way without *feeling* a certain way about it would not seem to be acting humanely. It certainly would not strike me as the best kind of decision making.

Contrast this view with the traditional view of economists, who have long based their predictions on the so-called "rational actor" theory of human behavior. Humans are assumed to make choices based on a cost-benefit analysis, maximizing their own utility (basically a word that means "pleasure," broadly defined) as best they can. This theory has been extremely influential, and not only in economics. The rational actor assumption has been used to craft rules in criminal law, corporate law, and family law. The problem is that it takes as its touchstone an extremely narrow view of human rationality.

Our Choices, Our Brains   55

Anyone living in the real world understands that people make decisions for reasons other than their own pleasure. To be fully human is to act with spite, compassion, confusion, love. Economists may not understand this, but the rest of us do.

In fact, scientists performed a study of people who had suffered brain aneurysms or tumors to their ventromedial prefrontal cortex, the area discussed above that helps people empathize with others.[15] As it turns out, people who had suffered such injuries tended to make decisions with less compassion and with more utilitarian "rationality." The scientists asked the subjects questions like the runaway trolley problem. Those with the injuries were twice as likely as those with undamaged brains to push someone in front of the train. The brain damage, the scientists hypothesized, "put a finger on the brain's conscious, cost-benefit scale weighing moral dilemmas." Those without proper brain function in that area ended up making decisions with a more "utilitarian cost-benefit analysis." The bottom line: a certain kind of brain injury makes its victims think like economists.

For the rest of us, to be a good thinker and a decent choice maker depends not only on the analytical and reflexive parts of our brains but also on our emotional abilities.

4.

In 1966, the nation was stunned by the news of a sniper in the clock tower at the University of Texas at Austin. The sniper, who turned out to be a twenty-five-year-old former Marine by the name of Charles Whitman, killed fourteen people and wounded thirty-two before he was killed by police. It was later discovered that Whitman had killed both his mother and his wife the night before. It was the deadliest campus shooting in the United States until the murders at Virginia Tech forty-one years later.

Charles Whitman.

Whitman left behind a letter, asking that an autopsy be performed on his body, hoping it would explain his increasing headaches and "unusual and irrational thoughts."[16] He wondered why he could not stop himself from doing what he was preparing to do, writing, "I don't really understand myself these days." He asked that his life insurance proceeds, if still valid, go to medical research "to prevent further tragedies of this type." When the autopsy was performed, doctors found that a tumor in his brain was putting pressure on his amygdala, one of the structures that regulate emotions.

Should this revelation affect how we think about Whitman's guilt? He certainly understood what he was doing, knew it was wrong, and nevertheless planned his rampage with care and sophistication. Sounds like the embodiment of evil. But perhaps his brain was sufficiently diseased that he had no emotional connection to what he was doing, no empathy for his victims or concern for his own future. The part of the brain that would have stopped a healthy person from committing such atrocities may not have been in working condition. Without the tumor, there might have been no violence. So was he evil? Or was he, like the others who died that day, a victim of the tumor?

This is where the law's traditional response does not map well with brain science. Traditionally, defendants can be found not guilty because of insanity only when they cannot distinguish between right and wrong. Whitman knew what he was doing was wrong, yet he was still compelled to do it. "You can have a horrendously damaged brain where someone knows the difference between right and wrong but nonetheless can't control their behavior," says Robert Sapolsky, a neurobiologist at Stanford. "At that point, you're dealing with a broken machine, and concepts like punishment and evil and sin become utterly irrelevant."[17] Calling the brain a machine may seem cold and overly scientific. But here it makes sense, since Whitman's defect was not that he was doing a bad job of thinking, but that he was doing a bad job of feeling.

It's important to distinguish between noticing that Whitman may have been impaired and deciding what to do with that information. Even if the science says Whitman had no control over his actions, how we determine moral responsibility or punishment is a different question, even though we often conflate them. As Sapolsky puts it, "Does that mean the person should be dumped back on the street? Absolutely not. You have a car with the brakes not working, and it shouldn't be allowed to be near anyone it can hurt."

I find it hard to be sympathetic toward Whitman, even if a neuroscientist could ascertain that portions of his brain were on the fritz. But one thing is clear: good choices depend not only on the rational, deliberative part of the brain but on the emotional part as well. Culturally we are more understanding when the brain defect is in the deliberative part rather than the emotional part, but there is little doubt that what goes on biologically in our brains affects how we make decisions. We may be unsure what juries and judges should do about it, but the fact is inescapable.

5.

Raelyn Balfour and Charles Whitman are only extreme examples of the broader point that good decisions depend on deliberation, reflex, and emotions all working together. Few of us have caused the death of our own child or used a sniper's rifle to pick off victims. But we've all made bad decisions. And the more we learn about the brain, and about why and how we make those decisions, the more we see how decisions can be manipulated. The people who seem to understand this best are those who want to sell us something.

Take the "bikini effect." You might not expect that giving a man a bra or panties to caress would make him want to drink beer. But you'd be wrong, according to studies that showed this very effect. Apparently the brain has a common appetite system, which—at least in the case of straight men—can be stimulated by the sight of beautiful, scantily clad women or the touch of their underthings. It can also be stimulated by the smell of baked goods or anything else that tips off the brain that it is time for pleasure. Once stimulated, the brain seeks to satisfy the craving, and the source of satisfaction need not correlate with the stimulation. What matters is that when the pleasure centers are put on high alert, the brain tries to answer the alarm. It seeks a way to satisfy the craving *now*. As the lead researcher in one study said, after seeing beautiful women "men valued the future less and the present more."[18] Long-term thinking be damned.

This is why the Miller Lite Girls, the Coors Light Twins, or the St. Pauli Girl work as marketing gimmicks. Men see attractive women and crave pleasure. In the absence of something better, they get their drink on. That's also why casinos dress their hostesses in scanty outfits, why car shows are staffed with sexy women, and why Tomb Raider Lara Croft has breast implants. At one level, this is no surprise. We all know that sex sells. But now we understand that it sells because of the way our brains work.

A fourth-century mosaic of a woman in a bikini.

Interestingly, the more men are satisfied in other ways, the less powerful the bikini effect is. In one study, men were told that their incomes were much higher than the national average. The bikini effect lost its influence, apparently because the men felt financially well-off. When men were told the opposite—that their incomes were low compared to society in general—they were much more likely to seek immediate gratification once they saw the sexy women. Again, the actual gratification can come in any number of forms. One study showed that people who were put into a state of "high desire" for money tried to satisfy that desire by eating more M&Ms.[19]

While the bikini effect causes men to seek immediate gratification, it does not turn them into idiots. Sexy stimuli can actually improve cognition and creativity. This should make sense to anyone who has watched men try to pick up women in bars, or been a teenager trying to figure out how to get beer. Many a movie is based on the reality that creativity is necessary to satisfy an immediate need. Remember *Superbad*? (If you haven't seen it, you should.)

These are male-centric examples, but women, too, are influenced by brain chemistry. Consider a 2007 study by brain scientists of purchasing decisions. They hooked up test subjects, both men and women, to a functional MRI machine and scanned their brains while they were shown a series of products and prices, and then asked whether they would buy or not.[20] The scientists learned that when the "shoppers" saw a product they wanted, the pleasure center of the brain, the nucleus accumbens, saw increased blood flow and lit up on the fMRI. When the price was shown, another part of the brain—the insula, which is activated when you anticipate pain or see something disgusting—lit up. What the scientists learned is that spendthrifts tended to have more activity in the accumbens and less in the insula. Tightwads had the reverse. Neither side made "rational" decisions, coldly weighing costs and benefits. Both kinds of shoppers were "guided by instant emotions."[21] The results were similar for both men and women.

Consider how this knowledge could be manipulated by those trying to get us to buy something. If the pleasure center can be activated more strongly—by the sight of an attractive spokesmodel or the smell of chocolate—the purchase is more likely. If the pain of paying can be suppressed—through credit cards, for example—then the purchase is more likely. It doesn't take a brain scientist to figure this out.

But here's the real kicker about the shopping study. We're so influenced by our brain chemistry that the scientists believe they can predict whether we will make a purchase *before we make the decision*.[22] Once they saw neurons in the insula light up, the scientists could say that a decision not to buy was on its way. The test subject's conscious choice to forgo the purchase happened later. Moreover, the brain scans did a better job of predicting the purchase decision than the subject's own self-reported preferences and price points.

Those of us who are not neuroscientists may find it difficult to admit how constrained and channeled we are by our own brain chemistry and biology. This is the cutting edge of science; we can be excused for being a bit skeptical or failing to recognize our lack of agency in our own decision making. But the science is increasingly clear: we are slaves to our brain chemistry more often and in more ways than we might like to admit. If a marketer is able to trigger our pleasure centers into a craving and suppress the pain center's response to paying, then psychologically we're more like sitting ducks than wise owls.

6.

The bikini effect is not the only way in which our brains are predictably susceptible to cognitive mistake and manipulation. Take the fact that men systematically overestimate the sexual interest of potential mates. This is probably based on the evolutionary need to reproduce, and "ancestral males who tended to read too much into the signals given by possible partners would have more opportunities to reproduce than would their more cautious counterparts, who likely failed to identify bona fide opportunities."[23]

Such an insight is useful in all kinds of situations where someone is trying to get men to spend money. Sexy female bartenders get bigger tips, probably because men at the bar misinterpret their attention as sexual interest. Pharmaceutical companies notoriously hire attractive female sales reps to market their drugs to mostly male doctors. Case in point: I came across a 2005 article describing how two dozen University of Kentucky cheerleaders had become drug reps over the previous few years; my guess is that they didn't land those jobs because of any particular understanding of pharmacology.[24] This effect also explains why I long ago bought a leather jacket I didn't need—I eagerly misinterpreted the attractive sales lady's pitch as interest in me rather than my money. As soon as she had the money and I had the jacket, I stopped getting any signals to misinterpret. I still have the jacket somewhere.

There are thousands of such studies showing various tendencies in the way we think and choose. Consider the "familiarity effect." We tend to like things that are familiar—whether people, beliefs, or products—and we like them even more when we feel threatened or stressed.[25] We also are guilty of "motivated reasoning," meaning that we scrutinize ideas we disagree with more than those we agree with. Our brains are prone to noticing facts that confirm what we already think—"confirmation bias"—and disregarding things that would tend to disprove our preexisting notions.[26] Our brains are biased toward attractive people, who we see not only as beautiful but also as more competent and more intelligent, even when judged on activities that have nothing to do with looks. Better-looking students get better evaluations from teachers. Also, attractive people who are observed doing something bad or illegal are more likely to be seen as having a bad day or acting aberrantly. Less-attractive people are judged more harshly, with worse motives projected onto them, and receive harsher prison sentences.[27] Remember this the next time you serve on a jury.

The way you think about a question or issue can be manipulated if you are focused on a component part of it. In one study, teenagers were asked how happy they were. If they were first asked how many dates they had had in the previous month, their self-reported happiness index fell.[28] The dating question focused the teenagers' thinking on one aspect of their happiness and skewed their answers. The preliminary question focused their thoughts in a predictable and manipulable way.

This kind of "mental contamination," to use Gary Marcus's term, occurs even if the focus is on something completely irrelevant. In one famous experiment, Nobel Prize winners Daniel Kahneman and Amos Tversky asked people to spin a "wheel of fortune" with the numbers 1 to 100 on it, and then asked them how many nations were in Africa.[29] The number the person spun affected his or her answer—a low number on the wheel meant that answers to the Africa question tended to be low, and vice versa. The numbers on the wheel had a kind of gravitational pull for those thinking about completely unrelated matters. This is called priming, since the brain is primed to think a certain way, like old water pumps that had to be primed before they worked.

Some of this mental contamination is benign and best used as fodder for brain teasers and jokes. One of my son's go-to jokes when he is at a table of grown-ups is to ask someone to say "toast" twelve times fast. He is priming his audience. Then he asks, "What is it that you put in a toaster?" Most people will say "toast," because their brains are primed to give that answer. He will then slyly explain that at our house we usually put *bread* in the toaster.

Other times, mental contamination can be more serious and can undermine good decision making. One study showed that when students taking a test were primed beforehand by being asked about their race, African American students did worse than when they were not so primed. The negative stereotype of African Americans as poor students was ingrained in the students, and the priming influenced them to meet that expectation.[30]

Mental contamination can also be used to manipulate people into thinking a certain way. In the 2000 presidential election between George W. Bush and Al Gore, the Bush team ran what looked at first to be a run-of-the-mill television ad attacking Gore's prescription drug plan. Bush used the rhetorical power of choice to contrast his drug plan with Gore's—in Bush's plan "seniors choose," while in Gore's "bureaucrats decide." As the word "bureaucrats" appears and grows larger, the word "RATS" floods the screen for one frame. Although "RATS" lasts only one-thirtieth of a second, it is in capital letters and larger than any other word in the ad. Democrats accused the Bush campaign of using a subliminal trick to influence viewers. The Bush campaign denied any malicious intent and eventually pulled the ad, though not before it ran over four thousand times at a cost of $2.5 million.[31] While it is difficult to know how big

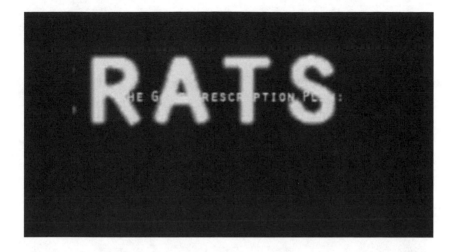

an effect such an ad could have had, I'll venture a guess that the word's appearance was not inadvertent. And you'll remember that the 2000 election was decided by a handful of votes in Florida, where voters would care quite a bit about a prescription drug plan for seniors. Moreover, at least one study has suggested that such a quick, subconscious association of a candidate with a negative word could significantly affect voters' perceptions of that candidate. The reason is our old friend the amygdala, which can respond to threatening stimuli even without our registering the threat consciously.[32]

7.

Mental contamination can work wonders for marketers of products. Consumer choice for an item is affected drastically by other items offered around it. For example, the prices of suits that shoppers will not buy affect their decisions about suits they *will* buy. As Barry Schwartz describes in *The Paradox of Choice*, in a fancy department store displaying suits costing over $1,500, an $800 pinstripe may seem like a bargain. In a store where most suits cost less than $500, that same $800 suit will seem extravagant and will likely be left on the shelf.[33] So one way to sell something is to place it next to something that costs more.

Another example comes from a mail-order seller of high-end kitchen equipment, which was offering a bread maker for $279.[34] The bread maker was not selling. So the firm added a deluxe version for $429. The company did not sell many of the expensive ones, but the sales of the $279 version almost doubled. One might expect that people looking to buy bread makers would be unaffected by extraneous information, such as the price of a product they wouldn't buy. But people's choices can be manipulated in predictable ways, and marketers take advantage of these irrationalities all the time.

All of these examples show the kind of tricks our brains play on us when we're doing something relatively simple—making decisions in the present. When we try to make decisions about the future, or remember the past, our brains do an even worse job. You might think that a mistake about the future or the past would not necessarily be a big deal, but it is. Our ability to make anything close to a good decision in the present depends not only on our judgments about what we want, think, and feel right now but on our memories of what we wanted, thought, and felt in the past and our predictions about what we will want, think, and feel in the future.

We have a hard time correctly keeping track of what made us happy in the past. The human brain collapses past experiences and stores them as memories in ways that distort their accuracy. According to some studies, humans remember past experiences by condensing them to their salient elements, which tend to be whatever was best or worst about the experience, and whatever happened first and last.[35] This significantly influences how people make choices, since their choices about the future are inevitably based on their poor memories of past choices. If they do not accurately remember how they felt in the past, then their choices will lead to poor results even by their own assessment. (One of my favorite movies is

Memento, about a man searching for his wife's murderer. His problem is that in the same attack that killed his wife, he suffered a head injury that makes it impossible for him to form new memories. The movie is told backward, to put the viewer in the same position of not knowing what just happened. Even if our usual memory problems aren't this extreme, we can relate.)[36]

The most colorful example of this difficulty comes from a study of patients undergoing colonoscopies.[37] Back when this was not done with anesthesia, the procedure was painful, particularly when the physician manipulated the probe. In the study, the doctors removed the probe from some patients as soon as the procedure was done. For other patients, the doctor would leave the probe motionless inside the colon for twenty additional seconds. While painful, these last twenty seconds were less painful than the earlier part of the procedure. This latter group of patients thus endured more total time with a probe inside their colon, and the total amount of pain they suffered was greater than the first group by any objective measure. But they *remembered* less discomfort than the first group, influenced less by the aggregate amount of discomfort than by what they felt during the last twenty seconds. This is more than just an esoteric point from medical research. Those who remembered less discomfort were more willing to return for annual screenings.

Similar defects in our abilities to remember our experiences accurately can explain why women who go through childbirth remember it being less painful than it actually was, and why people who end their marriages remember them as worse than they actually were.[38]

Our predictions about the future are even worse. As psychologist Daniel Gilbert tells us, "When we imagine future circumstances, we fill in details that won't really come to pass and leave out details that will. When we imagine future feelings, we find it impossible to ignore what we are feeling now and impossible to recognize how we will think about the things that happen later."[39]

The disconnect between the present and future is sometimes caused by our inability to predict our own preferences, usually because when we make predictions we think about the future, but when the time comes to put our preferences into action we're making judgments about the *now*. One example of this is a study that asked people at a conference to establish their preferences for snacks over several days, picking one kind of snack per day. When asked for such a prediction, they anticipated that they would want variety, so they ordered a variety of snacks. When the time came to eat every day, however, the attendees were offered the full panoply of snacks. Did people eat a variety of snacks? No. They selected their favorite every day. The future had become now, and in the present they wanted their favorite.[40]

I have started to use this insight in my grocery shopping. I used to buy a variety of frozen dinners to heat up and eat when I was eating alone and there was no time for a home-cooked meal. Usually, I would eat my favorite one—chicken parmesan and pasta—within a couple of days of bringing it home. The next time I opened the freezer, I was inevitably disappointed that my favorite was already gone. Sometimes I would just eat cereal. After I started buying *only* chicken parm I was much happier when I opened the freezer door. In the future I may have wanted variety, but in the now I want chicken parm.

8.

Here's the point to all of this. We don't have to be Raelyn Balfour or Charles Whitman to be led astray or limited by our brains. Parts of our brains are highly sophisticated, but other parts are still prehistoric. Our brains make mistakes, are easily fooled, and have tendencies to make us think, react, and feel a certain way. We routinely misremember the past and make horrible predictions about the future. In the phrasing of Dan

Ariely, we are "predictably irrational," with our minds playing tricks on us all the time.[41]

What's worse, we usually do not recognize these tendencies in ourselves, which leaves us open to manipulation. Sexual titillation makes us want to buy stuff; subliminal association influences our views of political candidates; a primed brain will think one way rather than another.

Does this mean we are not really choosing when we buy stuff when titillated, vote when subliminally influenced, or think the way we have been primed to think? The answer depends on what we mean by "choice."

On the one hand, influences are only that. They do not dictate behavior, and their effects can be moderated merely by our knowing they exist. On the other hand, our brains are pre-programmed to think and feel in certain ways, and it takes the analytical, reflexive, and emotional parts of our brains all working together to give us a fighting chance at making good decisions. Even when they do, we can fall into traps, and the pathways into those traps are well trod.

What do we do if it turns out that much of what we feel and think is not really intentional? It's a troubling insight, and one that most of us will rebel against. After all, we do not *perceive* our decision to buy beer or to prefer one candidate over another as out of our control. You may not experience a lack of free will, and most of the time neither do I. But despite our feelings, brain science is revealing that our decision making processes are much more bewildering than we ever imagined, and that our own perceptions of free will should not necessarily be trusted. Choice is complicated.

Instead of assuming that everyone is completely responsible for his or her decisions, we'd be better off recognizing the complexity of choice, in law and politics and life. We would be more forgiving of our foibles and understanding of others'. We'd be more likely to recognize the limitations we face and the constraints on our decisions, and better able to prepare for the times when decisions really do need to be made well.

4

Choice
and Culture

We don't live in a world that suffers from
doubt, but one that suffers from certainty, false
certainties that compensate for the well of
worldly anxieties and worries.
—Les Back, *The Art of Listening*, 2007

After all, what was adult life but one moment of
weakness piled on top of another? Most people
just fell in line like obedient little children, doing
exactly what society expected of them at any
given moment, all the while pretending that
they'd actually made some sort of choice.
—Tom Perrotta, *Little Children*, 2004

AN OLD JOKE: A bird sitting on a branch over a lake looks down and sees a fish swimming by.

"How's the water?" the bird asks.

The fish answers, "What water?"

Our cultural surroundings, like the fish's water, influence everything we do but often go without notice. They play a large role in constructing our views of possible and impossible, good and evil, luxury and necessity. Culture instructs us about who we can love, what kinds of jobs are open to us, what kind of family we can have, and how we should understand our environment and human nature. Culture teaches us what is "normal" with regard to the roles women and men should play in the family, how thin or fat we should be, what we should wear, how much we should consume, what sports we should care about, how we should spend our time, and which religions it is respectable to observe.

Culture creates norms. Culture enforces norms. And for many of us, much of the time, culture influences decisions so much that the scope of genuine choice is exceedingly small.

I.

It is much easier to recognize cultural constraints when they are not our own. Take, for example, the plight of fourteen women who were arrested inside a popular café in an upscale neighborhood of Khartoum, the capital of Sudan, in 2009. Their crime was wearing pants. They were among a crowd listening to an Egyptian singer when members of the government's public order police burst in and ordered all the women to stand up so the policemen could check what they were wearing. The women wearing trousers were arrested, even though they were otherwise dressed modestly in blouses and the traditional headscarf. The government charged the women with a violation of the country's indecency laws. These laws are based on a strict interpretation of Islamic doctrine and impose punishment on "those who commit an indecent act that violates public morale; or who dress indecently."[1] The penalty was severe: for most of the women, a flogging, which in this case meant being lashed ten times with a whip.

One of the women, a Sudanese journalist and United Nations employee named Lubna Hussein, decided to fight the conviction. She printed and distributed five hundred invitations to her flogging, attracting the attention of international journalists and human rights activists. Her trial was covered on CNN and in major newspapers. During her trial, scores of women came to protest outside, some wearing trousers. Police fired tear gas into the crowd and, according to the Associated Press, beat some of the protestors. Perhaps because of the attention, the judge in Hussein's trial declined to sentence her to flogging and instead fined her the equivalent of two hundred dollars. When she refused to pay, she was carted off to jail. Friends soon paid her fine and gained her release.

For most of us in the West, this episode shows the backwardness of Sudanese culture when it comes to gender roles and gender equality. We see the insistence on a certain kind of modesty in attire as a cultural and religious norm that operates to maintain a subservient role for women. Lubna Hussein and women like her are courageously trying to fight those cultural norms, sometimes at significant personal risk. We also recognize that women in Sudan have little genuine choice about what they wear in public. They might be able to fight the imposition or enforcement of the norm in a small number of cases, but for most women, most of the time, to wear pants is to risk public humiliation, arrest, fines, and even corporal punishment. That once in a great while there is a woman who can gain international attention for challenging the norm does not change the fact that the norm is strong and rigorously enforced. Hussein is the exception, not the rule, and she was jailed for her impertinence.

We also see the power of cultural norms when people from different cultures come together in the same space. A legal and social battle now going on in France concerns whether Islamic girls may wear hijabs, traditional headscarves, in school. France has a long tradition of public secularism, and many see the wearing of the hijab by students and teachers in public schools as conflicting with that tradition. Some French citizens consider the hijab a token of women's subservience and inequality.[2] On the other hand, many Islamic women and girls wear it as an expression of religious identity and argue that it should be their choice to do so. One side sees the hijab as evidence of cultural oppression and coercion, and the other side sees it as a free expression of cultural identity.

The burqa.

French law now prohibits the wearing of the hijab in public schools. Ironically, girls who wear it are suspended—thrown out of school without a choice—in order to protect their freedom to choose not to wear it.

The problem is even more pronounced with the burqa, the full-body covering with only a mesh screen over the eyes, worn largely by women in fundamentalist Islamic families. To see a woman wearing one in the West is jarring to our sensibilities.

One summer my wife and I visited Paris, where I had been invited to speak at an economics conference. Our first day there, we walked from our small hotel to the Louvre and sat enjoying the park and gardens that stretch away from the museum. People from all over the world strolled around, played games, rode bicycles, and licked ice cream cones. It was a bright, muggy July day, and most people were wearing shorts and T-shirts. Amidst this cacophonous microcosm of Western life, a man walked past us in clothing that would not have caused anyone to think twice: fine jeans, a white shirt. He was carrying a nice camera. Slightly behind him walked a woman in a burqa, clad head to toe in black veil. We could see no part of her skin. The sight of the woman, hidden as she was behind dark folds, was jarring to me and even more to my wife. It was difficult not to stare. The burqa seemed more like a sign of oppression than religious expression. To my wife and me, the woman clad completely in black cloth, sliding along behind her Abercrombie-dressed husband on a hot summer day, certainly did not appear to embody the potential of human agency and choice.

We are not the only ones to have had this reaction. French President Nicolas Sarkozy, addressing a joint session of the French Parliament a few weeks before, had argued that the burqa should be banned outside the home: "In our country, we cannot accept that women be prisoners behind a screen, cut off from all social life, deprived of all identity." He said that "the burqa is not a religious sign, it's a sign of subservience, a sign of debasement." The French parliament later voted to ban the burqa in public spaces.[3]

Of course we in the West have our own gender norms and assumptions, many of which are enforced by cultural rules about styles of dress. If "dress is code,"[4] then Western culture is hardly immune to discomfort at the hands of people who defy the dominant code. For example, in many public schools around the United States, girls are banned from dressing like boys, and vice versa. Ceara Sturgis, a senior at a Mississippi public school, found herself barred from the school's yearbook after she sat for her photo in a tuxedo rather than the open-necked drape that other girls were wearing. In Marion County, Florida, students are required to dress "in keeping with their gender." A more troubling example comes from Oxnard, California, where Lawrence King, an eighth-grader who occasionally wore gender-bending outfits and makeup, was shot to death in 2008 by another student while in class.[5]

We also have our own religious fundamentalists of various stripes who enforce strict gender norms in part by requiring women to dress extremely modestly: consider the Amish, some branches of the Mennonites,

The habit.

or the traditional garb of Catholic nuns. The Christian Bible does say that "the head of the woman is man" and "every woman who prays or prophesies with her head uncovered dishonors her head . . . A man ought not to cover his head, since he is the image and glory of God; but the woman is the glory of man. For man did not come from woman, but woman from man; neither was man created for woman, but woman for man."[6] The current Pope, when he was still a cardinal in 2004, wrote a Vatican document "urging women to be submissive partners, resisting any adversarial roles with men and cultivating 'feminine values' like 'listening.'"[7]

2.

One of the most powerful ways culture influences us is by telling us what our roles are, and how we may behave in those roles.

My father began his career as a minister in 1956, when he became the pastor of the Sugar Creek Baptist Church. He was nineteen and a freshman in college. The church, located on a long stretch of road outside Princeton, Kentucky, was surrounded by fields planted with sweet corn. It was small, with only forty-four members, making it a perfect place for my father to begin his work. The church folk took him under their wing, encouraging him, praying for him, and feeding him expansive Sunday dinners of fried chicken, mashed potatoes, and black-eyed peas.

Soon after my dad began his work at Sugar Creek, he met my mom at college. They fell in love and my dad proposed. Receiving a proposal from a man is one thing; receiving a proposal from a Southern Baptist preacher is another. Then as now, being married to a preacher was a job in itself. My mom had to be willing to step into a role.

A few months before their wedding, my mom received a gift from one of my father's friends, a book entitled *The Pastor's Wife*. The friend had added this inscription: "To the future Mrs. Greenfield, That she may know her job better." The norms of what it meant to be a pastor's wife had been written down in book form.

My mom recently pulled this book off her shelf and sent it to me, and it does indeed read like a rule book.

On marriage and motherhood: "If a girl says, 'Marriage does not interest me' either she is not normal or she is 'a gay deceiver'! Every normal girl looks forward . . . to having a home of her own, and to becoming a mother. The Creator made her so . . . At the heart of every parsonage he would have a woman who would rather live as a wife and mother than occupy any other position on earth." And "a Christian woman excels most of all as a mother," but be warned—"never should the wife make the husband feel that he has taken a second place."[8]

On housekeeping: "The first duty of the minister's wife is to make the home attractive. The same holds true for any woman. The wife of a farmer or a mechanic, a doctor or a merchant, looks on the home as her chief opportunity to do good in the world." More specifically: "I urge that you keep the bathroom immaculate day and night . . . How could a woman say her prayers if she knew that the bathroom needed a day's work to make it fit for human beings?"[9] (Now I understand why my mom would often stay up late at night doing housework.)

The norms expressed in these rules were powerful to my mother, and women who were not pastors' wives had books of their own, or books of general admonition such as Emily Post's *Etiquette*. Women were expected to focus on the home even if they had to find an outside job. They neglected their roles in the home at their peril, and few marriages could fairly be described as equal. The norms limited men as well, in ways that only later became clear to those of us who wanted a greater role in child rearing. Even now, most employers—including my own—provide little or no paternity leave for new fathers, even when maternity leave is generous.

These gender norms were only partly the product of law, but the law always lurked—reinforcing, reflecting, assuming. It was not until 1976 that a court recognized sexual harassment as a legitimate cause of action—before then, women who were sexually harassed at work had no right to sue. If a woman were raped by her husband, most states did not consider it a crime until the 1980s or later.[10] Employers who discriminated on the basis of sex were protected by law—it was considered a part of the freedom of contract to base employment decisions on sexual stereotypes. This changed as a matter of federal statute only with the Civil Rights Act of 1964, and the Supreme Court first interpreted the Constitution to invalidate a gender classification only in 1971.[11]

Rules and norms worked together to enforce cultural limitations. In the early 1970s, our family lived near Louisville when my mother and other female teachers wanted to start wearing pant suits to school. It was both a norm and a rule for teachers to wear skirts and dresses, and before the female teachers could feel comfortable wearing pants, they had to ask for a ruling from the county board of education to permit it. My mother would not have been flogged if she had broken the norm. But absent a board ruling she could have been punished or reprimanded. More precisely, she *feared* such punishment or reprimand, and that was enough to keep her from wearing pants.

It's easy to see from the distance of half a century that for many women, the norms defined what was possible and appropriate. In the era when my mother decided to take advantage of her skills and education to get a paying job, she had essentially three choices: secretary, nurse, or teacher. She became a teacher, and she taught for twenty-six years. I asked her recently when she saw her first female doctor, lawyer, or minister. She was a grown woman in each instance—the first female attorney she ever knew, in fact, was a woman who graduated from high school a year before me, went to college and then law school, and returned to our home town to practice.

Culture has a great capacity to define the possible or the impossible, whether the culture operates at the level of the family, school, business, ethnic or religious group, or society generally. If the culture tells you that you are not equal, valued, empowered, or full of potential, then you can hardly be accused of lacking personal responsibility if you act as if you were unequal, valueless, powerless, or empty of potential.

If we had asked my mother fifty years ago whether she had any aspiration to be an attorney, a doctor, or the president of the United States, she surely would have said no. Her aspirations at the time—like those of millions of women—were formed in a cultural context that narrowed what she viewed as possible. It would not be meaningful to say that my mother "chose" not to become a doctor any more than I "chose" not to become an NFL lineman. It is not a choice when we fail to do something that never occurs to us to do because we think it is impossible.

One implication of this insight is that we cannot base our public definition of discrimination only on whether certain people "feel" discriminated against, or whether they aspire to have different opportunities. Looking back, it would have been a mistake to make the women's rights movement or the civil rights movement depend solely on whether a majority of the people who eventually benefited from these movements rose up and demanded change. A view of racial and gender equality must be based on views about justice, equality, and human dignity that are not founded

"You can be anything you want to be—no limits."

only on people's preferences, because those preferences were developed in cultural contexts of inequality and injustice.

This means that we should not base decisions about, for example, whether burqas are a sign of religious expression or sexual oppression by asking the women inside them whether they aspire to be outside. To convince someone that they have no choice is the perfect coercion, and the most perfect coercion will appear as choice.

3.

When looking at other cultures, or at our own culture years ago, it is easy to recognize the constraints on choice created by cultural norms. It is harder to recognize such constraints when we look around us. We are fish who do not recognize the water.

What are the mechanisms through which culture affects our choices?

Culture affects us not only by defining what is possible and impossible, but also by influencing how we interpret the world. Our cultural assumptions influence which facts we find salient and convincing, make us more likely to ignore the views of people who differ from us, cause us to interpret contested situations to accord with our worldview, and make us miss our own blind spots while ascribing others' blind spots to bad motives or ignorance.

In May 1993, the Pennsylvania Supreme Court heard arguments in the appeal of Robert Berkowitz, who had been convicted of raping a woman when they were both sophomores at East Stroudsburg State University. Berkowitz was convicted after a trial in the lower court, but he argued on appeal that what had occurred between him and the woman was not rape. Appellate courts usually take no more than a couple of months to decide criminal appeals. The Berkowitz case, however, raised such difficult issues that the court could not decide it for over a year.[12] To make the point I want to make with this case—a point about the power of culture—I need to set out the facts in some detail.

In the weeks leading up to the incident that brought about Berkowitz's arrest, he and the woman in question (who is not named in the court opinions) shared a cadre of friends and socialized together informally a number of times. He was twenty, she was nineteen. Some of their interactions had a flirtatious and sexual tone, including conversations about the size of his penis. The woman visited Berkowitz in his dorm room a couple of times after she had been drinking. On one of those occasions, she lay down on the bed next to him and, according to Berkowitz, asked him to show her his penis.

On the day of the incident, in the early afternoon, the woman again showed up at Berkowitz's room after she had been drinking. He was on his bed, napping. After he awoke, she told him that she had come to see his roommate, who was also a friend of hers. The woman left a note for the roommate, and as she was about to leave Berkowitz asked if she would "hang out for a while." She decided to stay for a few moments. He invited her to sit on the bed and to give him a back rub, but she declined, saying she did not trust him. She instead sat on the floor, and they had a conversation about her problems with a boyfriend.

After a few minutes, Berkowitz joined the woman on the floor and, according to the woman, "pushed" or "leaned" her backwards with his body, straddled her, and started kissing her. The woman said, "Look, I gotta go. I'm going to meet [my boyfriend]." Nevertheless, Berkowitz lifted her shirt and bra and began fondling her, and the woman said, "No." Despite the woman's continuing protests that she had to go and her persistence in voicing "no," Berkowitz continued to fondle and kiss her. He also undid his pants and tried to put his penis into her mouth. According to the court, "The victim did not physically resist, but rather continued to verbally protest . . . in a 'scolding' manner."[13]

Berkowitz "disregarded the victim's continual complaints" and later claimed that he did so because the woman was responding passionately to his kisses. As the court explained, "He conceded that she was continually 'whispering . . . "no"s,' but claimed that she did so while 'amorously . . . passionately' moaning. In effect, he took such protests to be thinly veiled acts of encouragement." He then locked the door to the room and, according to the woman, "put me down on the bed . . . He didn't throw me on the bed . . . It wasn't slow like a romantic thing, but it wasn't a fast shove either." Once the woman was on the bed, Berkowitz straddled her again, took off her pants and underwear, and entered her. At no time did the woman physically resist or scream out, but she did say "'no, no' to him softly in a moaning kind of way . . . because it was just so scary." Berkowitz remained inside her for approximately thirty seconds, at which time he withdrew and ejaculated.

The woman quickly dressed and left to meet her boyfriend, who, upon learning what had happened, called the police. A jury convicted Berkowitz of rape, and he was sentenced to a prison term of one to four years.

The question on appeal was whether what had occurred was rape. At the time in Pennsylvania, the statutory definition of rape did not hinge on consent but on force. Rape was "sexual intercourse with another person not one's spouse"—note the spousal exception—"by forcible compulsion . . . or by threat of forcible compulsion that would prevent resistance by a person of reasonable resolution." For the Pennsylvania Supreme Court, since the question under the statute was not one of consent but of force, the question in the Berkowitz case was whether he had forced the woman to have sex with him. Ultimately, the court held that no rape had occurred because Berkowitz had not used force. The court was swayed by the evidence that she had not physically resisted, that he had not physically prevented her from leaving, and that even though the door was locked the woman "was aware" that the "door could be unlocked easily from the inside" and that "she never attempted to go to the door or unlock it." The fact that the woman continually said "no" throughout the encounter was, according to the court, "relevant to the issue of consent," but "not relevant to the issue of force."[14]

This decision caused wide controversy. Women's groups protested; court watchers issued scathing critiques, saying the opinion was "one of the worst setbacks for the sexual assault movement in the last several years." A newspaper halfway across the country asked of the "all-male Pennsylvania Supreme Court," "What is it about the word 'no' they don't understand? . . . Obviously the court has a difficult time comprehending the most unambiguous word in the English language." Many states, including Pennsylvania, changed their laws to define rape in terms of lack of consent instead of the presence of force.[15]

But here is why this case is important for our discussion of the role of culture: according to a fascinating study by Yale professor Dan Kahan, the most important determinant in whether someone thinks what Berkowitz did was rape is *not* the statutory definition of the crime. It is not even the gender of the person making the determination.

The most important correlate in whether a person believes "no" means "no" is his or her cultural beliefs about the role of women in society. The group most likely to think Berkowitz did not commit rape is *women* who hold traditional, hierarchical views of gender roles.

As Kahan reports, "Individuals who adhere to a largely traditional cultural style, one that prescribes highly differentiated gender roles and features a commitment to hierarchical forms of authority and social organization more generally, are highly likely to believe that 'no' did not mean 'no' in *Berkowitz*." Surprisingly, these cultural predispositions affect traditionally minded women more than traditionally minded men. Kahan theorizes that this is because, in the traditional view, women say "no" when they mean "yes" in order to avoid the social stigma traditional norms would otherwise impose on women who engage in casual sex. Norms offer "scripts of sexual behavior, conformity to which apportions status within the cultural groups that adhere to them." So traditionally minded women "who have earned high group status by conspicuously conforming to these norms are the ones most threatened by the prospect" that women who use the no-means-yes strategy will get away with it without suffering reputational harm.[16]

In other words, traditionally minded women who abide by the rules are the ones most likely to want to punish those women who do not. In the *Berkowitz* case, that means that a jury of traditionally minded women would almost certainly have voted to acquit.

4.

Kahan has done important work in describing the mechanism by which cultural predispositions and "formative identities" affect individuals'

views, not only on issues of sexual violence but on other legal and political questions, such as the decriminalization of drugs, the regulation of
handguns, and gay marriage.[17] He argues that a person's core values affect
what facts the person infers about the world based on his or her perceptions. Values also affect whose opinions and arguments we tend to listen
to, acknowledge, and appreciate. All in all, deep cultural values and assumptions create "strong psychological pressure" on us to perceive the
world in ways that fit our views of how the world *should* work.

All this sounds accurate to me. Kahan analyzes culture at a high level
of generality and along only two axes—egalitarian norms versus hierarchical norms, and communitarian norms versus individualistic norms.[18]
But he is persuasive in showing that "egalitarians" perceive the world—
and thus law and politics—quite differently from those who fall into the
hierarchical camp, and that "communitarians" view the world quite differently from "individualists."

At one level, this is unsurprising. We know that traditionalists greet
their surroundings differently from those who subscribe to more progres-
sive, egalitarian norms, and we can easily understand that those who consider themselves individualists (a group that includes people who cite the
free market as their guide) usually reach different conclusions about political and legal questions from those reached by people who promote communitarian values. Culture affects people's viewpoints, and we can all in-
tuit the power of deep-seated cultural values over one's views of a range of
issues. In other words, culture and politics usually march in lockstep. This
seems true whether you define these values in terms of hierarchy versus
egalitarianism or along the more informal axes many of us would come up
with: urban versus rural, traditional versus hip, religious versus secular.

What is surprising is that in predicting how people around us will
think about any given political, legal, or social question, their cultural
values will often swamp other characteristics—such as race, gender, or
class—that we tend to focus on more. This means that if you are an attor-

ney for either side in a rape case, a sexual harassment case, or perhaps even in a sex discrimination case, and it is time to pick a jury, you should care more about the jurors' cultural assumptions than their race or gender.

Kahan's research also suggests that an individual's views about a wide range of political and legal questions will be remarkably stable over time. Change will come when core values shift and evolve, but that kind of change generally occurs slowly, if at all. What's worse, if Kahan is right, then the widespread assumption that people can be persuaded on the basis of facts—an assumption that underlies our belief in the importance of juries, legislative debate, scientific research, and books like the one in your hand—may be too optimistic. There may be little hope of changing people's minds unless we change strongly held cultural values and assumptions. This is probably not done through factual argument.

I do not want to imply that culture is unchangeable. It certainly changes eventually—just ask my mother, or Barack Obama. And sometimes the courageous acts of individuals, such as Lubna Hussein in Khartoum or Rosa Parks in Montgomery, Alabama, can challenge the cultural norms around them. When culture does change, it evolves through the individual acts of scores, then hundreds, then thousands, then millions of people. Sometimes this evolution occurs steadily, if incrementally; sometimes the forces for change build up with little apparent effect, only to have the pressure hit a "tipping point" where the new norms cascade through society.[19]

But meanwhile, from the standpoint of most individuals, cultural influences are pervasive and overwhelming. Just ask the thirteen women flogged for wearing pants.

5.

Perhaps the most important lesson about the power of cultural norms and assumptions is personal. If culture really does influence us in ways we do not recognize, it is probably essential that we be skeptical of our own perceptions and opinions. We should ask of ourselves a bit of humility, especially when we think we are sure about something that draws on cultural predispositions (that is, concerning most things that people actually argue over). We should be willing to "check our work" by articulating our assumptions and values. And we should be understanding toward those who vehemently disagree with us.

I know this kind of humility is damned difficult. It is not natural, especially for professor types who have sufficiently inflated egos that they would write a book trying to persuade other people what to think. I am lucky to have a spouse who challenges many of my assumptions about gender roles. I am fortunate to have been able to travel in cultural settings other than my own. And I am lucky that my boyhood home town of Princeton, Kentucky, is sufficiently different from my current home town of Cambridge, Massachusetts, that I am sometimes culturally uncomfortable in both places, and that this discomfort forces me to recognize some of my own cultural assumptions.

But I am not setting myself up as anything more than a person with the same problem of cultural bias that you probably have. Like most people who will read this book, I have friends who share most of my values and essentially live in the same cultural group. I do not go out of my way to talk to people who disagree vehemently with me. Who needs the hassle?

But this insulation comes at a cost. If we fail to recognize our cultural predispositions, we are likely to make some bad decisions.

My wife was recently walking to the subway from her job in downtown Boston when she came upon a mugging in progress.[20] A middle-aged woman named Barbara Pero had just retrieved her car from the valet at her daughter's condo when a crazed, vacant-eyed man pushed his way into her car and pulled a knife on her. The valet saw what was happening and started banging on the car and on the assailant with an umbrella. The assailant jumped out of the car, ripping Pero's purse from her hands, and ran up the street. The valet chased the knife-wielding assailant, calling for help. When the valet caught up, the assailant turned and swung his knife at him. The knife missed its target, and the assailant jumped into a car idling nearby. A police officer arrived and placed the assailant under arrest.

My wife and another woman happened upon the scene as the assailant grabbed Pero's purse and ran away, followed by the brave valet armed only with an umbrella. My wife tried to comfort Pero while the other woman called 911. The other woman told the dispatcher that a mugging had just occurred, and that the police should be looking for an African American who had just fled the scene.

Here's where the cultural assumptions come into play: the assailant was white. It was the valet, who protected Pero with only an umbrella, who was black. But the woman who saw the commotion of men fighting and then running up the street had seen the African American man as the assailant. Pero and my wife immediately spoke up, and the caller corrected the description.

But how often do such mistakes occur? Studies repeatedly show that eyewitness accounts are seriously flawed, in part because as the brain tries to process information in a moment of stress, it takes shortcuts. One of these shortcuts is the use of cultural assumptions to shoehorn what we see into what we *expect* to see.[21] Our cultural assumptions play on some of the cognitive flaws described in the last chapter. We often see what we expect to see, not because it is actually what happens but merely because we expect it.

The woman who called the police acted with the best of motivations. But she's a member of this society like the rest of us, and it is a society where petty criminals are routinely depicted in the news media as men of color. Even though we have elected an African American president, we have not abandoned longstanding racial stereotypes.[22] These stereotypes influenced the woman—unknowingly and innocently—to interpret what she saw in a certain way.

Culture can also create blind spots—things other people see but you do not. An example occurred recently in a Supreme Court argument over the Establishment Clause, the provision of the First Amendment that prohibits the government from establishing a religion. Some constitutional scholars believe this provision creates a "wall of separation" between church and state (although this phrase comes from a letter written by Thomas Jefferson and does not appear in the Constitution itself).[23]

The case concerned a cross that had been erected in 1934 on federal property in the Mojave National Preserve in California to commemorate the veterans who died in World War I.[24] The Supreme Court's case law about displays of religious symbols on public property emphasizes whether the display makes it appear that the government is endorsing one religion over others, or over non-belief. In the Mojave cross case, the government refused to have other religious symbols erected nearby, and the American Civil Liberties Union brought suit, saying that the cross endorsed Christianity and therefore amounted to an establishment of religion. Lower courts agreed and ordered that the cross be encased in a plywood box while appeals continued. Congress fought back, ordering the Interior Department to convey the small patch of land around the cross to the Veterans of Foreign Wars. The question before the Supreme Court was whether this land transfer was sufficient to cure the Establishment Clause problem.

At the oral argument, however, Justice Antonin Scalia wanted to engage the ACLU's lawyer on whether the cross was an establishment at all. Scalia wanted the lawyer to admit that the cross could be a commemoration of all war dead, not just Christian war dead:

> Justice Scalia: "The cross doesn't honor non-Christians who fought in the war?"
>
> Mr. Eliasberg [Counsel for the ACLU]: "I believe that's actually correct."

Justice Scalia: "Where does it say that?"

Mr. Eliasberg: "It doesn't say that, but a cross is the predominant symbol of Christianity and it signifies that Jesus is the son of God and died to redeem mankind for our sins, and I believe that's why the Jewish war veterans—"

Justice Scalia: "It's erected as a war memorial. I assume it is erected in honor of all of the war dead. It's the—the cross is the—is the most common symbol of—of—of the resting place of the dead, and it doesn't seem to me—what would you have them erect? A cross—some conglomerate of a cross, a Star of David, and you know, a Moslem half moon and star?"

Mr. Eliasberg: "Well, Justice Scalia, if I may go to your first point. The cross is the most common symbol of the resting place of Christians. I have been in Jewish cemeteries. There is never a cross on a tombstone of a Jew." [At this point, the transcript just says "Laughter."] "So it is the most common symbol to honor Christians."

Justice Scalia: "I don't think you can leap from that to the conclusion that the only war dead that that cross honors are the Christian war dead. I think that's an outrageous conclusion."

Mr. Eliasberg: "Well, my . . . point here is to say that there is a reason the Jewish war veterans came in and said we don't feel honored by this cross. This cross can't honor us because it is a religious symbol of another religion."[25]

According to reports of those present, Justice Scalia became visibly angry during the exchange. (Usually he gets laughs at the expense of attorneys, not the other way around.)[26] He was angered by the suggestion that Jews would not feel honored by a Christian symbol, and he thought it was "outrageous" to argue that a cross could not honor the dead of other faiths.

Justice Antonin Scalia.

Justice Scalia is not a humble man, and in this exchange he seemed to be flaunting a cultural blind spot. To him, crosses are the "most common symbol" of respect for the dead. But of course the reason he believes this is that we live in a majority Christian country, where most dead people have graves marked with Christian symbols. I doubt that Scalia would think it outrageous if Christian war dead did not feel honored by a war memorial erected in Israel using a Star of David. But to Scalia, a devout Roman Catholic, Christianity is the neutral position; it is the water and he is the fish.

Others on the Court sided with Scalia in this respect when the decision was released. The Court allowed the cross to stand. Justice Anthony Kennedy wrote a plurality opinion (meaning he won a majority for the result but not for his reasoning) noting that "although certainly a Christian symbol, the cross was not emplaced on Sunrise Rock to promote a Christian message . . . Rather, those who erected the cross intended simply to honor our Nation's fallen soldiers."[27]

The meaning of the cross in the Mojave Desert case is subject to cultural bias much as the word "no" was subject to cultural bias in the Berkowitz case. The problem for judges—especially cocky judges like

Scalia—is that they readily see the cultural biases of others ("How can you say that the cross cannot honor all war dead? That's *outrageous*!") but don't see their own.[28]

This lack of self-reflection is especially troubling in a judge. As law professor Don Braman noted about the case: "It may be cognitively difficult for someone with the cultural commitments of Justice Scalia to understand the cross as anything other than a universal symbol [of] profound respect, and to struggle with evidence to the contrary. But struggling with cultural blindspots is something we expect judges to do . . ."[29]

On the other hand, perhaps we should not hold Justice Scalia to a higher standard than we apply to ourselves. If we all have blind spots, there is no reason he should not too.

6.

If I am correct in arguing that deeply embedded cultural assumptions and biases influence us in ways we hardly recognize, then we should worry a great deal if the culture around us bombards us with messages that do not correspond with what we would believe if we considered things from a distance. The task for us is to identify the elements of culture that have these influences. In other words, we're fish that need to discover the water. If we do, some of the power that cultural norms have on our decision making may evaporate.

Of course it is impossible for me to recognize all the influences around me, any more than you can identify all those around you. But let me mention a few:

Patriotism and nationalism. In 2009, a ten-year-old Arkansas boy named Will Phillips made waves in his Washington County elementary school by refusing to stand for the Pledge of Allegiance.[30] He did so to protest the lack of equality for gay and lesbian Americans—he said he would not say the pledge until there was truly "liberty and justice for all." Of course it was his right under the First Amendment to refuse the pledge, but that did not protect him from reprimands from teachers or ridicule and bullying from other students. Will deserves admiration rather than correction, since his act gives others a chance to snap out of the rote recitation of the pledge and listen to what it articulates: a promise of loyalty to our country's banner.

Not all of us may want to promise such loyalty, at least not unconditionally and out of habit. Patriotism is so customary for us that it sometimes disables critical thought. Yet the mere suggestion of that possibility would get you shouted down in most classrooms, public forums, or bars around the country. Laws requiring the pledge to be recited at the beginning of each school day, and the practice of singing the national anthem before the start of any significant sporting event, have the effect of instilling and celebrating national pride. That is a worthy goal. But such patriotism comes at a cost, especially when citizens of other countries are also socialized to believe in the exceptionalism of their own nations. The cultural norm of patriotism makes it much more difficult for citizens in each country to recognize the ways in which their respective nations have acted poorly toward others or would stand to benefit by learning from others.

There are, of course, benefits to socializing citizens to have pride in our nation—we have much to be proud of. These benefits erode, however, if patriotism is not only pervasive but unthinking.

Consumerism. Some of us call shopping "retail therapy" since we shop when we're happy, stressed, or depressed. Malls are our new public squares, where seniors power walk, teenagers cruise for flirtation, and middle-aged professors try out new electronic gadgets. We teach our children at an early age that one of their primary roles in life is as consumers—one of the newest children's stores spreading across the country is called BuyBuyBaby.

After September 11, our leaders asked us to express our patriotism by buying something. President Bush urged Americans to "fly and enjoy

America's great destination spots. Get down to Disney World in Florida. Take your families and enjoy life, the way we want it to be enjoyed." New York Mayor Rudolph Giuliani said, "Go to restaurants. Go shopping. Do things. Show that you're not afraid." Florida Governor Jeb Bush asserted that "we need to respond quickly so people regain confidence and consider it their patriotic duty to go shopping, go to a restaurant, take a cruise."[31]

As my colleague Juliet Schor has written, "In contemporary American culture, consuming is as authentic as it gets. Advertisements, getting a bargain, garage sales, and credit cards are firmly entrenched pillars of our way of life. We shop on our lunch hours, patronize outlet malls on vacation, and satisfy our latest desires with a late-night click of the mouse."[32]

If this focus on buying and consuming is the culmination of centuries of progress in determining our needs and desires and satisfying them with earned wealth, then this trend is to be applauded. If, however, it comes from Americans' being "manipulated into participating in a dumbed-down, artificial consumer culture, which yield[s] few true human satisfactions,"[33] then it is a significant social loss.

Religiosity. The most despised people in America are atheists. Notwithstanding the popularity that defenses of atheism enjoy at the bookstore (see *The God Delusion* by Richard Dawkins or *God Is Not Great* by Christopher Hitchens) or on Netflix (*Religulous* by Bill Maher), it is still the atheist who consistently tops the Gallup Poll list of people Americans would refuse to vote for. Another study conducted by the University of Minnesota found that respondents ranked atheists below Muslims, recent immigrants, gays and lesbians, and all other minority groups in who was perceived to share "their vision of American society." Americans are also less willing to allow their children to marry atheists than any other group.[34]

Religious belief is embedded in our everyday lives. Religious statements are inscribed on our money, and religious institutions occupy valuable real estate in our cities and towns. We begin sessions of Congress with a prayer, start Supreme Court arguments with a cry that "God save the United States and this honorable Court," and commemorate presidential inaugurations with a national prayer before hundreds of thousands of celebrants. Every calendar year culminates in the celebration of holidays—Thanksgiving and Christmas—that are religious in meaning and origin.

Most Americans have not moved from their childhood faith. If you include in this group people who have merely shifted from one Protestant denomination to another, more than 70 percent of Americans currently profess the religion in which they were raised.[35] Another study found similar results, concluding that "nearly three out of every four American adults said they are the same religious faith today as they were during their childhood. That means the most common faith journey that people take is to form spiritual commitments as children and teenagers that typically last for the duration of their life."[36]

The reason for this consistency may be that each of us believes he or she has found the Truth. The search for that truth, personal or collective, needs to be protected and encouraged. But the insistence on religiosity may be less a product of rigorous search than of multigenerational habit and socialization. No reasonable God would expect that, and no society is well served by it.

Gender roles. Notwithstanding the advances in gender equality over the past generation and the courageous ground-breaking by numerous men and women, our culture continues to serve up generous helpings of tradition and hierarchy when it comes to the roles of men and women inside and outside the home. Try this the next time you watch television: actually watch the commercials. Take special note of commercials about the home—anything about appliances, food, cleaning products, or children. *Every* one of them assumes that the woman of the house prepares the frozen pizza for the family, nurses sick children with motherly love and VapoRub, mops the kitchen floor with a Swiffer, and pretreats the kids' grass stains before she washes and dries the clothes. In commercials as well as television sitcoms and dramas, women drive cars only when men are not available. In crime dramas, women disproportionately are the victims rather than the heroes.

This does not affect only women. Men are assumed not to be caretakers of their kids. When I go to parent-teacher conferences with my son and his mom, most teachers address their comments to her. When he is sick and we take him to the clinic, most doctors talk to her as the principal decision maker. In divorce proceedings in most states, the presumption is that the kids will stay with the mother.

We have undoubtedly come a long way since my mother received *The Pastor's Wife* as an engagement gift. But we have a long way yet to go before we come close to genuine equality, even in our portrayals of our own culture. And these portrayals have an impact. Most women still mechanically adopt their husband's name when they marry, and those who do not are seen to be making some kind of statement. Meanwhile, when my wife and I were married not a single person asked me if I was going to change my name. Women are encouraged to develop their own careers, but they also have to make sure they keep the home in good condition (or hire other women to do so for them). If children come along, it is assumed that it will be the mother who presses the "pause" button at work to bring up baby. (When my son was born, a senior colleague boasted to me that he had never missed teaching a class after the birth of his children.)

Of course, people should be able to choose how they organize their family lives. The risk is that the culture of sex and gender roles is so pervasive that most people make automatic choices without considering the many possibilities.

Sexuality. The struggle for sexual autonomy and independence has been a part of the fight for women's equality for decades if not centuries. One of the touchstones of inequality is the lack of power to decide for yourself with whom you share your sexuality. This lack of sexual empowerment is a badge of inferiority.

My worry is that we have replaced a culture of sexual inhibition and inequality with one of sexual exploitation and inequality. Fast forward from the old days to 2009, when seventeen-year-old Miley Cyrus performs a stripper-like pole dance while singing her song "Party in the USA" on the nationally televised Teen Choice Awards in Los Angeles. In the words of author Ariel Levy, "An interest in [strippers and porn stars] used to seem like a way of resisting the status quo. Now it feels like a way of conforming." Levy answers Erica Jong's 1970s paean to female sexual freedom, *Fear of Flying*, by admitting that she "would be happier if my daughter and her friends were crashing through the glass ceiling instead of the sexual ceiling . . . Sexual freedom can be a smoke screen for how far we *haven't* come."[37]

Sexual freedom has to be a good idea, if by freedom we mean the ability to choose for ourselves how to display and enjoy our sexuality. But sexiness by itself may not be freedom. It depends whether it is done mindfully or mechanically. As Levy argues, "The proposition that having the most simplistic, plastic stereotypes of female sexuality constantly reiterated throughout our culture somehow proves that we are sexually liberated and personally empowered has been offered to us, and we have accepted it. But if we think about it, we know this just doesn't make any sense."[38] Choices need to be made available: "If we are really going to be sexually liberated, we need to make room for a range of options as wide as the variety of human desire. We need to allow ourselves the freedom to figure out what we internally want from sex instead of mimicking whatever popular culture holds up to us as sexy. *That* would be sexual liberation."

This chapter, like the last, ends with questions. Do all of our biases, assumptions, and influences constrain us so much that we have no genuine choice in the way we organize our family life, decide the guilt or innocence of a criminal defendant, or elect whether to stand to recite the Pledge of Allegiance? Sometimes I feel the presence of culture around me, but usually I do not. Sometimes I feel my own choices being constrained or coerced, but usually I do not. Yet culture is so powerful that my feelings about my own decisions may not be the best indicator of whether my choices are truly my own.

Once we acknowledge that we are subject not only to the cognitive defects and biases outlined in the previous chapter but also to pervasive cultural influences, we have to acknowledge that we are less autonomous than we would like to believe. We are subject to more influences than we easily admit. We should thus question the independence of our own decision making, especially when it coincides with the cultural norms of those around us.

The essayist Judith Warner has written about the constraints facing mothers in deciding whether to work outside the home: "Why this matters—and why opening this topic up for discussion is important—is very clear: because our public policy continues to rest upon a fictitious idea, eternally recycled in the media, of mothers' free choices, and not upon the constraints that truly drive their behavior."[39]

What Warner says about mothers applies more broadly. We should not comfort ourselves with the belief that we, and everyone around us, are choosing our positions in life. Instead, we should focus on the constraints that bedevil and bewilder all of us.

5
Choice
and Power

I'll make him an offer he can't refuse.
—Vito Corleone in *The Godfather*
(Mario Puzo, 1969)

When a man cannot choose, he ceases
to be a man.
—Alex in *A Clockwork Orange*
(Anthony Burgess, 1962)

IF YOU HAPPEN TO LIVE in a college town, you may sometimes see on your favorite café's bulletin board an advertisement from a scientist asking for volunteers to serve as test subjects for a research project. Some want smokers, others want insomniacs, still others call for any average Joe or Josephine.

Some time ago, one such advertisement in a small city asked for volunteers to help with a university research project about how people learn and remember. Volunteers were paid well for an hour of their time. Let's imagine you were one of those who agreed to participate.

When you arrive at the research facility, you are paired with another volunteer, whom you have never met before. A middle-aged, distinguished man dressed in a scientist's white lab coat explains that you and your partner will be participating in a project testing the effect of punishment on learning. He tells you, "One theory is that people learn things correctly whenever they get punished for making a mistake. Actually, though, we know very little about the effect of punishment on learning, because almost no truly scientific studies have been made of it in human beings."[1] This experiment, he explains, is designed to gather evidence about whether punishment affects the learning process in any way, and it calls for one of you to be the "learner" and one the "teacher." The teacher will be asked to teach the learner a series of word pairs, using punishment to encourage fast learning. You are told you can leave the experiment at any time.

If you're like me, at this point you'd be a little nervous. I certainly would not want to be the learner. Who wants to be punished for failing to remember some random word sequence?

The scientist says that the fairest way of determining your roles is to draw from a hat. You draw first, and "teacher" is written on your slip of paper. You breathe a sigh of relief. Your glance at your partner, who seems apprehensive but is not backing out.

The scientist then escorts you into the testing area, which has two small rooms. In one room, your partner is strapped into a chair and an electrode is attached to his wrist. The scientist explains that the punishment will come in the form of electric shocks, which might be "extremely painful" but will "cause no permanent damage." The researcher applies a small amount of paste to the learner's arm underneath the electrode "to avoid blisters and burns." He tells you that the electrode is attached to a shock generator in the next room.

You are then taken into the room with the shock generator. About the size of a stereo receiver, it sits on top of a desk next to a clipboard and microphone. On the clipboard is a series of word pairs running down the page. You are to recite the word pairs ("blue box," "nice day," "wild duck") into the microphone, which pipes your voice into the room next door. Then you are to go back through the list again, stating the first word

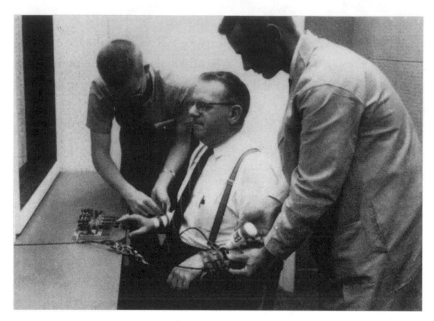

The experiment setup.

in each pair ("blue") and offering a multiple choice of words ("sky," "ink," "box," "lamp") as the second word in the pair. The learner is supposed to recall the correct second word, reciting it back to you through a microphone in front of him.

If the learner fails to remember a word pair correctly, you are to administer the punishment by flipping one of the thirty switches on the shock generator, sending a momentary current to the electrode on your partner's wrist next door. Each of the switches is labeled with a voltage designation ranging in 15-volt increments from 15 to 450 volts. The lowest four are labeled "slight shock." The next four are "moderate shock," then "strong shock," "very strong shock," "intense shock," "extreme intensity shock," and finally "danger: severe shock." The final two switches are labeled simply "XXX."

To show the reality of the shocks, the researcher gives you a "sample shock" by applying an electrode to your wrist and flipping the switch corresponding to 45 volts, a "slight shock" according to the diagram on front of the generator. A light above the switch flashes, an electric buzzer sounds, and you feel a shock that makes you sit up and take notice. It does not make your teeth clatter, but it is not pleasant. Incentive enough to get an answer correct.

So the experiment begins, and you read the word pairs, and you hope the learner is concentrating. You begin the multiple choice portion of the experiment, and the learner has difficulty remembering the proper responses. He gets more wrong than right. With the first wrong answer, the researcher instructs you to flip the first switch—15 volts. On each subsequent wrong answer, you are told to move up the board to the next switch: 30 volts; 45 volts; 60 volts. At 75 volts, you hear a little grunt come from the learner next door. Another mistake leads to a 90-volt shock, and another grunt.

By this time, you are probably not feeling confident about the research project. You certainly don't think it's cool to go around shocking someone just because they failed to remember a pair of words correctly. You turn to the researcher, sitting at a desk nearby, and ask whether you should continue. He says, "Please go on." So you do.

At 120 volts, the shock you administer is equivalent to sticking a fork in a household outlet. The learner shouts out that the punishments are getting painful. You hesitate again, and the researcher says, "Please go on. The experiment requires that you continue." At 135 volts, you can hear painful groans. At 150 volts, labeled a "strong shock," the learner shouts out, "Experimenter, get me out of here! I won't be in the experiment any more! I refuse to go on!" You look at the researcher and he says, "It is absolutely essential that you continue. You have no other choice, you *must* go on."

What do you do?

If you haven't done it already, you would call off the experiment, insist on freeing the learner in the next room, and walk out. You would then call the police and report the mad scientist to the authorities. At least, that's what I would *hope* I would do, and no doubt you do too. But we probably wouldn't.

I.

The experiment just described was the work of Yale scientist Stanley Milgram, who conducted hundreds of such tests in New Haven in the early 1960s. He was not actually testing the effect of punishment on learning. That was a ruse. The real subjects of the experiment were the teachers: Milgram wanted to see how willingly they would inflict pain on others when instructed by a person in authority.

The design of the experiment was brilliant, if ethically troubling.[2] The learner was in on the ruse and the role selection was rigged—both slips of paper in the hat said "teacher" so that the real volunteer would always become the teacher. The electrode attached to the learner's wrist in fact carried no current, and the learner's responses, both his mistakes and his reactions to the supposed shocks, were precisely choreographed. The researcher's instructions were also exact: any time a teacher hesitated or questioned the procedure, the researcher responded with a sequence of increasingly insistent verbal prods. If the teacher continued the experiment, the learner's pleas became more emphatic as well. After 150 volts, he was consistently to demand to be let out of the experiment. At 180 volts, labeled "very strong shock," the learner was to cry out, "I can't stand the pain." At 270 volts, there was to be an agonized scream. After 300 volts, an "extreme intensity shock," the learner refused to provide answers to the test, and the researcher insisted that a failure to answer should be considered a wrong answer and punished with a shock. At 315 volts, the learner violently shrieked and yelled again that he did not want to continue the test. After 330 volts, the learner was to act as if he had lost consciousness. The experimenter continued to insist that the test go on until all the shocks have been administered, all the way past "danger: severe shock" to the 435- and 450-volt switches that were labeled simply "XXX."

If you were the teacher in such an experiment, how far do you think you would go before refusing to administer more shocks? Would you give any at all? Would you stop once the learner cried out that the shocks were getting painful? When he shouted his refusal to go on? When he refused to answer the questions? Or after he fell silent? Are you confident that you would maintain your refusal even if the researcher insisted that you had no choice?

Is there *any* way you could see yourself administering shocks at the top end of the board, where the labels indicate that you are inflicting severe pain—or worse—on an innocent volunteer?

Milgram wondered about this too, and he asked a number of people if and when they would stop the shocks.[3] He explained the experiment to over a hundred college students, psychiatrists, and other middle-class adults. Every single one believed—as you and I believe—that they would stop the test at some point. Half said they would halt the shocks at 135 volts or below, soon after the learner started complaining about the pain. Only a handful predicted they would administer shocks above 210 volts, and no one thought they would continue past 300 volts, the point at which the learner refuses to provide any more answers. Milgram also asked people to predict what others would do. Most predicted that only a lunatic would administer the most severe shocks. The psychiatrists predicted that only one person in a thousand would obey the researcher all the way to the end.

Milgram's experiments have become famous mostly because of their disturbing results. Everyone he questioned vastly underestimated the willingness of the teachers to shock the learners. More than 60 percent of the teachers were willing to obey the researcher all the way to the end, where they shocked the learner three separate times with 450 volts, labeled "XXX."[4] Of the fewer than 40 percent who refused at any point, half nevertheless administered shocks labeled "intense" or "extreme intensity." In all, more than 80 percent of the teachers administered eight or more shocks of increasing severity even after the learner cried out in pain and demanded to be released from the experiment.

Milgram varied the experiments to see what would affect the willingness of teachers to administer the shocks. If the researcher left the room, the teacher was more willing to disobey his commands. The closer the victim was to the teacher, the less willing the teacher was to shock him.[5] If the teacher was forced to administer the shocks by holding the learner's hand to a plate of metal, the obedience level fell by half. Even so, almost a third of the teachers were willing to administer the highest shock on the board by physically forcing the learner's hand to a shock plate.

One of the most significant results had to do with the impact of group pressure.[6] In one version of the experiment, the teacher worked with two other teachers who were actually confederates of the researcher. One of the fake teachers read the word pairs; the other said whether it was correct. The one teacher not in on the ruse—the real subject of the experiment—was to administer the shocks. Above 150 volts, when the learner shouts out his refusal to take part, one of the fake teachers rebels and stops participating in the experiment. The second fake teacher defies authority a few shocks later. In this situation, only 10 percent of the subjects continued to administer shocks until the end, compared to 60 percent when the subject teacher was working alone.

Group pressure worked the other way, too. In one design, the teacher-subject worked with another teacher—in on the ruse—who seemed to be administering the shocks. The teacher-subject performed subsidiary acts necessary for the experiment to proceed, but never administered the shocks himself. In this design, more than 90 percent of the teacher-subjects willingly participated in an experiment they had reason to be-

How far would you go?

lieve was causing lethal harm to an innocent person. Fewer than 8 percent rebelled.

One remarkable thing about Milgram's experiments is how constrained the subjects reported feeling. The teachers were not physically compelled to participate and could have left at any time. If they objected to administering the shocks, they only had to face the stern voice of the researcher, telling them to go on. Yet in interviews after the tests, many explained their actions by saying they had no choice. One subject said that he "had to follow orders," another said she "had to do it," another noted he felt "totally helpless" and in an "impossible situation."[7]

Milgram's experiments have become famous because of their obvious implications for our thinking about the role of authority in decision making. His motivation for this study was the still-fresh memories of Nazi Germany. How could so many seemingly good people acquiesce in the mass murder of millions of Jews and others? In our own day, we cannot study Milgram without thinking about the role of authority in the mistreatment of prisoners at Abu Ghraib prison in Iraq, or in the use of terror against innocent civilians in London, Madrid, or New York City. (Milgram died in 1984, at the age of fifty-one, before seeing these modern implications of his work.)

In the words of Milgram's former colleague Jerome Bruner, who wrote the foreword to the 2004 reissue of Milgram's book *Obedience to Authority*, Milgram showed us "that there are predisposing conditions in our culture, perhaps in any culture, that prime us to 'follow orders,' however those orders may seem on second thought. Not all of us go along, to be sure, for there are always competing impulses to stick to one's own inner convictions—as there were in Milgram's experiments. But for all of that, we follow orders."[8]

One might think that Milgram's test would not work today. His experiments were performed before the cultural upheavals of the 1960s, before Watergate, before the nation's fixation on personal responsibility and autonomy. But two present-day researchers (working under modern ethical guidelines) confirmed his basic findings in separate studies at Ohio State and Santa Clara University.[9] A British television special also reconstructed the experiments in 2006 and came up with largely similar results. While television should never be mistaken for science, the episode did make for interesting viewing because it showed its subjects administering what they believed to be extreme shocks to another person. In 2010, a French documentary filmmaker staged a fictitious game show in which "contestants" posed questions to a man strapped in what looked to be an electric chair. Neither the contestants nor the raucous audience knew the electric chair was a fake, but nearly 80 percent of the contestants continued to shock the man for wrong answers even after he begged to be released. Some participants shocked the man until he appeared to die, all the while being egged on by the audience.[10]

"The most remarkable thing," wrote Dr. Jerry Burger, who headed the Santa Clara study, "is that we're still talking about [Milgram's] work, almost 50 years after it was done." His experiments are both troubling and enlightening. Most people obeyed, but some did not. Obedience rates can be manipulated. The situation matters, as do the people around you and what they're doing. We might not be able to say what any particular individual will do, but we have a good idea of what most people will do most of the time. We follow orders.

2.

As I write this chapter, it is winter. My wife, son, and I have just returned from a hike through a local forest with our dog Murphy. During the hike, we made our way across a frozen pond, where some enterprising kids had cleared the snow from a part of the ice to make a place for ice skating. While we were there, another father was enjoying the spot with his son, who looked to be about six years old. I noticed them only when I heard the father call out urgently to his son: "Move away from there!" The boy had eased up to one edge of the pond, where the water falls over a spillway in summer. The flow was only a trickle, but the ice there was noticeably thinner—gray-brown rather than blue-white. The son looked up at his father quizzically but didn't move. The father was probably fifty feet away, and now moving quickly toward his son. His second command was even more urgent: "Don't question me now. The ice is thin there. Come here now!" The son still looked confused, but he started walking toward his dad away from the spillway. The crisis was averted.

It was averted because the son followed an order.

Obedience is often a good thing, and our individual urge to obey certainly has deep roots in our respect for and trust in our parents. More broadly, the tendency to obey surely has an evolutionary source.

Moreover, much of the socialization that occurs in school emphasizes the importance of respecting elders, following directions, and pledging allegiance.

As a parent, one of the most difficult lines to draw is how to encourage personal accountability but also respect and deference. We do not want our children to "decide for themselves" if they are standing on thin ice, running after a ball thrown into a busy street, or bantering with a creepy stranger on Facebook. As long as the subject is not electronic gadgets, music, or sixth-grade math, parents usually do know best.

A key decision for parents is when to allow questions and when to require obedience from our children. Which situations demand obedience, and which are opportunities for children to decide things for themselves, make their own mistakes, and learn personal responsibility? I have no easy answer. Different parents, different cultures, and different generations may answer this question differently. My guess—based on my own experience—is that a good number of parenting disagreements between spouses (or, worse, ex-spouses) are about this very thing.

As we think about the nature of choice, it is important to recognize that this parenting decision is simply the question Milgram's subjects were asking themselves about their own behavior. When should I obey? When do I have the freedom to question? As adults, we are our own parents.

We face this issue daily in various ways and talk about it in various guises. "Go along to get along." "Pick your battles." "Don't rock the boat." Sooner or later, these norms are sufficiently internalized that it takes real courage to question authority. And when we do, authority does not always take kindly to it.

A friend of mine—let's call him Pete—was recently in New York's Penn Station after a night on the town with friends, waiting for a late-night train to his home in the suburbs. Pete and his buddy noticed a twentysomething woman nearby, clearly drunk. She appeared to be waiting for a train of her own, along with a couple of other young women. But the friends ambled off, leaving the first woman passed out on a bench.

If you met Pete, you'd probably want him as your friend. He's a personable, smart, and athletic guy in his twenties who works hard and plays hard. He has a job on Wall Street, but its ethos of "me first" seems not to have seeped into him yet. He's the kind of guy who'd return a found wallet, help an older gentleman find his glasses on the subway, or back you up in a bar fight. You would want him on your side.

And if your daughter were passed out on a bench in Penn Station in the middle of the night, Pete is the kind of guy you'd want sitting close by. He would unobtrusively keep an eye out for her, without being creepy.

On this night, Pete noticed that a disheveled, shoeless man was standing over the drunk woman, rubbing himself inappropriately. Pete and his friend yelled at the man to get away. He ignored them. Pete saw a policeman nearby and walked over to let him know what was happening. The cop said something to the effect that he couldn't take care of everyone passed out in Penn Station.

At this point, Pete had a choice. Go along to get along? Or rock the boat?

Armed with the courage of several beers, Pete questioned the officer. "Well, you should take care of her." When the officer again refused, Pete grew angry. "That's fucked up."

From the policeman's standpoint, Pete and his friend became the threat, not the man standing over the passed-out woman. Pete was angry and failing to sit down and shut up. Two other cops arrived. The first officer threatened to give Pete a citation for disorderly conduct. When Pete protested, one of the new cops pointed to a plate glass window and told Pete: "You see that window? I am going to put your head through that if you don't shut up."

"Are you kidding me?" Pete responded. "May I have your badge number?" The cop told Pete and his friend that if they didn't walk away they'd be arrested.

Pete finally backed down and went back to his seat. The homeless man by this point had walked away. The woman's companions came back, and thanked Pete and his friend profusely for looking out for their passed out friend. Pete and his friend caught their train.

The point is that in the real world, questioning authority takes real courage and has risks. It is no wonder that questioning was so difficult in Milgram's laboratory.

One can understand why police officers are so insistent on obedience. They often must seize control of a situation that could quickly spin dangerously out of control. The best way for them to seize control is to assert their authority by using a commanding voice and imposing physical presence. Unfortunately, however, they often internalize the norm of requiring obedience, so that any questioning of them brings reflexive pushback. And then they sometimes go too far. Pete got off easy.

Others have created more of a stir. Harvard Professor Henry Louis "Skip" Gates was arrested on his own porch for loudly questioning the behavior of Cambridge police officers who came to investigate a supposed break-in at his house. The charge was disorderly conduct for "exhibiting loud and tumultuous behavior, in a public place"—his front porch— "directed at a uniformed police officer . . . [which] caused citizens passing by this location to stop and take notice while appearing surprised and alarmed."[11] The charges were quickly dropped, but Gates's experience became a national lesson in how police officers do not take kindly to boisterous questioning and opposition. (When President Obama initially took Gates's side in the conflict, it also became a national lesson in the *political* costs of questioning the actions of the police. Obama recanted within forty-eight hours and then hosted the famous "beer summit" between Gates and the arresting officer.)

Of course police officers are not the only people in authority who insist on obedience and make it difficult to question them. You may remember the story about my third-grade teacher, with which I began this book. She would tell it differently, I'm sure. To her, it was about a headstrong kid who refused to play by the rules. To me, it is a story about how questioning authority brings costs.

It is also worth emphasizing that the costs of questioning increase if you are already marginalized or at risk. A friend of mine—Ivy League educated, a graduate of Harvard Business School, a business executive in Chicago—tells me that he's warned his children that they should *always* obey whatever a police officer tells them to do, even if they think it's incorrect. *Do not question.* The reason? He and his children are African American. He says he learned this lesson while in college, the hard way: face down, on the sidewalk, in handcuffs.

3.

Given the way we are socialized to obey by our parents and schools, and seeing the many costs we must bear when we disobey, it is no surprise that the urge to play by the rules is so strong. Indeed, the tendency is so strong that we often obey even to our detriment.

In October 2009, self-help guru James Arthur Ray hosted an event in Sedona, Arizona, which he entitled "spiritual warrior" training. In his early 50s, tan, and ruggedly handsome, Ray has quite a following. He describes himself as a "catalyst for personal transformation."[12] He has appeared on Oprah and Larry King, and his book *Harmonic Wealth: The Secret of Attracting the Life You Want* is a best seller. He stars in countless self-help seminars around the country, speaking to thousands of people who pay to hear his motivational message of self-empowerment. The business magazine *Inc.* named Ray's company one of the nation's fastest growing, with revenues approaching $10 million.

For the Spiritual Warrior event, fifty or so participants paid almost $10,000 to spend five days learning from Ray. The culmination of the training was a "vision quest" in which the "warriors" were to stay alone in the desert without water or food for thirty-six hours, followed by a return to camp for a two-hour "purge" in a sweat lodge. The sweat lodge, about 24 feet wide and 4 1/2 feet tall, was "a makeshift structure covered with blankets and plastic and heated with fiery rocks" vaguely modeled after similar structures used in some Native American religious ceremonies.[13]

There was space—just barely—for the fifty "warriors" to squeeze in around a fire pit, kept hot by fresh coals brought in by Ray's assistants over the two hours. Ray sat beside the tent flap, keeping it sealed.

What happened next is a perfect case study of the power of authority.

About halfway through the ceremony, some of the participants started to become ill from heat and dehydration. Ray urged them to press on. The heat grew more and more oppressive. A man named James Shore, a forty-year-old from Milwaukee, tried to lift up one of the walls of the lodge to allow fresh air to circulate, but Ray chastised him, saying he was being "sacrilegious." Some people vomited. Ray explained that vomiting was good for them, and that it was part of the purging process. Others started to pass out. James Shore dragged out a woman who had fallen unconscious, but he returned. As people became more distressed, Ray repeatedly told participants, "You are not going to die. You might think you are, but you're not going to die."[14]

A few people struggled out, but most stayed. "There were people throwing up everywhere," said one participant. Ray hovered by the door, intimidating people if they tried to leave. "Play full on" was his catchphrase. "You have to go through this barrier." One man pushed his way out of the lodge, thinking he was having a heart attack and was about to die. According to reports, Ray did not summon medical help and instead commented that "it's a good day to die."[15]

At the end of the two-hour ordeal, several of the participants were indeed near death. One of them was James Shore. Another was a thirty-eight-year-old woman from New York named Kirby Brown. Both died later that evening. A third, Liz Neuman of Minnesota, forty-eight, was taken to a hospital, where she fell into a coma and died a few days later. In all, almost half of the participants ended up in the hospital, suffering from injuries as severe as scorched lungs and organ failure.

What happened? Why did people stay in the lodge, risking their health and even their lives? Any one of them could have left at any time— just as Milgram's teachers could have done. Ray "highly encouraged" them to stay, but he did not exert physical force. The police report simply explains: "Participants thought highly of James Ray and didn't want to let him down by leaving the sweat lodge."[16] Ray was arrested in connection with the deaths and, after a four-month trial, convicted of negligent homicide.

Knowing what we know about the human tendency to obey orders and respect authority figures, we should not be surprised that so many participants put themselves at risk by staying in the lodge. The irony is that this was a self-help event ostensibly designed to help participants take control of their lives. Instead they were put in a situation where they were physically and emotionally weakened, subjected to undisclosed risks of physical injury and death, and intimidated by an authority figure whose validation they cherished.

The "warriors" may have seen the sweat lodge purge as a test of courage. *Do I have the strength of will to withstand the heat? Am I brave enough to take the pain of the purge?* In hindsight, we understand that the purge was seen as an act of courage only because Ray had identified it as such. Staying in the lodge was in fact dangerous and harmful, with no real benefit. It was courageous only in the way that forcing yourself to break your own finger with a hammer is courageous. In hindsight, the genuine act of courage was to question Ray's methods, ask about the risks, demand care for those in distress, and leave the sweat lodge. But that demanded the emotional and psychological wherewithal to challenge the authority figure. It is a measure of the difficulty of such a challenge that most people in the lodge were more willing to risk injury or death than push their way through the tent flap.

I attended a self-help event in the late 1990s, held in one of the World Trade Center towers. The two-day seminar, for which I paid several hundred dollars, was focused on helping participants make better decisions and take control of their lives. Thinking back on it now, I realize that much of the training was not about teaching people to act from strength but intimidating them to act from weakness. At the beginning of the event, people were asked to stand up if they were not committed to the process. Those who stood were then challenged to explain to the hundreds of people in the room why they had doubts. It did not take long for most people to sit down. (I never stood up. I remained seated not because I was committed to the process, but because I was not sufficiently committed to my skepticism to stand up and explain it.)

After a few hours of self-help medicine, we were asked to promise to return from lunch at the appointed time and not be tardy. It was ostensibly a measure of how prepared we were to take responsibility for our decisions and actions. I remember hurrying back from getting a sandwich. But I wasn't motivated by self-empowerment or a sense of responsibility. I was scared of being ridiculed by the leader if I was late.

Many self-help experts are truly focused on helping people take control of their lives and make better choices. Unfortunately, many gurus and religious demagogues do the opposite—take advantage of our tendency to respect authority and obey rules in order to build a following and to assert an intimidating influence over those followers. When churches or self-help businesses become more about the charisma of the leader than about the needs of the audience or congregation, there is a risk that people are in fact being led *away* from self-empowerment and toward dependence on an authority figure.

Of course, behavior sometimes needs to be changed. We might need the harsh words of a physical trainer to prepare us for a race, or the demands of a drill sergeant to prepare us for combat. We might need a doctor in a lab coat to instruct us to eat less fatty food. We may need a parent to tell us to move away from thin ice. And we may need the words and charisma of a self-help guru to help us build habits that are emotionally, socially, and physically healthy.

But we now know that these beneficial effects take advantage of the same tendency to respect authority and follow orders that allowed Ray to incite people to risk their lives. It is the same tendency that allows police officers to induce confessions from suspects without overt coercion, or to get people to agree to have their luggage searched. It is the same tendency that caused hundreds of people to follow cult leader Jim Jones to Guyana and commit suicide at his command. It is the same tendency that makes sexual harassment by bosses in the workplace a serious concern. It is the same tendency that allowed the sexual abuse of children by members of the clergy to remain hidden for so long.

4.

Like cultural norms and influences, our tendency to obey rules and respect authority undermines our ability to make genuine choices. Without recognizing it, we tend to follow along in situations when we should not. We obey in times when we should dissent. We remain silent when we should speak up.

But also like culture, the influence of authority is not so great that we are under its spell all the time. Influence is not coercion. We cannot predict with certainty when we will succumb. And we *should* succumb much of the time. Police officers, teachers, parents, and stop signs, for example, generally deserve respect and obedience.

Having said that, what each of us experiences as an exercise of will is often a product of more than our own atomistic processing of values and analysis. Our will is also partly a product of the influence of authority and rules, along with cultural norms and assumptions, processed within the limitations of our cognitive biology.

I want to make sure I am not misunderstood. I am not saying that the teachers in Milgram's studies had no choice but to shock the learner, and I am not saying the spiritual warriors in Sedona were coerced by their own psychology into staying in the lethal sweat lodge. What I am saying is that the influence of power on our decision making is significant, and it often acts without our recognizing it, often to the detriment of ourselves or others. We should be wary of the sway authority has on our decision making, so that we are less likely to be manipulated by those who understand its effects and use it for selfish purposes. It also makes sense to institute protections against the influence of authority in contexts where its misuse might be particularly harmful. Protections against sexual harassment in the workplace, bans on teacher-led prayers in school, and Miranda warnings after the arrest of a suspect, to pick just three examples, make eminent sense. The same reasoning points toward greater protections against the use of "consensual" searches by police. At present, there is not even a requirement that the person searched be informed that he or she has the right to refuse.

More importantly, we would be better off if we established more room for dissent in our daily lives. Even though it would create some difficult moments in our schools and families, we should try to engender in our children the insight and strength of character necessary to speak up when something does not sit right with them.

There are models for this kind of behavior. I am thinking of not only famous dissenters and questioners such as Martin Luther King, Jr., or Edward R. Murrow. Role models do not have to be so lofty. They can be people like my friend Pete, whom we met earlier challenging a police officer to do his job.

Or they can be like Jan Rensaleer, an industrial engineer who was one of Milgram's original subjects more than fifty years ago. Described as "mild mannered and intelligent" by Milgram,[17] Rensaleer provides a wonderful counterexample to the teachers who blindly obeyed the researcher and then sought to shift responsibility for their actions to the situation. Rensaleer began the experiment and obeyed the researcher during the early stages. At the 150-volt level, when the victim complained and cried out, Rensaleer paused and asked the experimenter what he should do. The experimenter told him to continue, and he did, with hesitation. He administered several more rounds of shocks, but then at 255 volts, he pushed away from the desk and turned to face the experimenter. "I can't continue this way," he said. "It's a voluntary program . . . the man doesn't want to go on with it." The experimenter told him that the "experiment requires that you go on." Rensaleer held his ground: "The man, he seems to be getting hurt," and "I know what shocks do to you. I'm an electrical engineer, and I have had shocks . . . and you get real shook up by them . . . I'm sorry."

Clearly, Rensaleer was conflicted, and he was apologetic to the authority figure. But his empathy for the victim caused him to overcome his discomfort.

The experimenter pressed on: "There is no permanent tissue damage," and "It is absolutely essential that you continue." Rensaleer maintained his disobedience. The experimenter finally countered with "You have no other choice."

Rensaleer turned indignant. "I *do* have a choice," he asserted. "Why don't I have a choice? I came here on my own free will. I thought I could help in a research project. But if I have to hurt somebody to do that, or if I was in his place, too, I wouldn't stay there. I can't continue. I'm very sorry. I think I've gone too far already, probably."

After the experiment was called off, he was asked who was responsible for shocking the learner, before he had refused. Many of the other subjects had projected the responsibility onto the experimenter—it was his experiment, they said, and he insisted that the shocks continue. Rensaleer refused to do this. "I would put it on myself entirely . . . I should have stopped the first time he complained . . . I think [it] is very cowardly . . . to try to shove the responsibility onto someone else."[18]

This is personal responsibility in its most genuine form. It is worth emulating.

"I *do* have a choice," we can say.

6
Choice
and the
Free Market

There's small choice in rotten apples.
—William Shakespeare, *The
Taming of the Shrew*, c. 1590

Money, it turned out, was exactly like sex, you
thought of nothing else if you didn't have it and
thought of other things if you did.
—James Baldwin, 1961

WE ALL KNOW THE CONVENTIONAL WISDOM: the free market is the embodiment of robust, unlimited choice. That's why it's called the *free* market. In its current state, it lets us choose among approximately 45,000 items in the typical grocery store, millions of songs on iTunes, scores of vacuum cleaners at Best Buy, and more than twenty different flavors of Coca-Cola available in the United States alone. (The list includes such favorites as Coke Lime, Diet Coke Black Cherry Vanilla, Coca-Cola Citra, and Coca-Cola with Raspberry.)[1] The free market allows us to spend our money on Snuggies to warm us while we watch television, nose-hair clippers to keep us well groomed, orthopedic dog beds to keep our pets comfortable, child-sized treadmills to ensure our offspring get their exercise, and products like the Electronic Feng Shui Compass that "locates and calculates energy fields," allowing buyers to "align [their] physical surroundings to match [their] intentions."[2]

The ability to buy or sell products without the approval of a feudal lord, parish priest, or mob boss is a mark of modernity and liberty. The ability to buy what we want is tied to our individualism; we define ourselves in part by what we buy. We can be a Hummer or a Prius; Old Navy or Brooks Brothers; Bud Light or Amstel Light; Xbox or Wii. I am a Suburu Outback, Banana Republic, Guinness, Playstation kind of guy. Once you know those preferences, you can guess many other things about me. After all, these market choices not only help us decide who we are, they also identify us to others.

The story of markets, whether supermarkets, flea markets, or capital markets, is a story of choice. The conventional wisdom is that markets embody and nurture choice, and choice embodies and nurtures markets. Often ignored is how markets constrain and limit choice.

I.

Here is the typical narrative of the free market. If people can freely choose, the theory goes, then they become better off over time. In a free market, no one forces us to buy the Snuggie (OK, I actually bought one), fancy dog beds (we bought one of those, too), or nose-hair clippers (no, although my son thinks I need them). Conventional free market economic theory says that because all such purchases are voluntary, rational people will buy these products only if the purchase makes them better off. If having the Big Mac makes you happier than keeping the four dollars in your pocket, then you buy it. You are then, by definition, better off after the purchase.

A mark of success for an economic system is how well it produces an abundance of choices for buyers and sellers and thus allows more people to satisfy more of their preferences more perfectly. By this measure, our economy is wildly successful. You or I can walk into our local Target or Costco and purchase anything from raisin bread to car wax. If what we want is not available in a physical store, we can go online and browse for hours on Amazon.com or other sites. Compared to the limited consumer choices available to billions of people around the world, we in the United States and other rich nations are surrounded by abundance.

The right to buy and sell is important not only for products. The right of individuals to sell their labor to those who would pay them a wage is such an important ideal that you could even say the United States fought a civil war over it. Slavery is, among other things, a ban on the selling of one's own labor. With a free market for labor, you are assured that if you can add value by way of your effort, knowledge, or charisma, then you can derive additional income. The free market allows us to earn millions of dollars as hedge fund managers or NFL quarterbacks.[3]

So the market is a powerful and beneficial thing.

One of the almost magical effects of the free market is the "price mechanism"—the translation of the preferences and choices of millions of us into prices and wages. If we like a product, we are willing to pay for it. The more of us who are willing to pay, the more the supplier can charge, and vice versa. In this way, prices themselves embody information about people's desires and tastes. If we value something, it has a high price; if we don't, it doesn't. That in turn means that resources flow, as economists say, toward "their best and highest use." The free market allows finished products to be purchased by those who value them the most, since if someone else valued the product more they would simply outbid the other buyers. That prices fluctuate to reflect the preferences of potential buyers means that products end up, almost by operation of an invisible hand, with those who want them most.

The same can be said about raw materials, investment capital, or human labor and expertise. As long as the prices for those things are allowed to reflect the choices and preferences of those who want to buy them, these goods will flow to those who are willing to pay most for them. And as long as those willing to pay the most are the people who value them the most (although this is a problematic assumption), then all of those resources will flow to their best and highest use.

This story about the markets helps explain why economic libertarians hold up free choice as a fundamental value. Markets embody choice—look at how many things you can choose! And equally, markets depend on choice—if we all are free to choose, the market allocates resources to those who desire them. If choice is limited, the story goes, then people are less able to satisfy their preferences and thus worse off. What's more, if choices are limited or certain preferences declared off limits, markets themselves work less efficiently because prices—and therefore resource allocation—will be skewed. The moral of this story is that we should not, say, impose rent control on apartments or ban marijuana. If we did, apartments would become too hard to find, and people would have to pay a black-market premium for their glaucoma medication.

But much conventional wisdom about the glory of unfettered markets is simply wrong.[4] We should be less confident about the benefits of markets bestowing choice, or of choice empowering markets, than economic theory would suggest. The market also *limits* choices. Rather than being the locus of freedom and individual empowerment, markets may be constrictive, manipulative, and invasive. Perhaps ironically, markets need to be controlled in order for people to enjoy genuine choice.

At one level, this point is mundane. Even the most ardent free marketeer would acknowledge that some limits on markets are necessary. The most uncontroversial of these limits is an insistence on disclosure and truthful information. The price mechanism does not work if market participants can lie to one another with impunity, so anti-fraud laws and disclosure laws are a common market constraint. They are justified by arguments about choice—our market decisions are not genuine unless we know what we're buying.

But it would be a mistake to depend on disclosure and anti-fraud requirements as a cure-all. Sometimes, information can be overwhelming, so more disclosure of arcane data can hurt as much as it helps. (The best way to hide a lie is to bury it in a mass of inconsequential truths.) Sometimes, disclosure is meaningless, especially if there is nothing you can do with the information. I seem to get disclosures from my credit card companies all the time. Do I do anything about them? No. Could I if I wanted to? Maybe, but probably not. I have to have credit cards to move through this modern world of ours, so my ability to opt out of a credit card agreement is subject to my ability to find another card with better terms. And given the market power of credit card companies and the lack of market power of most credit card consumers, that's difficult. At the very least, it's difficult enough to see that disclosure cannot be a panacea for lack of market choice.

In any event, lack of information is not the most fundamental constraint on choice that markets bring about. Let's talk about a few others.

2.

I only knew one of my grandfathers, and he actually wasn't one. Albert Carroll, whom my siblings and I called Abby, was my mother's stepdad. He married my mom's mother, Noona, about the time my mom started college. He brought stability and a tireless work ethic to the household, but also the gruffness and severity of a man who had worked his entire adult life as a coal miner. Starting when he was seventeen, he began each work day by riding a tram, conveyor belt, or elevator deep into the earth, where he dug the black ore that fueled the nation's furnaces and steel plants. He never had another job.

One of my earliest memories is shopping with Noona at her small town's general store, which was owned by Abby's employer. When it came time to pay, Noona retrieved from her purse a booklet of coupons,

Noona and Abby.

emblazoned with the coal company's name and various dollar amounts. She used the coupons to pay for her groceries and sundries. I asked about the coupons, and she explained to me that they were a kind of money that she could use only at the company store.

Only later did I come to understand that those coupons were what was called scrip, a medium of exchange often used in mining communities. The mining companies would pay the miners in scrip instead of cash, and the scrip was redeemable for goods only in stores owned by the company. Because of the closed system, the company could charge a premium for its products. If a miner ran out of scrip, he could ask for an advance on his wages, which was also paid in scrip. The system often drove miners deep into debt to the company: low wages paid in scrip, scrip used to buy overpriced goods from the company, loans from the company paid in scrip. This cycle created an obligation on the part of the miner to continue working to pay off the debt.

The problem of scrip was made famous in the United States by the singer Tennessee Ernie Ford, whose "Sixteen Tons" was the Billboard number one song in the nation for six weeks in 1955. The chorus went:

> You load sixteen tons, and what do ya get?
> Another day older and deeper in debt.

Saint Peter don't you call me, 'cause I can't go.
I owe my soul to the company store.[5]

My dad sang this song to me growing up; I use it with my own children as a lullaby. (The song was actually written by Merle Travis, whose version I prefer to Ford's. I only know this because I found it among the millions of choices on iTunes.)

Coal companies cannot lawfully pay wages in scrip any longer. It even may have been illegal to pay Abby in scrip back in the 1960s, when I saw Noona carrying her coupon books.[6] Scrip was outlawed because it was exploitative. The power the coal company exerted over its employees was too great.

But notice something. The scrip system was not a market perversion but its perfection. No one was coerced, and economists would say that no one was acting irrationally. The coal miners were not prisoners—they could quit at any time. And because they were acting voluntarily, the theory is that they were better off working for scrip than whatever the alternative was, which probably was not working at all.

This is why economic reasoning often seems obtuse and out of touch. To say that coal miners in the days of scrip and debt servitude were acting voluntarily is a misunderstanding of what "voluntary" means. There was coercion everywhere. Miners were not prisoners marched at gunpoint to the mines. But Abby had to feed his family; there were few other jobs to be had, and no better ones for someone with his skills; he had no way to move on; and the wage came in the amount and form the company offered. "Take it or leave it" is not a real choice when "leave it" is not an option. Abby was in the same boat as Henry Lamson—he of the hatchet-in-the-head case in chapter one.

Abby's example shows why markets do not necessarily provide a way for people to improve their lot. They simply enable people to engage in exchanges. Those exchanges inevitably benefit the parties that are already more economically powerful, because they can extract more from the exchange. If you have little economic power, there is nothing inherent in the market exchange that makes you better off than before. All an exchange ensures is that the deal you "voluntarily" agree to is better than your other options. If you have no other options, then an exchange can make you *worse* off. You can spiral downward, little by little, as the unfavorable exchanges add up. You have to make some kind of deal, and all the choices are bad. There is nowhere else to sell your labor, nowhere else to go, and no way to subsist on air and dirt.

In other words, if you're given a choice between being pushed down an open elevator shaft or pushed down a staircase and you rationally pick the latter, it doesn't mean that you weren't pushed, aren't going down, and won't get hurt on the way to the bottom.

3.

Markets are amoral. There is no good or evil in markets, no just or unjust. There is only "willing and able to pay for" and "not willing and able to pay for." You don't get out of markets what you deserve—you get what you can negotiate for, based on the information you have and what you have to offer in exchange. And if you don't have much or know much, you don't get much.

Your wage is not based on what you need but on what your employer is willing to pay you. And your employer's willingness to pay may not depend on the added value you create for the company. If markets have their say, your wage would depend not on what you produce but on how much the company would have to pay your replacement. If you're a coal miner, your wage does not depend on the value of the coal you dig but on what the company would have to pay the guy standing outside the gate looking for work. If you're an associate at a law firm, you make the market rate for associates, not what the firm bills from your work. And if you're a recent liberal arts graduate, you might be lucky to make a couple bucks an hour plus tips at Joe's Crab Shack. Wages are competitive only in a competitive market, and a worker is not guaranteed anything other than what he or she can get by threatening to walk away.

This applies whether we are talking about your labor or your money. What we have to pay for bread and milk is not based on how much we need them but on how much everyone else is willing and able to pay. Just as your wage is pushed down if someone will do your job for less, the costs of things you buy will go up if someone will pay more.

So markets are not the perfect embodiment and celebration of choice. What we have to pay for things is dependent on others. What we earn is dependent on others. What products are available is dependent on others. What jobs are available is dependent on others. Moreover, an empty wallet is not a problem that markets race to fix. By definition, if you have nothing to trade in an exchange, markets ignore you. If your resources are thin, the market is no longer a source of abundant choices. Since markets allocate even basic necessities according to our ability to pay for them, if you cannot pay then the market does not provide them. The market becomes a way to limit choice.

In fact, if we remove the hazy presumptions of economic deism from our eyes, the world around us reveals the limits of markets. There is nothing magical about markets that raises the living standard of any given person over time. Billions of people are desperately poor and not getting better off as markets reach them. As Jon Jeter notes, "With more cash spinning the globe faster than ever, 1.3 billion people now live on the equivalent of less than $1 per day. Half the world's population—3 billion people—survive on only twice that, or about 25 cents less than each cow in the European Union receives per day in government subsidies."[7]

The problem of market-created scarcity and inequality does not just affect the developing world. Even in the richer nations, scarcity is real. In the United States over the past generation, the richest of the rich have seen their wealth and income skyrocket, both in absolute and relative terms. Meanwhile, working people in America are struggling, often working longer, in less secure jobs, for pay that has been largely stagnant in real terms since the early 1970s. More and more working Americans are crushed by financial obligation, and the poverty rate recently hit a new high, with nearly one in seven Americans qualifying as poor.[8] After each day of work, they are another day older and deeper in debt.

All this is to say that markets provide choice only if you have something to pay with. Nothing limits choice like scarcity. For millions of people in the United States and billions throughout the world, markets are a source of powerlessness.

4.

If you've ever been in a casino, you know that both money and hours can vanish without much apparent help on your part. Windows and clocks do not exist. Lighting does not change: it could be 3 o'clock in the afternoon or 3 o'clock in the morning. Attractive young women in sexy outfits offer free drinks as long as you play. Fresh air is pumped in continuously. When you win at the slots, lights flash and bells ring, and the slots that the casino calibrates to pay out at a higher rate are placed in high-traffic areas where more people will witness your victories. Brain scientists have shown that when we win at slots, our brain experiences a rush of pleasurable dopamine, and because of the randomness of winning our brain is unable to adapt to reduce the dopamine the next time.[9]

When you win at craps, other gamblers around the table win too, so you're cheered onward and slapped on the back. Casinos track how much you gamble and give you extra benefits (such as free rooms) if you're a high roller, like airlines giving frequent flier miles. Casinos are laid out like mazes, difficult to navigate, so you can't walk through quickly. Ceilings are low, giving gamblers a sense of safety, intimacy, and privacy. Some casinos reportedly use "mood-influencing" aromas, to make us more open to the suggestion that we release our grip on our cash. Everything about the casino environment is crafted with sophistication intended to separate us from our money.

Perhaps the cleverest tactic is the use of chips. When you step up to a blackjack or craps table to gamble, the first thing you do is exchange your cash for chips. Then you bet with chips, in various denominations. I don't gamble much, but when I do, I quickly stop thinking of chips as money. I throw down a twenty-five-dollar chip on a craps table much sooner than I would ever put down twenty-five dollars in cash. The cash seems real to me—and why risk my hard-earned cash on a roll of the dice?—but a chip is just a piece of plastic. I'm much more likely to gamble longer and for higher stakes than if I had to put cash on the table for each bet.[10]

There is no coercion in casinos (setting aside gambling addiction). Everyone there chooses to be there. But everything about the environment is constructed with the knowledge that people can be manipulated. Perhaps not every one of us, every time. But enough of us succumb often enough to make running a casino a winning proposition, and going to casinos a losing one. Casino owners drive Bentleys; habitual gamblers take the bus.

Casinos understand that human decision making is done in the contested space of our conscious and subconscious, habit and intention. Our rationality is a battleground, and casinos are smart and greedy enough to fight hard on that field.

Casinos are markets perfected, but choice perverted. Rather than being places where people coolly measure their options and make decisions based on the various costs and benefits, markets are often places where people make unreflective decisions that are the product of manipulation and habit. Manipulation is a genuine source of constraint on choice in markets.

To economists, this is not a problem. To economists, markets depend on rational actors who use their own preferences to make choices. The theory of efficient markets depends on this notion because markets allocate resources properly only if people's choices are voluntary. As long as choices are voluntary, they are rational to economists' eyes.

It's worth pointing out how thin the economists' view of rationality really is. Something is rational because you choose it. If you voluntarily cut off your finger because the pain you feel is outweighed by the pleasure you will receive from showing off your new scar, then you have acted rationally. Economists do not consider it their business to question the substance of your choices, just that you made them voluntarily. Economists also do not care whether you used your higher faculties to make your choice. In fact, Richard Posner, perhaps the leading thinker in the field of scholarship called law and economics, wrote in his seminal book *Economic Analysis of Law* that it would not be a mistake to "speak of a rational frog."[11] To an economist, a frog is acting rationally when it chooses to sit on this lily pad rather than that one. If it preferred the other, it would move. Because it hasn't, we assume it has chosen this one. Because the frog's choice is voluntary, it has acted rationally to satisfy its preferences.

Economists are not terribly worried about manipulation within markets. Unless the manipulation consists of someone physically forcing you to buy, sell, consume, or produce something, your act is voluntary. You have made a choice, and your choice, by definition, is rational.

Thankfully, most of us are not economic theorists. We understand that rationality should mean more than sitting on this lily pad rather than that one. People's choices can be better or worse, and voluntariness is something of a sliding scale.

One of the classic methods of manipulation in markets is creating or taking advantage of various compulsions. The cigarette companies' infamous manipulation of nicotine levels is an obvious example—creating demand by creating a physical need in smokers for the next nicotine hit.[12] A cousin of mine who worked for a large cigarette company told me once that making cigarettes was like printing money. This rings true, simply because the product they sell creates the need for more of the product.

But cigarettes are not the only product for which people develop physical or emotional dependency. Alcohol, of course, is another example, and gambling addiction is a real phenomenon. Also, scientists are increasingly worried about the addictive characteristics of various foods, especially fast foods. The craving that many of us get for a Big Mac when we drive by a McDonald's is in part a physical reaction to the salt, starch, and sugar in the sandwich.

Of course this raises the question of what compulsion is. If it means that a person has no control at all over his or her physical actions, then compulsion and addiction are very limited problems. Even heroin addicts have *some* level of control over whether they continue to use.[13] But we can recognize that our choices are the outcome of a range of inputs, many of which we're not conscious of. These factors might not force our behavior as strongly as true compulsions do, but nonetheless they constantly pressure us toward irrational decisions. And here we can recognize why companies spend so much on advertising and marketing.

From a company's perspective, if it can create compulsions for its product, great. But influences that fall short of compulsion also work. Marketers know that we are more likely to buy products presented at eye level than placed elsewhere on the shelf. They know that we're more likely to buy a product if it's near a more expensive product, so the latter item becomes the "frame" in which we compare prices. They know to put a product on sale, so that its old price becomes the comparative frame for the new price. When we shop for goods that have variable prices, like homes or cars, sellers know to provide a high "anchoring" price that keeps our bargaining within a narrow band.

Marketers know that if they tell us a product is in short supply, that we need to "act now," or that the product is available only to a select few, then we will rush in, elbows out.[14] (Remember the craze for the Wii, Cabbage Patch Kids, or initial public offerings of common stock in 1990s-era Internet start-ups? We *really* want what we cannot have.) They know that associating their products with a celebrity who has a positive image will mean that customers will subconsciously link their positive feelings toward the celebrity with the product advertised. And let's not forget the bikini effect, where marketers spark a craving in the brain's pleasure centers with a visual or other sensory cue, and then offer a way to satisfy the craving that may have little to do with the original cue.

5.

You may be thinking at this point: "Hey, being an addict is one thing. Buying a product because it's at eye level or because it's on sale is another." You're right. We have to ask: in thinking about constraints on choice, should we care about influences that fall short of compulsion but affect our decision making most of the time? Or even some of the time?

I think we should. While some decisions we make in the marketplace are conscious, deliberative acts using our higher brain functions, many are based on habit or subconscious influences that we are not aware of and thus cannot easily evaluate. It makes complete sense that our brains do this. If I weighed every possible option for every possible purchase each time I shopped for groceries, I would never leave the store. The fact that my brain acts out of habit or looks for cognitive shortcuts when sorting through thousands of choices is a good thing. It saves me hundreds of hours a year.

In fact, we often look for shortcuts to improve our decision making. Think about all the instances when you pay someone to make decisions for you, or to use their expertise to limit your choices to a manageable few. My wife and I are renovating our kitchen as I write this, and we are at the stage of choosing a faucet, sink, appliances, and tile. If these decisions were left to me it would likely be a disaster. So my wife takes the lead, with the advice of experts, whom we pay. Much of the benefit the experts provide amounts to limiting our choices to a handful of options, or making the decisions themselves.

The more complicated the decision, the more I want someone else to make it. A couple of years ago, I went to a specialist for advice about some headaches and weird sensations in my inner ear. After an examination, the doctor asked if I wanted an MRI. She would order it if I wanted, but would not insist on it. I did not want to make the decision—I wanted to say, "Look, you're the doctor. *You're* supposed to tell *me* whether I need an MRI." Sometimes we want to be told what's best. (I ended up having the MRI, which showed that my head was fine.)

We can be overwhelmed by much simpler and more mundane decisions than whether to get a brain scan. You'll remember the jam experiment I mentioned in chapter two. Some shoppers were offered a large variety of jams to sample; others were offered only a few.[15] The shoppers offered more options actually decided to make a purchase less often. They had more difficulty choosing. Shoppers offered fewer choices not only bought more jam, they were happier with the jams they chose. They worried less about whether they might have liked the boysenberry more than the raspberry. Even where our biology and situation give us a good amount of freedom, we are easily overwhelmed by choice.

It is only natural for our brains to look for shortcuts, to make as many decisions as possible without involving our higher faculties. In a complex world, worrying about everything is a recipe for mental illness. To avoid this, our brain understands the adage "Don't sweat the small stuff." When choices are complicated, unfamiliar, numerous, or overwhelming—from decisions about jam to brain scans—we need cognitive shortcuts and aids to make decisions.

Here is where advertising and other marketing efforts have their effect. In the free market, companies do not care whether we buy their product after making a cool, rational decision, balancing all the pros and cons. In fact they would prefer that we act out of compulsion, habit, or craving. If they can push our purchase decision from the conscious into the subconscious, from the considered to the habitual, they can rake in the cash.

Thus they have every incentive to find better ways to influence us. If they are really good at it, then the influences will be invisible to us. We'll feel like we're acting autonomously when we experience a Big Mac attack or put another coin in the slot machine. And if they are *really* good, they will not only influence us about ways to satisfy our preferences, they will create completely new preferences that only they can satisfy. They can manufacture our desire and then manufacture ways to satisfy it. How many of us knew we wanted iPhones before they existed? Now it's hard to think of oneself as a member of the middle class without one.

My point here is that, contrary to economic theory and the rhetoric of marketers everywhere, markets are not a Garden of Eden of choice. Each of us depends on mental shortcuts, and we all delegate to our subconscious as much decision making as possible. In response, our subconscious becomes a battleground for all kinds of influences. In the free market, people and companies have every incentive to fight hard for this contested ground.

It is not that we have no control over what we buy, or that all of our tastes are manufactured. But the feeling of free will we have when we purchase something is often misleading. In fact, that feeling itself may be manufactured. From the standpoint of marketers, the perfect product is one that is purchased out of habit or compulsion, but which the purchaser feels he or she has exercised free will and rationality in choosing.

6.

In discussing how the so-called free market limits choice, we've thus far focused on scarcity and manipulation, both of which are inherent in markets. Markets also restrict choice because of their pervasiveness. Markets are so powerful that it is virtually impossible to opt out of them, even for things that our society does not want to allocate based on ability to pay.

I've mentioned several times by now my home town in Kentucky. My childhood memories include Norman Rockwell scenes of perusing Superman comics in the downtown magazine store, shopping for baseball pants at Finkel's General Store, and eating the blue plate special at the lunch counter near the courthouse. (I try not to whitewash my memories completely—our downtown movie theater was still racially segregated when I was in high school, fifteen years after the Civil Rights Act.) About the time I went away to college, Walmart opened a store on the outskirts of town, and it was an instant sensation. Their prices were lower. They had everything in stock. And it was all under one roof, from comic books to baseball pants to lunch counters. The effect was exactly what you would imagine. The family-owned businesses downtown could not keep up, and eventually most of them failed. In effect, the town's center of gravity moved from the courthouse square to the Walmart parking lot.

This was not completely a bad thing. Many people were able, in the words of Walmart's current slogan, to "save money" and "live better" because Walmart was there. Sometimes businesses *should* fail, especially when faced with competitors that are better.

But consider this: the change in the town brought about by everyone shopping at Walmart was not a choice in any meaningful sense. It was the result of thousands of individual decisions about where to buy things. The nature of markets is that the decision about what kind of town you want is chopped up into thousands of individual decisions about, for example, whether to get a twenty-dollar hammer at the downtown hardware store or a fifteen-dollar hammer at Walmart. The ultimate effect of the two decisions—you keep a lively downtown with the twenty-dollar hammer and end up with no downtown with the fifteen-dollar hammer—is invisible until it happens. And then there is no going back.

Markets allow you to "vote" with dollars (or Euros, or rupees), and that's fine when you're voting on which hammer offers the most value. But sometimes, your vote on the hammer is also a vote on the nature of your hometown. That's not a decision that should be atomized. It should not be the unintended product of thousands of individual purchasing decisions, especially when the cost of each decision is hidden and borne by others. Markets elbow aside collective decision making with their focus on individual decision making. Even if we wanted collectively to object, the market does not offer us a mechanism to voice that objection other than with money. And no one wants to be the chump who spends twenty dollars for a hammer in the hope of saving his hometown if everyone else is buying fifteen-dollar hammers anyway.

This problem of markets chopping up big decisions about important things into little decisions about money is known as a "collective action" problem. Markets do not provide ready ways for people to act collectively, to make decisions about big things. There are thousands of other examples. Clean air and water, adequate public transportation, and access ramps for the disabled—to pick just three—are choices that markets simply do not provide. Absent government regulation, a company that pollutes will produce its products more cheaply. Absent government subsidies, public transportation will be too expensive for people to use. Absent a government mandate, no business will spend the money for wheelchair ramps. If we want to live in a society where we have clean air and water, public transportation, and the ability of the disabled to be part of society, we have to elbow markets aside and make those decisions in another way. On its own, the market will commodify everything, including the decision to have a hometown or not, to have clean air or not, or to treat people fairly or not. The "prices" of those decisions will be hidden in products and services all around us, whether we like it or not.

Markets not only commodify decisions that ought to be made in other ways. They also commodify things that ought not be bought and sold at all.

For one example, consider the horrible choice facing Rab Nawas.[16] Nawas is a farmer in rural Pakistan who fell into debt to his landlord. He had asked for a loan because he owed money for his wedding and he needed cash to pay off medical bills for his wife and six children. His poverty would make it impossible for him to pay the bills on his own, so a loan from his landlord was his only option.

Then his landlord demanded payment, and Nawas had only two things of any value to sell: his children or his own body parts. He chose the latter. He contracted with a local broker to sell a kidney to a "transplant tourist," most likely someone from Europe, Australia, or the United States who needed a kidney and was willing to pay. Nawas now sports a foot-long scar on his lower back, acquired at a "kidney center." In return, he was paid around $1,600. But he's now less able to work, because his strength and stamina are not what they used to be.

Nawas explained his decision this way: "I am helpless. Should I sell my children? Should I go sell my children? So, it's better I sell my kidney."

Nawas's decision is not unusual. Organ selling has become prevalent around the world. In Pakistan, a poor farmer can sell his kidney for $1,600. In Brazil a kidney can fetch $10,000, more than a decade's wages for some. Some newspapers in Africa carry classified ads offering cash for organs. The broker stands to make substantial income, since organ recipients pay as much as $150,000. Organ brokerage is such a lucrative business that, according to the World Health Organization, about a fifth of all kidneys transplanted worldwide come not from charitable donors but from the black market. This market has even gotten a toehold in the United States: in 2009 the FBI arrested a New Jersey man for matching organ "donors" in Israel with recipients in the United States.[17]

Even though it is illegal in most countries, organ trafficking is a thriving business. In the words of *Newsweek*, "Most of that trade can be explained by the simple laws of supply and demand."[18] The market values what people are willing to pay for, and it is no surprise that some will pay a lot of money for a desperately needed kidney. Where the market has its say, even our bodies become commodified.

It is thus no surprise that Nawas's other choice was to sell his children. The sale of children, especially girls, has become a sickening fact of life in many areas of the world. In Malaysia, baby selling is "big business" for crime syndicates.[19] The syndicates run prostitution rings staffed with poor peasant women, deny the women the use of contraceptives, then steal the resulting babies. The babies are then sold for as much as $50,000, presumably to couples unaware of how they came to be.

But Nawas's children would not have been sold to couples in the West who wanted children. In all likelihood they would have ended up as prostitutes. The trafficking of both girls and boys into prostitution is rampant. According to UNICEF, more than a million children a year are trafficked for sex, and more than half of the children who are forced into sex slavery are under sixteen. In Pakistan, the sale of Afghan refugee girls is "thriving," with prices ranging from $80 to $100, depending on the color of their eyes and skin and whether they are virgins. In some villages in Thailand, as many as seven out of every ten families have sold at least one daughter into the sex trade, at prices ranging from $100 to $900.[20]

Trafficking is not just a problem in developing countries: about 25 percent of the world's sex tourists are from the United States, and news reports of American parents selling or pimping their children are becoming more common. In 2010, two parents in Georgia allegedly offered their fourteen-year-old daughter to a local car dealer. They were late on their payments on the family minivan, so the parents forced their daughter to perform sex acts on the dealer in lieu of their car payment. The parents and the dealer were arrested.[21]

It might be easy for us to think of this as a faraway issue. I do not fear that my own children will ever be sold, notwithstanding the occasional cinematic thriller that presents the horrible possibility.[22] I also do not worry much about the need to buy a kidney, although that might change quickly if I or a loved one contracted kidney disease. But whether or not you feel that sex slavery or organ trafficking touches your life, the fact is that markets have a persistence that is virtually impossible to resist. Eventually, everything gets monetized. If children and body parts have market value, it is no surprise that the market also monetizes sex, votes, wombs, and lives.[23] (My son told me that people sell their souls on eBay. There is a soul for sale as I write this, with an opening bid requirement of $500. No one has placed a bid yet, with nine hours remaining in the auction. Another soul has a current bid of ninety-nine cents. That soul's owner was thoughtful enough to offer free shipping via email.)

In one sense, the market's pervasiveness—its insistence on monetizing *everything*—is a measure of how much it prizes choice. If you want to sell your daughter, rent out your womb, or buy sex services, a free market will provide you that choice. We can also choose *not* to sell a daughter, rent a womb, or buy sex.

What a market does not offer is the choice to not have these things monetized. By their very nature, markets cannot give us a choice to protect our most prized and sacred things. And once they become monetized, something important is lost—their pricelessness.

We cannot use markets to limit the things markets can buy and sell. We have to use law. In order to have the choice to live in a society where children, organs, or sex services are not sold, we have to limit the kinds of choices people can make in the market.

It is undoubtedly true that the market provides us with an incredible range of choices. Just walk into your local superstore and witness the abundant options available to you. At the same time, the market restricts choice in ways that are just as profound, if more often ignored. Because it allocates everything according to who can pay, you don't have choice if you don't have money. The market gives marketers incentive and opportunity to exploit our tendency to make unreflective decisions. It monetizes everything—including our children, our sexuality, and our decisions about what kind of society we want to live in—whether we want to commodify those things or not. The pervasiveness of markets makes it nearly impossible to opt out of them.

Like the constraints on choice posed by the makeup of our brains, the power of culture, and our tendency to obey authority, pervasive markets operate to keep us within narrow bounds. We revel in the choice we have when we shop at Target or surf through hundreds of television channels. But the offering of so many consumer choices makes it difficult to see how we're constrained and left open to manipulation.

There is one choice the market will not provide: a way to limit markets.

III

What
to
Do

7
The
Problem with
Personal
Responsibility

Bartender, make it straight and make it two—
One for the you in me and the me in you.
—Melvin B. Tolson, *An Ex-*
Judge at the Bar, 1944

It is not the responsibility of knights errant to
discover whether the afflicted, the enchained and
the oppressed whom they encounter on the road
are reduced to these circumstances and suffer
this distress for their vices, or for their virtues:
the knight's sole responsibility is to succour
them as people in need, having eyes only for
their sufferings, not for their misdeeds.
—Don Quixote, in *Don Quixote*
(Miguel de Cervantes, 1605)

ONE OF THE ODDEST POLITICAL firestorms of Barack Obama's first
year as president began with his announcement that he would address

the nation's children on the morning after Labor Day, when most of the country's schools began the new year. His speech, delivered at a school in Virginia, would be beamed live into classrooms, auditoriums, and gymnasiums across the country. Schools set aside time for children and teens to assemble to hear the president's message.

The outcry began almost immediately. Parents demanded that their children be allowed to skip school assemblies. Fox News led its online coverage of parental concerns by quoting a Florida parent saying that the speech was "a form of indoctrination . . . indicative of the culture that the Obama administration is trying to create . . . It's very socialistic." Jim Greer, chairman of the Florida Republican Party, said the speech was an effort to "spread President Obama's socialist ideology." One conservative blog called the day of the speech "National Keep Your Child at Home Day" and urged parents to take "responsibility" to protect their children from the views of "a socialist with a radical agenda."[1]

To quell the furor, the White House released the text of the president's speech ahead of time. The message was as benign as they come. Urging the nation's schoolchildren to do their homework, pay attention in class, and stay in school, the president told them that they needed to take responsibility for their own success: "That's what I want to focus on today: the responsibility each of you has for your education."[2]

The president said he understood that not everyone had it easy. He reminded the students that he was raised by a single mother who woke him each morning at 4:30 to do his homework. He did not want children to use their own tough situations as an excuse: "At the end of the day, the circumstances of your life—what you look like, where you come from, how much money you have, what you've got going on at home—none of that is an excuse for neglecting your homework or having a bad attitude in school . . . There is no excuse for not trying." Obama linked the message of responsibility with the iconic symbolism of the American Dream: "Where you are right now doesn't have to determine where you'll end up.

No one's written your destiny for you, because here in America, you write your own destiny. You make your own future."

In the end, the controversy about Obama's address was simply partisan hysteria (although he hasn't done it again). He did not indoctrinate the minds of the nation's youth with visions of socialism. He used his bully pulpit to emphasize a core tenet of the American narrative: the need for personal responsibility.

Like many hinterland politicians before him, Obama came to Washington wanting to build and rely on a new era of bipartisanship and common ground. In his first news conference as president-elect, he said that he was "not going to anticipate problems" and that he was "going to go in there with a spirit of bipartisanship."[3]

If that was in fact an honest hope at any point, it had been smothered by the realities of Washington before his first year in office was done. We live in an era when a member of Congress can yell "You lie!" at the president in a speech about health care and a Supreme Court justice can mouth "Not true" during the State of the Union.[4] In this political context, Obama's speech to schoolchildren took advantage of the one thing that politicians of all stripes seem to agree on: personal responsibility.

"Personal responsibility" is the safest of political mantras. It is the last foothold of bipartisanship. Its focus on the power of individuals to make their own way is linked to the American Dream, the belief that "here in America, you write your own destiny."

No one disagrees with the idea of personal responsibility. That is, no one but me. Before you run to get your tar and feathers, let me explain.

I.

When I graduated from college, back in the 1980s, I headed west to San Francisco. As a small-town kid from Kentucky, I was a little wide eyed in such a beautiful and worldly city, and the four years I lived there were pivotal for me in learning how to be a grown-up. I had a decent job but only a handful of friends. For the first time in my life, I was on my own.

So I bought a motorcycle. I needed transportation and did not have money for a car, so I asked around and found a used Kawasaki street bike, red and fast. I had ridden dirt bikes as a teenager, but navigating Nob Hill and the Pacific Coast Highway on a crotch rocket was another matter.

I wish I could say I always wore a helmet, but I didn't. California had no helmet law at the time, and as I grew more comfortable with the bike and my skills, I increasingly rode with my head exposed. I particularly enjoyed doing this when I could entice a date to ride along—she got the helmet while I played the daredevil with a leather jacket, sunglasses, and flowing locks.

Of course it was stupid. There is nothing I should have wanted to protect more than my head. I was aware of the risks of riding motorcycles, especially in San Francisco. I had a couple of near-accidents. But I refused to think about the risks, instead focusing on the joy of helmet-free adventure. The risks were abstract, and the benefits were immediate and concrete.

Let me ask about personal responsibility in this context.

We should start by assuming that the phrase "personal responsibility" means something, and that it is meant as a guide not only for individuals but for public policy. Let's try to figure out what the phrase could mean in the context of my stupidity about motorcycle helmets, and also ask whether the law should care.

On an individual level, the answer seems pretty easy. To ride without a helmet is daft and shortsighted, putting me at risk of massive injury in exchange for fleeting benefits. Moreover, the risks flow not only to myself but to others, even if no one else would likely be physically harmed. The risks that others bear because of my stupidity are indirect but no less real. Those who love me—my family and friends—are at risk of suffering emotionally if I am injured. Emotional harms will also occur to those who witness any accident, whether they know me or not. Someone will have to pay for my injuries, and if I am insolvent or do not have sufficient insurance, then hospitals or taxpayers will foot the bill. If I am laid up, society temporarily loses whatever benefits I would normally provide others through my productivity at work, voluntary activities, life at home, and general good humor. If I die, society loses those benefits forever. So if I was bound for glory as the mapper of the human genome, but I die in a motorcycle accident, then someone else has to do that. Society suffers the costs of the difference between my abilities and the next genome mapper's.

So if personal responsibility indeed means being responsible, then we should act with due attention to the costs our behavior imposes on ourselves and others. This is the kind of personal responsibility that President Obama exhorted children to remember as they began their school year. Act with responsibility. Do your duty to yourself and your family. Remember that the one most responsible for taking care of you is you.

If that's what we mean, then it's clear that a person who cares about personal responsibility should wear a helmet. The sight of a motorcycle rider without a helmet is a counterexample to personal responsibility, an affront.

Or maybe not. Perhaps personal responsibility is best understood to mean that individuals get to make the choice for themselves about wearing a helmet. In this sense, personal responsibility is not necessarily about maturity but about who gets to decide. People make their own choices; they are masters of their fate. They can decide to be stupid or thoughtful, shortsighted or mature. They can care about risks or care about looking cool. It's up to them. It's their responsibility. In other words, choice itself is personal responsibility.

If that's what we mean, then a motorcycle gang rolling down the street without helmets is the epitome of personal responsibility. They are making their own choices. If I choose to look cool on a motorcycle by not protecting my skull, I am exercising personal responsibility because I have made my own choice.

Notice how odd this is. If I *choose* to be immature and shortsighted, then I am exercising personal responsibility because it's my own choice to be immature and shortsighted. When couched in this way, the idea makes little sense. If personal responsibility means that I get to do whatever I want, then it is a truly misguided use of the term. If it means choice and choice alone, it doesn't have any connection to the term "responsibility." That's not personal responsibility at all.

To make sense of this kind of personal responsibility—personal responsibility as pure choice—the person who chooses has to suffer the consequences of the decision. If I choose not to wear a helmet and I get hurt, then I have to pay for the consequences of my choice. The only way it is coherent to link the notion of choice, regardless of its quality, with the notion of responsibility is to focus on the costs of those choices. "Responsibility" does not mean maturity. It means accountability.

In this view of personal responsibility, the worst thing is to protect people from the costs of their own choices. They have to pay.

So let's return to my original question. Let's assume that I believe in personal responsibility and want to decide whether to wear a helmet. If we take the view that personal responsibility means being responsible, then the answer is clear: I should wear a helmet. If on the other hand we take the personal-responsibility-as-choice perspective, the framework offers no guideline for the substantive decision. A belief in personal responsibility of this stripe does not help me decide whether to wear a helmet. All it says is that the choice is mine to make, and I should bear whatever costs flow from the decision.

Now we can see something peculiar about the kind of personal responsibility defined by choice. It is completely indeterminate as a guide for individual decisions. It is not a guide for personal behavior at all. It helps me not a whit in deciding whether to wear a helmet or, for that matter, whether to eat a Big Mac, buy health insurance, or stay in my home in the face of an imminent hurricane. All it means is that those decisions are mine to make.

This brand of personal responsibility is *only* a guide to public policy. It is simply another name for leaving people to their own devices, allowing them to make their own decisions, and then making them suffer the consequences.

This brand of personal responsibility rhetoric seems to be in the ascendancy. It is used to oppose health care reform, support tort reform, and explain away problems of homelessness or delays in hurricane response. This brand of personal responsibility builds on the rhetoric of respect for individual choice to make the political point that government should be small, uninvolved, and deferential to individual decisions.[5]

And the point is not exactly soft-pedaled. A 2010 opinion piece in a prominent national publication argued that health regulations on food undermine "what were once considered quintessential American characteristics—personal responsibility and freedom of choice" and that such regulations have "sent us barreling down the slippery slope toward authoritarianism."[6]

The rhetorical link between personal-responsibility-as-choice and governmental and legal inaction is quite powerful. But it is also fundamentally flawed as a concept, and it collapses with only a bit of poking and prodding.

2.

We can easily recognize the differences between personal responsibility rhetoric that advocates maturity in decision making and personal responsibility rhetoric that is a placeholder for a respect for individual choice. The former is a guide for individuals; the latter is not. Instead, personal-responsibility-as-choice is about public policy. It says that government should avoid making decisions for individuals, and that individuals should suffer the consequences for their own decisions. Politicians of all stripes can agree on "personal responsibility" only because they can choose which brand of personal responsibility ("maturity" or "choice") they mean. But when the rubber meets the road, the policy prescriptions of the two brands are vastly different.

Let's look again at the helmet choice, this time asking what the law should be, not whether an individual is wise to wear one. If I believe in personal responsibility, should I vote in favor of a law requiring people to wear a helmet? (The question can also be asked about seat belt laws, bans on texting while driving, or indeed any government regulation.)

The answer, of course, depends on which brand of personal responsibility I subscribe to. If I believe that people should act maturely, it need not offend my sense of personal responsibility to require motorcyclists to don helmets. If, on the other hand, I believe people should make their own choices, then I will think the government should not be involved. People should choose for themselves.

But not so fast.

Remember the key to the personal-responsibility-as-choice framework is that people have to pay for their decisions. They have to suffer the consequences; the government should not protect them. How does this requirement play out?

Let's say that one evening as I return from a night out on the town I lose control of my motorcycle and hit a tree. I would be seriously injured even if I were wearing a helmet, but my injuries are even worse because on this night I was not. I lie unconscious at the base of the tree until an ambulance arrives. The paramedics look at my broken body and notice the lack of helmet. As a policy matter, what does a respect for personal-responsibility-as-choice require of them? Should they help?

To ask the question is to answer it. Of course they should help. The same goes for the doctors and nurses in the emergency room and indeed any bystander. They should not only care for the injuries that occurred through no fault of my own, but also for the injuries that my choices brought about. We simply do not live in a society where we leave injured people at the side of the road, whether they brought the injuries on themselves or not. Personal-responsibility-as-choice does not require others to be Hard Hearted Hannahs.

If respect for individual choice did indeed require hard-heartedness from others, this itself would be a cost that many would not freely accept. Many of us do not want to live in a society where we are required to turn away from people in need, even if that need is brought about by poor individual choices. If personal-responsibility-as-choice requires ambulance drivers, bystanders, or neighbors to turn away when I am suffering because of my own choices, that forced insensitivity is itself a cost that should not be forced onto them.

This means that without some kind of legal rule, there is no option to insulate my decision from imposing costs on others, even if we believe in personal-responsibility-as-choice. Others either have to suffer the psychological cost of looking at my broken body and doing nothing, or they themselves have to be willing to pay for my care. In other words, a libertarian framework creates a choice for bystanders, but neither choice is good.

It is not an answer to this concern to say that any Good Samaritans' decisions to help me are their own, and they should bear personal responsibility for them. This answer does not avoid the point that absent some kind of governmental or legal intervention, my decision not to wear a helmet will undoubtedly impose costs on any potential Good Samaritan who comes my way. Either they suffer financially from helping me out or psychologically from turning away.

Here's the point. The notion of personal-responsibility-as-choice is empty without some kind of legal rules surrounding it and governmental enforcement to police it. Without government intervention of some kind, my choice of not wearing a helmet is bound to impose costs on others.

What does it mean, then, to require me to suffer the consequences of my choice? At the very least, it means I should pay the financial costs of my own care. But medical care is expensive, and few of us could afford to pay for weeks of hospital care and rehab out of our own pockets. Those costs will quickly make me insolvent, meaning that in fact I will not be forced to suffer the full financial costs of my decision. As a matter of public policy, then, perhaps the best way to make sure I pay for the financial costs of my accident is to require me to buy insurance ahead of time. That way, the cost of my behavior is factored into my decisions before the fact, not afterward, and those who care for me after an accident are more likely to be paid.

Notice where we are. A respect for choice, if taken seriously, does not translate into the simplistic libertarian prescriptions often trotted out on the heels of personal responsibility rhetoric. It is impossible to have accountability for choices with no legal or regulatory mechanism to enforce it. What's more, an insistence on personal-responsibility-as-choice means that individuals can be required to buy insurance, to make sure the financial costs of their decisions are not borne by others.

This brings me to the nation's recent debate over health care. Throughout the fight over national health care reform, its opponents consistently attacked President Obama's plan as inconsistent with notions of personal responsibility and personal freedom.[7] They argued that we do not need government to take care of us—people should exercise personal responsibility and take care of themselves. If they wanted to buy insurance, fine. But the government should not make them do so.

With the motorcycle illustration fresh in our minds, the flaws in the personal responsibility argument opposing health care reform become clear. If personal responsibility involves actually being responsible, then it is consistent with that notion to require people to make the mature judgment to purchase health care for their families. If personal responsibility means that people can choose and then pay for their choices, then insurance is the best way that payment can be assured. If people are allowed to make bad health choices and also refuse to purchase health insurance, it essentially forces the rest of us either to foot the bill financially or to live in a society where we are forced to watch our neighbors suffer.[8]

President Obama's plan could have easily been called the Personal Responsibility in Health Care Act. To allow people to avoid paying for their own health care is inconsistent with both visions of personal responsibility. Purchasing health insurance is not only the responsible thing to do; it is also the best way to ensure that people actually pay for their choices. Instead of defending health care reform as an act of redistribution, cost saving, or altruism, the president should defend it on the grounds that it is the only way to make people take personal responsibility for their health care decisions.

3.

Respect for choice does not mean an absence of legal or governmental involvement, even for decisions as personal as whether to wear a motorcycle helmet. Most of our actions impose costs on others. Sometimes a respect for the autonomy and choice of others means that lawmakers or regulators need to step in, if only to make sure we pay the cost of our own decisions— either after the fact through judgments or fines, or before the fact through insurance. So the notion that personal responsibility means the law or government has nothing to say about our decisions is flat wrong.

And it's wrong for another reason.

Let's say there is a referendum on the ballot asking for a vote on whether to ban text messaging while driving. And let's assume that I believe in personal-responsibility-as-choice. That is, I believe that wherever possible, the government should let me decide my own fate. Let's also say—and this is true—that I text while driving sometimes, though I am embarrassed by the habit and avoid it when someone else is in the car (especially my wife, who won't suffer it).

Is it obvious which way I should vote on the referendum? One might think that because I believe in personal-responsibility-as-choice, the last thing I want is for the government to tell me what to do, especially with my cell phone in my own car.

But the answer is not so easy. I may be convinced that texting while driving is almost always a poor decision. Like the decision to not wear a motorcycle helmet, it ignores significant risks in favor of immediate gains that are rarely worthwhile. I may also recognize that my habit of texting is just that—a habit, a compulsion. It is usually done without reflection or deliberation. In this situation and in some others, I recognize in myself the capacity for, and indeed the propensity for, making substantively poor decisions. I know the limits on my own ability to make good decisions, perhaps because I have read the previous four chapters. I believe in my right to make my own choices, but I also recognize that I will sometimes make poor ones. I have a set of preferences about texting while driving, and my preferences differ according to whether I am driving or sitting at my desk thinking about the dangers of texting. In a sense, I have preferences about my preferences.[9]

What are my options? I can choose not to buy a mobile phone, or not to carry one. I can throw it in the trunk each time I drive. I can ask my wife to hold it for me. I can install software (now available) that will block my ability to text when the phone senses that it is moving at highway speeds. Like Ulysses, I can bind myself to the mast in order to resist the siren song of the iPhone.[10]

There is yet another option—I can vote in favor of the ban on texting. It is not inconsistent with my belief in personal-responsibility-as-choice to recognize the limits of my own ability to choose well, and to ask for help. Binding myself to the mast may include asking the law to punish me if I make a bad decision. In fact, I may recognize that the only way I will have the ability to choose well in each situation is to make a more global choice, as a voter, to ban the specific situational choices I would otherwise make.

Ulysses and the Sirens by Herbert James Draper.

My choices as a voter may not align with the choices I would make in any given situation. But that's okay. To think differently as a voter than as a driver, consumer, drinker, or credit card user is not a failure of personal responsibility, even personal-responsibility-as-choice. It is simply a different way to exercise my choice.

All this is to say that an insistence on personal responsibility does not necessarily help in crafting regulatory policy. Personal responsibility does not inevitably result in a hands-off governmental stance, because people may *want* to have the government's assistance in making good decisions. My way of exercising personal responsibility (of either kind) may be to call on the law to nudge me in the right direction.[11]

Another problem with the rhetoric of personal-responsibility-as-choice is that it allows some people to *avoid* responsibility.

The story of Nicole Eisel is a nightmare for any parent. Nicole was a thirteen-year-old middle school student in Montgomery County, Maryland, when for some reason she became obsessed with satanism. She became fixated on death and self-destruction, and she ultimately entered into a murder-suicide pact with a similarly obsessed friend.[12] Other friends heard about the pact and notified two school counselors, who met with Nicole to ask about her plans. Nicole denied the existence of any suicide pact. The counselors let the matter drop without informing other school officials or Nicole's parents.

About a week later, Nicole and her friend consummated the pact in a local park. Her friend shot Nicole to death and then turned the gun on herself.

Who was responsible for Nicole's death? If we take a simplistic view of personal responsibility, then the answer is simple: Nicole. She could have avoided death by not entering into the pact. We might also put her parents on the list—they are, by definition, responsible for the safety of their minor children. And let's not forget the girl who pulled the trigger.

Was Nicole's school also responsible? Nicole's father thought so. He sued the school, alleging that officials failed to warn him that his daughter was a suicide risk. The school defended itself by saying that Nicole's suicide was a "deliberate, intentional, and intervening act."[13]

This is the kind of question that the law knows how to handle. In a suit like this one, the law balances questions of duty (did the school have a duty to warn the parents?), seriousness of harm (here, pretty damn serious), and causation (if the school had warned the parents, would Nicole have committed suicide?). The law gives these decisions to juries or judges, and the parties have to make their best arguments. In Nicole's father's suit, the first judge dismissed the case against the school, but Maryland's highest appellate court reinstituted the suit, saying that the school system had a duty to use reasonable care to prevent the suicide, which could have included a warning to parents.[14]

But let's set aside the legal arguments and use Nicole's case to question the political arguments around personal-responsibility-as-choice. Notice the contours of the school's defense. It argued that Nicole's act was an intervening act that protected the school from responsibility by breaking the chain of causation from any negligence on the school's part to the ultimate event—Nicole's death. It is fair to say that the school was asserting that Nicole's choice—her "deliberate, intentional" act—meant that the responsibility for the suicide was hers and not theirs.

The school has a point. Nicole's decision was certainly the most immediate cause of her own suicide. She would not have lost her life if she had refused the pact with her so-called friend, asked for help, admitted her despondency to her parents or counselors, or avoided the park that day.

But this argument misses something important. Many events have multiple causes and influences, and the responsibility for creating them is dispersed. Sometimes responsibility is shared. That was probably the case with Nicole's suicide. She certainly made bad choices. But in all likelihood, so had her parents and so had school officials.

If our dedication to personal responsibility focuses our attention on Nicole, that's fine. But if that focus causes us to ignore the role played by others in her suicide, then we're allowing others who ought to share responsibility for the catastrophe to avoid that responsibility.

This is indeed what happens in much of the political discussion about personal responsibility. The last person in the causal chain—the last person to make a "deliberate, intentional" choice—is seen as holding all of the responsibility. To let the last person avoid all responsibility by pointing a finger upstream is usually a mistake. But it is also a mistake to allow the choosers upstream to avoid responsibility by pointing at the last chooser.

This is not an idle point. Recall the teenagers who sued McDonald's for contributing to their obesity.[15] The case was thrown out, and the suit was ridiculed in the media. The United States House of Representatives got so riled up about the suit—even though it was solitary and unsuccessful—that it drafted and passed a bill to stop copycat suits. Our national legislature thought that these suits were sufficiently dangerous to our country's best interests that it rushed to the aid of fast-food companies. The bill was named the Personal Responsibility in Food Consumption Act, also known as the Cheeseburger Bill. Its text included a congressional finding that "fostering a culture of acceptance of personal responsibility is one of the most important ways to promote a healthier society" and that such lawsuits were not only "legally frivolous" but "harmful to a healthy America."[16] The bill passed the House in both 2004 and 2005 but never reached the floor in the Senate. Meanwhile, at least twenty-three states have passed their own cheeseburger bills protecting fast-food companies.[17]

Now let's talk about shared responsibility. No one doubts that obesity is a severe problem in the United States. Recent studies show that perhaps two-thirds of Americans, 190 million people, are overweight or obese. Childhood obesity has tripled in the past thirty years. The problem is getting worse, not better.[18]

It seems to me that this problem cannot be laid solely at the feet of those of us who eat french fries, drink soda sweetened with corn syrup, and watch Dancing with the Stars rather than exercising. Don't get me wrong—the fact that I carry more pounds than I should is indeed my responsibility. But the responsibility is also shared. Our decision to eat really bad food is affected by what happens around us and inside us.

Fast-food executives bear the responsibility for the choices they make in developing foods that take advantage of human cravings for fats and sugars, and pushing their foods through ad campaigns that activate those cravings. Congress bears responsibility for subsidizing corn and other crops important for the fast food industry but not fresh produce. It is agricultural subsidies, not the free market, that make a super-sized meal cheaper than a salad and a bottle of water.[19] Communities bear responsibility for making it difficult to ride bikes safely or failing to provide parks that are inviting and safe. Schools bear responsibility for serving lunches of pizza and Tater Tots rather than beans, fresh vegetables, and lean meats.

If we take personal responsibility seriously, either in the sense of maturity or in the sense of choice, we cannot let people who make decisions avoid responsibility just because they aren't the last person in the causal chain. Too often, the rhetoric of personal responsibility is a way for those who ought to admit to shared responsibility to point the finger at someone else.

In December of each year, the City of Boston performs an annual census of the city's homeless population. Much effort goes into persuading the homeless to come in from the winter cold. After the 2007 census, the mayor's words were a headline in the *Boston Globe*: "Some folks, no matter what we do, don't want to come inside."[20]

Pause for a moment on these words. At one level, they are undoubtedly true. Some homeless people are mentally ill. Some have been victimized in local shelters. Some may actually want to die.

The mayor's comments also contain a tinge of blame. By emphasizing individuals' own choices, the story becomes a morality tale about personal responsibility, making it much easier to read as I sip my coffee and eat my blueberry pancakes. If we have any responsibility at all toward the homeless, it is to ask them if they want to come in from the cold. If they do not, it's their own fault for freezing to death, and I can go on with my life.

The emphasis on the last choice in the chain ignores the constraints on those choices, not to mention the choices of myriad others who created

"Only __I__ can prevent forest fires? Don't you think
you should share some of the responsibility?"

the situation in which people freeze to death in the world's richest nation. As legal scholar Joseph Singer reminds us, "People do not voluntarily sleep outdoors in wintertime if they have a family to be with or a safe place to go."[21]

The rhetoric of personal responsibility is often a cover for the avoidance of shared responsibility. A fixation on the choices of the last person in the causal chain allows us to feel comfortable with a lack of charity springing from our hearts or wallets. It also allows the rhetoric of personal responsibility to provide a cover for simplistic libertarian phobias of government regulation, whether of motorcycle helmet laws or health care reform.

Too often, the rhetoric of personal responsibility essentially urges the rest of us not to care about our fellow citizens. It avoids any sense of shared concern, of shared responsibility for others.

And that's why I am against it.

8

Umpires,
Judges,
and
Bad Choices

All his life he tried to be a good person. Many
times, however, he failed. For after all, he was
only human. He wasn't a dog.
—Snoopy, 1991

Storytelling awakens us to that which is real . . .
Stories bind . . . They are basic to who we are.
—Terry Tempest Williams,
Pieces of White Shell, 1987

ON JUNE 2, 2010, a mild, cloudy Wednesday night, the Cleveland Indians were in Detroit for a baseball game against the Tigers. There was no reason to expect anything special. The Tigers had lost seven of their last nine, and the Indians were already twelve games out of first place with less than a third of the season gone. The Tigers decided to start Armando Galarraga, a tall, thin, twenty-eight-year-old Venezuelan pitcher in his third major league season. Galarraga had enjoyed a blistering rookie year but had faded in his second, recording only six wins against ten losses. In 2010, he had been sent down to the minor leagues in spring training. In May, he was called up again to the big leagues but was not burning up the stat sheet, going 1–1 for the month with an earned run average of 4.50. In fact, Galarraga's previous outing was not as a starter but as a reliever.

So on June 2, fans did not exactly flock to the game. The ballpark was less than half full.

But Galarraga had the night of his career. Batter after batter strode to the plate for Cleveland, only to fly out weakly or hit a ground ball to an infielder. Not only was no batter getting a hit, no one was getting on base by way of error or walk. By the time Galarraga walked to the mound to start the ninth inning, he was three outs away from pitching a perfect game.

A perfect game is a spectacular feat. In comparison, a no-hitter happens in the major leagues about three times a season.[1] When it does, it leads off the national sports reports and is the kind of feat that will ever after get listed among a pitcher's greatest achievements. Many top-flight pitchers never get one. But a no-hitter need not be perfect. A pitcher can walk batters and his teammates can commit errors. Some pitchers have even lost games in which they no-hit the opposing team.

A perfect game is much tougher and rarer: it means that every batter the pitcher faces is put out in order. Three up and three down, nine innings in a row. There is no room for error on the part of the pitcher or his fielders behind him. Over the 135 years of major league baseball, only twenty pitchers have managed it, and none did it more than once. More people have orbited the moon than have pitched perfect games in the major leagues.[2]

So the eyes of the baseball-watching public turned toward Detroit as Galarraga took the mound to start the ninth inning. Baseball broadcasts around the country were interrupted so viewers could look in on Galarraga's effort.

The umpire at first base that night was a well-respected veteran named Jim Joyce. He had been an ump for more than twenty years, and was so consistent and fair that an anonymous poll of a hundred players rated him as the best umpire in baseball.[3] He twice umpired the All-Star game and the World Series. On that Wednesday in Detroit, Joyce had been busy. Galarraga threw only a handful of strikeouts, so many of the outs were ground balls ending with a throw to first. The ninth inning started with a fly out to center field and yet another ground out. So, having retired the first twenty-six batters in a row, Galarraga faced the Indian shortstop Jason Donald.

Every fan was standing.

Donald watched two pitches go by, one a ball and one a called strike.[4] He slapped the next pitch to the gap between first and second base. First baseman Miguel Cabrera ran to his right and fielded the ball cleanly. He threw to Galarraga, who had meanwhile sprinted toward first base to receive the throw for the out. The ball reached Galarraga, and Galarraga reached first base, about a half step before Donald made it to the bag. The television announcer anticipated the call, yelling, "He's out!"

Then Joyce made the mistake for which he will be long remembered.[5] He stretched out his arms, emphatically signaling safe. He seemed to have no doubt. The crowd cried a collective "Oh no!" and the television announcer howled, "No, he's safe! He's safe!" The call shocked even Donald, who stood up the first base line with his hands on his head. First baseman Cabrera also put his hands on his head in disbelief. The television analyst voiced the nation's bewilderment: "Are you kidding me? Why is he safe?" The crowd booed. As replays showed that Joyce had clearly blown the call and with it Galarraga's perfect game, the television analysis was little more than a groan: "Oh my goodness. Jim Joyce, no!"

And then something remarkable happened.

Armando Galarraga turned and smiled at Joyce. He cocked his head slightly, gave a bemused look, and walked back to the pitcher's mound.

He did not argue; he did not explode into a rage. He went back to his job. He faced the next batter and got another ground out, completing what amounted to a twenty-eight-out perfect game.

Then another remarkable thing happened. Joyce said he was sorry. Umpires rarely acknowledge mistakes, but as soon as the game ended and Joyce saw the replay of his call, he knew he had screwed up. He immediately asked to see Galarraga, and, in tears, hugged him and apologized. He explained that in the moment, "I thought he beat the throw. I was convinced he beat the throw, until I saw the replay . . . It was the biggest call of my career, and I kicked the shit out of it. I just cost that kid a perfect game."[6]

For his part, Galarraga was gracious and empathetic. "He probably feels more bad than me. Nobody's perfect. Everybody's human. I understand . . . I gave him a hug."[7]

The next night, Joyce was given the option to not umpire the last game of the series. Instead, he went back to work, taking his turn behind the plate. The Tigers' manager sent Galarraga to deliver the night's lineup card to Joyce at home plate. They spoke for a moment. Joyce, tearing up, gave Galarraga a pat on the shoulder while the crowd offered warm applause.

Joyce's mistake is almost incomprehensible. It was a routine call. ESPN baseball analyst Tim Kurkjian said that it was the kind of call that umpires get correct 100,000 times out of 100,001. Joyce said in an ESPN interview that his "instinct" had taken over, but that he could not explain the mistake: "I don't know how I got that call wrong."[8] Perhaps it was nervousness. Perhaps he was trying unconsciously to correct a tendency to err on the side of the pitcher in such a situation. One theory was that Galarraga caught the ball in the webbing of his mitt, so that Joyce did not hear the usual "pop" of the ball hitting the glove. But whatever the reason, Joyce made the wrong decision.

We can all identify with Joyce, though most of us have not made our bad decisions in front of millions with access to instant replay. Indeed, it's easier to identify with Joyce than with Galarraga. Few of us have achieved the kind of success Galarraga did that night, but each of us has chosen poorly. Some of our mistakes are made quickly, like Joyce's. Others are made after deliberation, discussion, and debate. We are all human, and to err is human.

The question for us is whether James Joyce—the writer, not the umpire—was correct when he wrote that errors "are the portals of discovery."[9]

I.

Some scientific evidence suggests that people who have developed expertise in a certain area may know or sense something before they can articulate it or even bring it to consciousness. Malcolm Gladwell's book *Blink* became a bestseller by popularizing this notion, arguing that we should learn to trust our first impressions and snap judgments. Gladwell begins his book using the example of art historians whose "intuitive repulsion" gave them clues that a statue purchased by the Getty Museum was a fake.[10] In his book *How We Decide*, Jonah Lehrer uses the example of New England Patriots quarterback Tom Brady, whose membership in the NFL elite depends primarily on his instantaneous reads of defenses and quick decision making in the face of onrushing behemoths.[11] Umpires like Jim Joyce provide additional examples. If they are good—and (it pains me to say this) most of them are—they get it right much more often than not.

The idea of trusting your snap judgments has become so popular that it is something of a fad. Massachusetts Senator Scott Brown, one of the fresher faces of the Republican party, told the 2010 graduating class at his alma mater (and my employer) Boston College Law School that new lawyers should, when facing career decisions, "go with their gut."[12]

But snap judgments may also lead to disastrous results; sometimes first impressions are wrong. Frequently the impulsive gut instinct is mistaken. No one is an expert in all things, and even in our area of expertise we are fallible. Tom Brady throws interceptions (though I am proud to say not very often); Jim Joyce gets calls wrong; even Gladwell's art historians were wrong before they were right.

It would be reassuring if we could guard against bad decisions through reflection and analysis. But even there, we are immensely fallible. Marriages are notoriously unsuccessful in the United States these days, but no one I know enters those arrangements lightly. The war in Iraq was an extraordinarily poor decision, but it was not made on the spur of the moment. The Supreme Court is insulated from the hottest part of the political kitchen to allow it space to deliberate and reflect, but the history of the Court contains massive mistakes. (My own list of worst Supreme Court cases ever would include *Dred Scott*, upholding slavery; *Korematsu*, upholding the Japanese internment during World War II; and *Bush v. Gore*, deciding the 2000 presidential election.)

Maybe we can guard against bad decisions by involving others. There is something to the notion of the "wisdom of crowds," and some studies show that groups can be better at making decisions than even the smartest individuals in the group.[13] But here too, we are human—we err. Individuals in groups are often swayed by the opinions of others in the group—even if clearly wrong. Sometimes this influence causes individuals to squelch their own opinions, and sometimes it results in individuals' changing their opinions even without realizing it.[14] Peer pressure is a real phenomenon. Remember how the subjects in Milgram's study were most willing to punish the "learners" when others in the room went along, and were most willing to object when others objected.

Groups also can fall into habits of thought that reinforce members' assumptions and insulate them from contrary notions. This is called groupthink, and it can be dangerous.[13] For example, at the beginning of this century most of the finance industry believed that housing prices would never, ever fall. They bet the farm—our farm, in fact—on this assumption. We are all still paying the price of that piece of groupthink.

The persistence of error, regardless of our decision making technique, is a symptom of the human condition. It is as certain as death and taxes.

We are therefore faced, on a personal and social level, with a choice about bad choices. Do we blame the people who stayed in their homes in the face of Katrina? Do we allow an obese Big Mac eater to sue McDonald's? Do we allow someone injured at work to sue his employer when the injury came from a known and accepted risk? Do we seek to understand the situation of the guards at Abu Ghraib as we allocate moral and legal blame for torture and mistreatment of prisoners?

In our personal lives as well as our legal system, we are required to figure out what to do about bad choices and poor decisions. We have to choose when we give or take a "do over." We have to choose whether to punish. We have to choose when to forgive or, as Armando Galarraga did, simply smile and get back to work. We have to make choices about our own bad choices and others'.

2.

The bad choice choice is, in a sense, a central question of law. Much of law is the establishment of rules, and much of it is the establishment and implementation of punishments for when rules are broken. Both rules and punishments depend on the choice we make about bad choices.

Sometimes rules can be clear and clean. The speed limit is 55 miles per hour. The drinking age is twenty-one. You have to be thirty-five to be president. It is easy for police, judges, or juries to determine whether such sharply defined rules have been broken. They check the radar gun, the driver's license, or the birth certificate. In those situations, the legal decision maker has an easy task. He or she simply compares the legal requirement to what was done.

Non-lawyers are often surprised to learn how few laws are this clear. Sometimes, lack of clarity comes because the drafter of the law in question—the legislator or regulator—was unkempt with language. Sometimes the actual text of a law is the product of compromise, and both sides would rather leave things unresolved than fight for clarity. Sometimes a law is unclear because we are trying to apply it in a situation that was beyond the expectations of its drafters.

Sometimes lack of clarity is necessary. Language is inherently limited. It's not easy to capture certain kinds of obligations in a clear linguistic formula. In tort law, for example, sometimes the best we can urge is to "be careful," or more precisely, to "not act negligently toward someone to whom you owe a duty to be careful." In deciding whether someone is liable for an accident, what constitutes negligence depends on the situation. In commercial law, no matter how finely negotiated a contract is, the various negotiated terms cannot substitute for the legal duty to "act in good faith." What amounts to good faith depends on the situation. Another example comes from property law, where the "duty of habitability," implied in landlord-tenant leases, requires the property to be "habitable." Habitability depends on the situation. In business law, officers of a corporation owe a "fiduciary duty" to the corporation. What satisfies that duty depends on the situation. A police search is legal only if "reasonable"—which depends on the situation. And so on.

When we have to decide what the law actually requires, we have to consider the situation in which the law is being applied. This mindfulness is required whether we are trying to figure out our responsibilities before the fact (lawyers would say *ex ante*), or trying to determine legal responsibility after the fact (*ex post*) as a judge or jury member.

We must also consider the situation after guilt or liability is established, when we are determining punishment. The law of punishment and remedies demands attention to particularities of each case. In criminal law, federal court judges are required to base punishments on the "real conduct" underlying the conviction. The Supreme Court has struck down congressional efforts to impose mandatory, uniform penalties for federal crimes that would make it difficult for judges to take into account the circumstances of each conviction.[16] Even when it comes to areas of law such as contracts and tort, the amounts of liability often depend on particular judgments that are hard to pin down ahead of time. Contract damages turn in part on what the parties' rightful expectations were if the contracts had been honored. Tort judgments depend not only on the total amount of the injuries but on who caused them and whether the victim (that is, the plaintiff) should bear some blame.

All this is to say that law is much less precise than non-lawyers might think. (One of the joys, and challenges, of teaching first-year law students is getting them comfortable with the ambiguity of law.) Rarely are both the rule and punishment clear. By its very nature, the law requires that there be some dialogue between the situation and the legal decision maker. The rule and punishment only become precise once the contours of the situation in which they are applied are understood.

Here we return to the choice about bad choices.

Usually, the law gets involved only after someone has screwed up, or after someone believes someone else has screwed up. You sue someone in tort if you've been injured by, say, a hit baseball or a falling ax. You sue your former employer to be reinstated in your old job even though you signed a contract to resign. You are accused of murder when you forget your child in the car and, God forbid, he dies of exposure. You accuse a fellow student of rape, on the basis of an incident in which you repeatedly said "no" but did not physically resist, while also engaging in behavior that the accused claims he misunderstood. You suffer charred lungs while in a self-help guru's sweat lodge, others lose their lives, and the guru is charged with negligent homicide.

In each of these situations, what the law demands depends on what the legal decision maker believes about the choices made. You will lose your tort suit if the judge or jury believes that your choice to put your head in the way of the ball or ax was more blameworthy than the choice of those who failed to protect you from those risks. You will win your old job back if the jury would recognize that your choice to resign was made under undue pressure. You will be acquitted of murder if the jury believes your bad choice of leaving your child in your car is understandable, if horribly tragic. The accused will be convicted of rape if the jury believes his choice to continue the encounter after you said "no" was blameworthy, given the specifics of the situation. The guru will be convicted if the jury feels his authority vitiated the free will of those in the sweat lodge.

In each situation, there is indeed law to apply. You must act with due care. You must abide by contracts. You may not cause the death of another. Sex without consent is rape. But the actual implication of the law—has there been a tort? is the contract valid? should someone be punished?—is not clear until we know a lot more about the situation. The law has substance only in its application.

Every time politicians talk about judges—especially when the president has nominated someone to the Supreme Court—it seems we are reminded that judges are not to "make law." But law is made each time it is applied, since (in most cases) there is no way to articulate what the contours of the legal requirement are without reference to the immediate situation. Judges make law all the time, and so do juries.

One might think that this lack of clarity in the law is a defect, and sometimes it is. If ambiguity arises because of ham-fisted legislative drafting, failure of foresight, or political unwillingness to make the difficult regulatory choices, then lack of clarity is indeed a legal flaw. It is also a serious problem if judges use vagueness to impose their own prejudice onto the parties. But forcing judges and juries to listen to stories in order to make choices about the choices that other people have made is a fundamental purpose of law.

The law's vagueness can have surprising benefits. Gray areas force legal decision makers to look at the nuances and particularities of situation before issuing legal edicts or making determinations of blame.

3.

Let's get back to umpires.

The story of Jim Joyce and Armando Galarraga is an example of how even experts make flawed decisions, and how we all need a dose of humility in responding to the mistakes of others. But there is a more famous use of umpires as metaphors, and it relates to the clarity or ambiguity of law.

When John Roberts was nominated by President George W. Bush to be chief justice of the United States, he began his confirmation hearings by saying he wanted to be an umpire. "Judges are like umpires. Umpires don't make the rules; they apply them . . . And I will remember that it's my job to call balls and strikes and not to pitch or bat."[17]

Roberts, by all accounts, is a very intelligent man. (Once, when he was an attorney, I watched him argue a very complicated case about admiralty law before the Supreme Court. He argued without notes, even quoting the applicable statute from memory when he was asked about it.) But the metaphor of judge as umpire is jaw-droppingly simplistic. Precision in the law is the exception, not the rule.

When the law demands situational judging, it is not particularly enlightening to compare a judge's work to that of an umpire. A judge should be impartial, to be sure, like an umpire. But judicial judgment is immensely

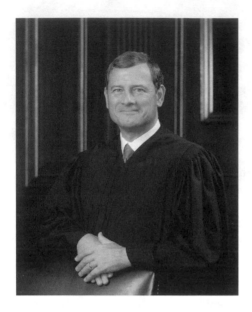

Chief Justice John Roberts.

more complex than umpiring judgment. Calling balls and strikes is relatively straightforward, and one thing every baseball player knows is that you cannot argue balls and strikes. There is no quicker way to ejection. But the very purpose of law is to hear arguments, to contextualize the application of law by hearing stories and making the bad choice choice.

Four years after Roberts took his place, Associate Justice David Souter resigned, giving President Obama his first chance to nominate a justice. Obama articulated a strikingly different conception of the role of judge, saying that he would look for a replacement who would bring "empathy" to the Court:

> I will seek someone who understands that justice isn't about some abstract legal theory or footnote in a case book; it is also about how our laws affect the daily realities of people's lives—whether they can make a living and care for their families; whether they feel safe in their homes and welcome in their own nation.

I view that quality of empathy, of understanding and identifying with people's hopes and struggles, as an essential ingredient for arriving as just decisions and outcomes.[18]

Obama's critics pounced, saying that empathy was code for liberal judicial activism. They denounced Obama's formulation for good judging, arguing that empathy allowed judges to impose their own opinions on the law rather than merely calling balls and strikes. Prominent law professor Steven Calabresi warned that asking judges to be empathetic was like removing the blindfold from Lady Justice, allowing the judge to decide in favor of whichever perspective elicited his sympathy.[19]

Liberals came to Obama's aid. They liked empathy because they equated it with compassion, and compassion with mercy. Liberals like mercy, at least when it comes to tort plaintiffs or criminal defendants who are not corporate CEOs.

Both the liberals and conservatives have it wrong.

I will admit that if empathy did mean compassion, the conservatives are probably right. If the law depends on whether the judge feels sympathy for one party or the other, the judge might be too quick to base judgments on unacknowledged bias or prejudice. Liberals would not like that either.

But that is not what empathy means in the judicial context. Conservatives are wrong to see empathy as a kind of feeling. A better definition of empathy for the judicial context focuses not on how judges feel but how they think. Empathy is a dedication to listening to the particularities of the stories embedded in the cases being heard.[20] As we've seen, the role of law is to offer room for people to tell stories about their bad choices, and to ask for an understanding of the contours of the situation in which bad choices were made. This kind of empathy is not only beneficial but crucial. More than an add-on to a judge's list of responsibilities, it is a core obligation.

Judges need empathy to guard against bad choices and cognitive mistakes. We've discussed throughout this book the predictable traps humans fall into when making decisions. We are susceptible to the familiarity effect. In difficult times, new ideas get short shrift, and the status quo gets an advantage unrelated to its merit. We are guilty of motivated reasoning and confirmation bias. We are overconfident about our own predictive or analytical judgments. We trust authority. We are blind to the influence of culture. We assume the decisions of individuals acting in the marketplace are indicative of their preferences, rather than created by the market itself.

These pitfalls can be magnified when we make decisions in groups. Humans tend to herd with others, which makes us less likely to speak up in dissent unless there is a critical mass of other dissenters. If we identify too much with others in the group, we can succumb to peer pressure (even without knowing it) and tend to reinforce rather than correct the mistakes of others in the group. These defects in decision making are more pronounced in groups that are more homogeneous.[21]

This means that Obama's emphasis on empathy is especially important for a nomination to the Supreme Court. By any measure of homogeneity, the Supreme Court is a dangerous decision maker. In 2010 the Court seated just the fourth female justice in its history. It has had two African Americans and one Hispanic in more than two centuries of existence, and no Asian Americans. Other aspects of its sameness are less obvious and perhaps more important. As of 2011 it is dominated by jurists from Harvard and Yale who served on lower courts in the "Acela corridor" between Washington and Boston. It has only one southerner (Clarence Thomas), and none of its nine justices were born away from the coasts. All are either Jews or Catholics.

In such a homogeneous group, a justice's ability to imagine and appreciate the situation of someone from a different background or in a different situation is essential. This kind of empathy is not a feeling but a method of thought, a habit of questioning one's perspective long enough to "check one's work." Empathy also allows the group to avoid the "herding" that accentuates the flaws of group decision making. It is critical not because of the need for compassion or sympathy, but because of its role in producing the only thing the Court is supposed to produce: good decisions. It protects all of us.

In a world in which law can never capture the complexity of human beings, intellectual empathy is the only way that the stories the law requires will produce fair outcomes, rather than outcomes that are receptacles for the bias and prejudice of judges and juries.

Obama was right to emphasize empathy in discussing David Souter, because Souter embodied the kind of empathy I am defining here. He is a Harvard- and Oxford-educated New England Republican, but his contributions were often in the understanding of people completely unlike him. Early in his career as a justice, the Court heard a case about a down-on-his-luck African American man named Curtis Kyles, who had been on death row in Louisiana for almost a decade.[22] Kyles had been convicted of the murder of a white woman in a supermarket parking lot, for her groceries and her red Ford LTD. The evidence against him looked strong. His appearance matched some eyewitness accounts, and he had been found with a revolver, which turned out to be the murder weapon, hidden in his apartment. A man named Beanie also claimed that Kyles had sold him the victim's LTD the day after the murder.

Kyles was as different from Souter as any party to a Supreme Court case I know about. Notwithstanding that fact, and despite Souter's experience as a state prosecutor, Souter pored over the record of the case, which increasingly gave him the sense that something was not right. The evidence against Kyles was not nearly as strong as the police had made out, mostly because the police had failed to give the defense some eyewitness descriptions that didn't match Kyles. They had also failed to disclose their chummy relationship with Beanie, who should also have been a suspect

Justice David H. Souter.

since he matched some eyewitness descriptions and had a history of criminal activity around the grocery store in question.

Justice Souter's attention to detail, and his openness to seeing the facts from vantage points distinct from the accepted official version, allowed him to understand that the evidence did not point unequivocally to Kyles. Beanie should have been a suspect too, but the police took a "remarkably uncritical attitude" toward him, perhaps because of his history as an informant.

Souter wrote a detailed and tightly argued opinion arguing that Kyles deserved a new trial, not because he believed Kyles was innocent but because the police had hidden evidence that might have created a reasonable doubt as to his guilt. He won four other votes on the Court, meaning that Kyles won a new trial by a vote of five to four. It was the first time Kyles had won any of his cases or appeals in a decade of state and federal court proceedings.

Souter's attention to detail in the case was striking. He could have taken it lightly or not thought to challenge the arguments of the state officials, with whom he might have identified. His contribution was not feeling a certain way, but thinking differently from what his background might have suggested. This kind of empathy did not lead him astray or make him "activist," but helped him see the facts in a way that no other court had seen them. It also meant that the Court could articulate an important rule of constitutional law: prosecutors cannot hide evidence. Without such empathy, Kyles would have been put to death for a murder he probably did not commit, and it would be easier for any of us to be falsely accused.[23]

Another example came in a search and seizure case called *United States v. Drayton*, which I discussed in chapter two.[24] A bus was stopped in the middle of the night, far from its destination. Police boarded and stood at the rear and the front. An armed officer walked up and down the aisle, approached two seated passengers, and asked them to open their luggage. The officer stood over them, blocking their exit, and did not say they had a right to refuse. The passengers "agreed" to let the police look in their bags, and a significant amount of cocaine was discovered. The Supreme Court majority held that this was a consensual search, since the passengers had a choice—they could have gotten off the bus.

There was no reason for Justice Souter to sympathize with a couple of drug dealers with kilos of cocaine in their carry-on bags. But his dissent made the important point that the consent forming the basis of the search was manufactured rather than genuine. In analytic but powerful prose, he described the power of police in situations that we can reasonably assume he had never faced: "When the attention of several officers is brought to bear on one civilian the balance of immediate power is unmistakable. We all understand . . . that a display of power rising to . . . [a] threatening level may overbear a normal person's ability to act freely, even in the absence of explicit commands or the formalities of detention." For Souter, taking a different point of view was not an emotional exercise but an intellectual one.

Understanding the importance of empathy for judges reveals the comparison of judges with umpires to be so unhelpful that it appears calculated to mislead. Judges rarely decide any case, much less a difficult one, by performing the judicial equivalent of calling balls and strikes. Good judging requires that the parties be given the opportunity to tell their stories, and that the judges and juries be intellectually empathetic enough to imagine themselves in the situation described, in the role of either or both of the parties. Only then can they reach the correct legal outcome.

4.

Why should all this discussion about judging matter to those of us who will never be judges? Of course it matters if we're in court. We want judges to hear our stories and try to empathize with the situation in which we faced our choices.

But more important, the habits of good judging are important to the rest of us as we judge the choices of those around us. In our roles as spouse, parent, friend, or colleague, we would do well to listen to others' stories, pay attention to particularities, and practice intellectual empathy. We need to understand the influences of biology, culture, authority, and markets on the decisions of those around us.

If you're like me, you're excellent at seeing this influence of situation when evaluating your own actions. We humans are terrific at absolving ourselves from blame because of what is going on around us. Every excuse we offer makes perfect sense to us.[25] We even put ourselves in situations where we know we will be tempted, *in order* to absolve ourselves. It's why Mardi Gras in New Orleans, spring break in South Beach, or any random Tuesday in Las Vegas becomes a morality-free zone. We recognize our susceptibility to the situation and take advantage of it. This is why "What happens in Vegas stays in Vegas" is a powerful slogan and why "Lead us not into temptation" is a brilliant prayer.

But we are much less sensitive to the influence of situation when we evaluate the choices of others. As scholar Jon Hanson might say, we tend to be "situationalists" when we judge ourselves, recognizing the constraints we act under, but "dispositionalists" with others, thinking that decisions flow from pure free will.[26] We probably could be more thoughtful before we release ourselves from blame—think of Jim Joyce's willingness to admit his mistake—and we could use an extra helping of understanding when it comes to the mistakes of others. We might think of Armando Galarraga and be quicker to smile a bemused smile and go back to work.

Sometimes we're pretty good at it already. When Hurricane Katrina devastated New Orleans and its environs, most Americans understood that those who stayed behind were not particularly at fault. The right-wing talk show hosts who tried to blame the victims of the hurricane were essentially shouted down by the Americans offering an outpouring of help and compassion.

But most of the time, we're pretty bad at empathy. Our nation's shunning of the obese and overweight allows little room for understanding the cultural, biological, and economic situation of those who overeat and under-exercise. Our demonization of the guards at Abu Ghraib allows us little room to understand the effect of authority in that setting. Our dependence on the marketplace adage "caveat emptor" makes it easy to ignore the myriad limitations embedded in the marketplace.

We could also stand to be more empathetic when we consider the acts of those accused of crimes. We look at bad behavior and see acts of free will worthy of punishment. We tend to ignore the constraints of circumstance, the influence of biology, and the areas of shared—rather than personal—responsibility. Because of our insistence on the personal blameworthiness of each individual, we can collectively shake our pitchforks in anger, demanding restitution and revenge. The bad people have made bad choices, and they deserve to be locked up. In percentage terms, Americans incarcerate five times more of their own than Britain, nine times more than Germany, and twelve times more than Japan.[27] One in every hundred Americans is behind bars; one in every thirty-one is under some kind of "correctional" supervision.

Are Americans really five times more criminal than Brits? Nine times more prone to bad behavior than the Germans? Twelve times more worthy of punishment than the Japanese? Of course not. But we are probably five, nine, or twelve times more willing to translate a cultural insistence on individuality into a basis for punishment. We turn our fetish for choice into a reason to ignore shared responsibility and disparage the full stories of those accused. We end up over-punishing and under-understanding.

Two points are worth clarifying. First, intellectual empathy— understanding the limitations others face—is necessary for both conservatives and liberals. Liberals like to think they are good at this, since tolerance is such a touchstone belief for progressives. But the truth is—and yes, I am talking to myself here—there is no one more judgmental than a good liberal. George Bush is a moron, corporate CEOs are evil, gun owners are rednecks, and religious people are idiots. Conservatives certainly could be more understanding of the situation of the poor, criminal defendants, sexual minorities, and religious dissidents. But liberals too could use a dose of humility in evaluating the beliefs and behavior of those they usually target, keeping in mind the influence of culture, markets, biology, and authority. Corporate executives, for example, work within a marketplace that mandates a short-term fixation on profit. Many gun owners were raised in communities where hunting is a common pastime and gun ownership is part of the transition from boyhood to manhood. In communities where the flag is deified and God is nationalized, it is only natural for people to pledge allegiance to God and country.

Here's the second thing worth clarifying. An understanding that we all err, the creation of space to tell one's own stories, and the commitment to intellectual empathy do not require letting people off the hook for their bad choices. Sometimes an understanding of one's situation allows room for a recognition of the nature of shared responsibility, or even for forgiveness. I might be convinced that the prison guards at Abu Ghraib deserve to share the blame with the people who helped create the situation that promoted a mindset of hatred and dehumanization of their victims. Raelyn Balfour, the mother who left her child in the car, probably merits forgiveness.

Other times, an understanding of the contours of situation allows us to recognize that blame is appropriate and punishment should be increased. The climbers caught in the storm on Mount Hood deserved more blame than they received. Self-help guru James Arthur Ray will be more blameworthy to a jury the more they understand the situation he created in the sweat lodge. The executives at fast food companies who knowingly take advantage of human frailty in order to sell unhealthful food do not deserve to be protected from lawsuits. Individuals and institutions who manipulate cultural iconography for selfish ends—politicians hiding pork barrel projects behind flag pins, the Vatican hiding pedophiles behind church robes, or professional athletes hiding sexual assault behind team logos—should be held accountable.

How do we tell when people should be let off the hook, given a "do over," or forgiven, and when they should be punished, held accountable, or ostracized? How do we make a choice about other people's bad choices? How do we make a choice about our own?

These are tough questions, and the answers will not be the same for everyone. But I can say with certainty that we could all stand to be a little more like David Souter and Armando Galarraga.

Like Souter, we could remember that decisions are much more complex than we usually assume. Most of us, most of the time, are being pushed and prodded in various ways, some obvious to us and some not. We can understand the limitations and situational influences on our own choices, but it's not a bad idea to cultivate the habit of opening our eyes to the constraints on others, too. We could all use a little of the intellectual empathy that Souter showed when he was charged with evaluating the choices of others.

And we all make mistakes. Few of us have reason to expect that we could throw a baseball as well as Armando Galarraga. But most of us could be more like him when it comes to cutting others some slack when they screw up. Especially when they fess up, as Jim Joyce did.

At the very least, people who make bad choices should be given the opportunity to tell their stories. They should have the chance to ask for—and sometimes gain—our understanding.

9
Building Choice in a World of Limits

Everybody thinks of changing humanity, and
nobody thinks of changing himself.
—Leo Tolstoy, *Pamphlets*, 1900

And this bird you cannot change
And this bird you cannot change
Lord knows, I can't change
Lord help me, I can't change
Lord I can't change
Won't you fly high, free bird, yeah?
—Lynyrd Skynyrd, *Free Bird*, 1973

NEIL JORDAN'S FILM *THE CRYING GAME* tells the story of a British soldier named Jody, played by Forest Whitaker, who is kidnapped by members of the Irish Republican Army. Over the few days of his captivity, he develops a bond with Fergus, a soft-hearted Irish volunteer. As days pass, Jody comes to believe he is about to be murdered and tells Fergus the ancient parable of the scorpion and the frog.

Ever heard of 'em? A scorpion wants to cross the river but he can't swim. Goes to a frog, who can, and asks for a ride. Frog says, "If I give you a ride on my back you'll go and sting me."

Scorpion replies, "It would not be in my interest to sting you, since, as I'll be on your back we both would drown."

Frog thinks about this logic for a while and accepts the deal. Takes the scorpion on his back, braves the waters, halfway over feels a burning spear in his side and realizes the scorpion has stung him after all. And as they both sink beneath the waves, the frog cries out, "Why'd you sting me Mr. Scorpion? For now we both will drown."

Scorpion replies, "I can't help it. It's in my nature."[1]

The next day, Fergus's bosses require him to kill Jody, but Fergus hesitates. Jody bolts but flees into the path of onrushing British armored troop carriers, which run him over and crush him. Fergus avoids the troops and escapes to London, where he finds and eventually falls in love with Dil, Jody's girlfriend. In the most famous scene of the movie, Fergus and Dil prepare to make love and Fergus discovers that Dil is a biological male. The revelation does not go well, and Dil eventually learns of Fergus's role in Jody's death. As the movie ends, Dil kills one of the IRA fighters trying to track down Fergus, but Fergus takes the blame and goes to jail. Dil visits him in prison and asks why he took the fall for her. "As the man said," he explains, "it's in my nature."

The ancient parable of the scorpion and the frog, sometimes attributed to Aesop, and the very modern story of *The Crying Game* both illustrate the belief that we are who we are, and there is little we can do. The scorpion stings even when it is not in his interest to do so. Dil battles with the differences between her identity and her biology. Fergus cannot kill, and takes on Dil's punishment even when tremendously costly.

It's a common refrain. Popeye claims, "I yam what I yam." In this view, we are our natures. We go through our lives remarkably stable in personality, value systems, and worldview. As the saying goes, "People don't change, they just become more so." The more we know someone— *really* know someone—the less they surprise us. The choices they make in any given circumstance flow naturally from their nature.

Aligned against this notion is the belief that people are products of their environments. We may believe that we make our own decisions based on our character and belief systems, but in reality we are products of situation and circumstance. This is the nurture side of the nature-nurture debate, popularized in movies such as *Trading Places*, where old tycoons switch the circumstances of up-and-comer Dan Aykroyd and homeless loser Eddie Murphy to see what will happen.

You could also include as an opposing viewpoint the belief that behavior has external rather than internal motivations. If you're of a certain age you might remember comedian Flip Wilson's character Geraldine, whose signature line was "The *Devil* made me do it!" I was reminded of this when I read of a sixty-two-year-old woman who stole over $70,000 from the church where she worked. She told prosecutors that "Satan had a big part in the theft."[2]

In this view, the more we know about people's circumstances and the external forces acting on them, the less they will surprise us. The choices they make will flow inexorably from their situation.

In a way, the view that we are chained to our natures and the belief that we are products of external forces are diametrically opposed. One sees each human as a product of his or her own static character and disposition. The other sees each individual as an object on which circumstances act. But these views have a lot in common. Both see human behavior as constrained rather than free. One can be agnostic about whether internal or external forces are more influential in any given case and still acknowledge that the end result is limit rather than choice. We need not decide the debates over disposition and situation, internal and external, or nature and nurture to recognize constraint.

And recognize it we must. Ignorance of how we are cabined by our biologies, blinded by our cultures, seduced by our authorities, and manipulated by our markets simply makes those influences more powerful, invisible, and intransigent. In a world of limits, an insistence on the rhetoric of choice is, at best, Pollyannaish. At worst, it's a public opiate.

What, then, shall we do?

We can build choice. We can make it more real, for more people, more of the time. In order to do this, we will have to talk about both disposition and circumstance, internal and external, nature and nurture. Let's talk about the internal side first.

I.

Choice is good. We all like it; our brains crave it. As Sheena Iyengar explains in her book *The Art of Choosing*, our brains "respond more to rewards [that we] actively choose than to identical rewards that are passively received."[3] In other words, we tend to live better if we choose our lives than if they are given to or imposed on us.

The problem is that choice is sometimes empty, ephemeral, or false. We may experience our behavior as the result of choice and ascribe the behavior of others to the result of choice even when such behavior is largely predetermined by situation or disposition. If neither is under our control, then there is not much choice. What's worse, our feelings may not be our best guide to whether choice has occurred. In addition, we may be too distracted by the options at our grocery stores and on our television sets to recognize the dearth of choices in our politics and culture, or our inability to choose differently.

So building the ability to choose entails building the ability to control our choices. As Iyengar points out, "In order to choose, we must first perceive that control is possible."[4] It is terribly easy to feel overwhelmed or under siege. How do we find the control necessary to build the ability to make real choice?

One thing I am absolutely sure about: this control is not innately robust. It takes effort, and we can be good or bad at it. We can develop our choice "muscles" or let them go flabby.[5] There are things we can do to improve our abilities to make good choices.

First, we should acknowledge the power of situation and circumstance—the context for our choices. One of my middle-aged friends has been married to his college sweetheart for many years. He is terribly devoted to her and to their children. He is a successful businessman, a pillar of his community, and a friend of Barack Obama. He's also gregarious and charming, and women find him attractive. I once asked him his secret to staying happy in his marriage for so long and maintaining faithfulness to his wife through thick and thin. His answer was, "I don't put myself in situations in which I would be tempted or my behavior would be misunderstood."

I think that was a wise answer. Even though my friend is a very disciplined person, with unquestionable integrity, he did not allow his family life to depend solely on his discipline and integrity. He acknowledged the risk that bad situations might pose. This might strike some readers as weakness, a failure of my friend to trust himself or to "take personal responsibility" for his actions. But I think the most powerful thing we can do to gain some semblance of genuine control over our choices is to recognize our tendencies to relinquish control and to succumb to the influences of our environment.

Those of us who are parents know what this awareness is like—we worry about our kids being around other kids who are "bad influences."

We worry about where they are, what they are seeing, and what they are being pressured to do. We understand that one of the most difficult things about growing up is building the capacity to resist bad influences and accept good ones. That is, growing up is about developing the ability to make one's own choices rather than mimic the choices of those around us.

The more I understand the contours of human choice, the more I believe that this process of growing up should continue long past age eighteen. Even as adults, we are wise to pick our friends carefully, to be aware of the influences of our surroundings, and to be humble about our abilities to resist the pull of bad choices once we're in bad environments. Jesus was onto something when he included in his most famous prayer the supplication "Lead us not into temptation." He is not reported to have said, "Give us strength to resist." Perhaps he knew we would be better off not to be tempted in the first place.

A second way we strengthen our capacity to choose is by acknowledging our limitations and "irrational" tendencies. We've seen in several places in this book how humans are irrational from an economic perspective, in that they do not always make decisions in ways that make sense to economists. Many of these tendencies are laudable, such as acting altruistically. But some irrational tendencies constrict our choice making abilities. For instance, the fallibility of our memories poses real problems for how we make choices, since our decisions about the future are inevitably based in part on our memories of the past. We tend to collapse our memories into a Reader's Digest version of our history. We'll remember the first part of an event, the high points and low points, and the last part. If the last moments of a medical procedure are particularly unpleasant, if the last day of a vacation is unusually stressful, if the last moments of an interaction with a friend are awkward, or if the dessert at a fancy restaurant is disappointing, it will disproportionately color our memory of the experience. The quality of our choices about going back to the doctor, saving money for another vacation, seeing the friend again soon, or returning to the restaurant will suffer.

Here's the good news. Most of the power of this memory "defect" is likely to vanish simply by making people aware of this tendency. Once we are aware of our fallibility, we can adjust our thinking about the past. I have started using this insight when my family plans our vacations. I understand that the last day of the vacation is probably the most important in creating a positive memory of the trip for the family. And you know how the last day of a vacation is often the worst? You're tired and cranky. Traveling is stressful. You're going back to work or school the next day. So our strategy is to reduce the length of our vacations by a day. We can be more relaxed in our return, be in better spirits, and have a transition day at home before the work or school week starts. We do this because we have a greater likelihood of *remembering* the vacation more favorably if its last day was pleasant rather than characterized by collective exhaustion and mutual ill humor. I offer this example not to suggest how to plan a vacation but to show that my understanding of my own tendencies in remembering the past has helped me make better choices.

Other choice making tendencies, cataloged in earlier chapters, can be accommodated and allowed for. For example, humans tend to believe that beautiful people are more trustworthy and that ugly or obese people are less so, but we can mitigate the effect simply by being aware of the tendency. We tend to believe factual assertions or opinions that match up with our own cultural and political beliefs, but if we're conscious of it we can inject a dose of skepticism about views that match up with ours, and openness toward those that conflict. We are susceptible to frames and anchors that trick our minds into making certain comparisons ("This suit is half as expensive as that one!" or "If you will buy this car today I will give you a 10 percent discount off the Manufacturer's Suggested Retail Price!"), but we can learn to recognize those influences and protect ourselves against them.

What I am suggesting is a little humility about our choice making powers. If we're not careful, we can be nudged in all kinds of different ways by those who know our tendencies better than we do. It may be counterintuitive, but the more we know about our own fallibility, the better choosers we are likely to be.

A third way we can become better choosers is to be mindful of our habits. We've discussed in several places in this book our how brains crave shortcuts. We love routine, familiarity, rote. Our worlds are so complex that we would go insane if we deliberated about every decision and every purchase. So our brains develop habits that save us time, energy, and sanity. We also develop schemas—rules of thumb—that help us make quick decisions in the face of complexity.

So habit, routines, and schemas can be extraordinarily helpful. But whether they are a positive or negative influence on our lives depends on the habits. If they make us happier and healthier, that's an advantage. If they make us miserable, less wise, or more physically fragile, they're a bad thing.

Here's how we can be better choosers when it comes to habits.

Sometimes I hear talk of the importance of a considered life, of constant awareness of the world around me, of the need for vigilance to recognize markers of beauty and meaning in the world. Henry Miller urged that "the aim of life is to live, and to live means to be aware, joyously, drunkenly, serenely, divinely aware."[6] Far be it from me to criticize the importance of thoughtfulness and awareness. But I think we are bound to be better choosers if we also acknowledge our need for habit. Our brains are hardwired to *escape* awareness and deliberation. We will be better choosers if we acknowledge this and learn to harness our habits as well as our considered behavior.

We should try to be more intentional in creating our routines and in monitoring the ones we have. Habits that "just happen" are as likely to be destructive as constructive, and as likely to be the product of some marketer's manipulation as of considered thought. It's probably worth taking stock of our habits and schemas once in a while, to check in with ourselves (or someone we trust) and deliberate about whether our routines of mind and behavior should be adjusted. Once, when I was in high school, my mom was driving me to school as I complained about how I didn't want to go. She pulled to the side of the road and told me that it was my decision whether I would go to school or not, that she would drive me back home if I wanted. It was a brilliant parenting move. I realized I needed to go to school for this or that, and asked her to drive on. Her stopping the car jarred me out of my habit and forced me to make a fresh choice. Not a bad strategy once in a while.

As we examine our habits, if we find ourselves making habitual mistakes, we should try to make some *different* mistakes. "Make a new mistake," my friend Jeff sometimes says. He means that when we get in a rut we should be willing to try something new, even if we are clumsy or inelegant in the attempt. We can also be on the lookout when we create new habits—when we go into new jobs, new schools, new stores, new homes, new relationships—because that's when we can most easily create good routines and avoid bad ones. Here's an example: my wife and I just bought a new stove, and I am using the change as the reason to learn how to cook something other than scrambled eggs. I am using the new stove as an opportunity to create a new habit—cooking better and more often.

Writers John Seymour and Joseph O'Connor say that "once a response becomes a habit, you stop learning. Theoretically, you could act differently, but in practice you do not. Habits are extremely useful, they streamline the parts of our lives we do not want to think about . . . But there is an art to deciding what parts of your life you want to turn over to habit, and what parts of your life you want to continue to learn from and have choice about."[7]

A fourth way to build our choice making power is to develop an awareness of how culture influences us. This suggestion is, in a sense, a subset of the guideline that we should acknowledge the influence of circumstance and situation, but I think it merits its own discussion. As I discussed earlier in the book, culture is like water to a fish. We live in it and depend on it but aren't always conscious of its presence. Our political and social culture is the sum of our public habits and routines—it short-circuits deliberation and is very difficult to break.

Just like personal habits, culture can be good or bad, empowering or debilitating. We need not be such cultural skeptics that we question everything all the time. Just as an insistence on constant awareness is a recipe for insanity in our personal lives, constant skepticism and challenge to cultural norms is a recipe for quick ostracism at our next cocktail party or PTA meeting.

But we become better choosers if we learn to recognize how our choices are influenced by cultural and political norms. Once we see where and how the norms operate, we are better able to choose whether to operate within them or outside them. The more we see the influence of societal habits on sex and gender roles, views of race, the status of religion, entertainment, styles of dress, patriotism, consumerism, and so on, the more we can gain sufficient detachment to have a shot at making our own choices, more of the time, about cultural matters.

This is much easier said than done, but I believe exposure to other cultures can move us in the right direction. The best ways to gain some understanding of the power of our own culture are to travel more among others and to read more about others. Occasionally watching a good movie from a different cultural point of view isn't a bad idea, either. Excursions need not take us far away; they can be a trip to the Mississippi Delta if you're from Los Angeles, or a visit to Castro Street in San Francisco if you're from Des Moines. I could stand to test my own assumptions by walking across a cultural chasm once in a while.

These four ideas—*recognize the power of situation, acknowledge our irrationalities, be mindful of habits,* and *cultivate an awareness of cultural*

*"No, I don't want to change you, Darryl. But sure, it
would be great if you were completely different."*

influence—can only do so much. We can become better at making choices,
but I do not believe the improvement is likely to be large. Most people do
not significantly change the way they think once they reach adulthood,
unless they suffer a catastrophic event, a religious conversion, or the end
or beginning of an addiction. It is a humbling lesson for authors of books,
preachers of sermons, and facilitators of ethics seminars to learn that people don't generally change as a result of their entreaties.

A recent study asked seminary students to give a talk about either
the parable of the Good Samaritan—where the Samaritan helps a person hurt on the side of a road—or a morally neutral topic about careers.
They were each to study their topics, prepare their talks, and then walk
across campus to another building to deliver it. On their way, they passed
a person in apparent need of help, who was actually a confederate of the
experimenters. Some seminarians had been told that they were late for

their appointment, and some were allowed to walk more leisurely. Fewer than half of the seminarians stopped to assist the person in distress. Those who were in a hurry were less likely to help; those who were not in a hurry were more likely to help. But the content of the talk they had been asked to give mattered not at all. Those who were about to deliver a message about helping those in need were no more likely to provide succor than those who were to give a talk about careers.[8]

I am bemused but not surprised by this finding. Our situation is likely to matter quite a bit. But we're not likely to change our natures much, whether we're scorpions or Samaritans.

2.

The hard question, then, is whether we can be any more successful building choice through external rather than internal means. Can we build choice by adjusting public policy? Can we make people better choosers by changing the circumstances in which they choose?

In thinking about this challenge, there is an important distinction to keep in mind. We are not only talking about encouraging people to make better decisions. We also need to ask whether and how we make it possible for individuals to *build the capacity* to make better decisions. These are different challenges.

Encouraging people to make better decisions is a large part of law. On one end of the spectrum of public policies are criminal punishments. These punishments are more than encouragements—they're mandates. To be a part of society you have to be willing to engage in specific behavior, whether you want to or not. You must pay taxes, drive on the correct side of the street, and provide clothing and shelter to your children. If you don't, you will be subject to criminal punishment. Also, society sets some decisions off-limits by way of bans or exclusions, backed with criminal penalties. A ban on prostitution, heroin, or backyard incinerators is simply society's way of saying that a decision to sell sex, use heroin, or burn household garbage is bad enough, enough of the time, to justify prohibiting the behavior.

Libertarian eras come and go, but even when libertarianism is "in," as it seems to be now, it is difficult to find someone who believes that this category of bans and criminal punishments should be empty. People might disagree on specific issues such as marijuana, handguns in the home, or late-term abortions, but all but the most unreasonable believe that the government should occasionally step in and overrule some individuals' choices. There is an implicit balancing between the desire to protect the autonomy of individuals and the desire to protect individuals from themselves and others. The question is where to draw the line.

Short of these mandates, law has a number of tools for encouraging good choices. The government can subsidize good decisions (installing home insulation or replacing your clunker with a new car) and tax bad ones (smoking cigarettes or refusing to buy health insurance). It can require us to disclose certain information necessary for others to make good decisions about such things as stock trades, chemical exposure in workplaces, and the side effects of prescription drugs. And the government can require that you take sufficient time to think through your choice, whether it be a big purchase (lemon laws give buyers a certain number of days to make a return) or a major life decision such as whether to get married (roughly half the states require some kind of waiting period before issuing a marriage license).[9]

Increasingly, public policy experts are urging governments to take advantage of so-called choice architecture in order to nudge individuals toward better decisions. Cass Sunstein and Richard Thaler have popularized the notion of "libertarian paternalism," the idea that even if government should not *require* certain decisions, it need not be neutral in whether they should be encouraged. Public policy can be used "to move people in directions that will make their lives better."[10] An example of a nudge is putting fruit at the beginning of school lunch lines rather than at the end. This action does not require school children to eat fruit, but it uses our known tendency to select food early in a food line to encourage more healthful eating. Another example is to create a default rule in favor of organ donation whenever someone renews a driver's license. Individuals can still opt out, but our tendency to stick with the status quo will result in a greater number of organ donations, thus saving lives. Another nudge is disclosure, usually about costs, so that consumers can do a better job choosing financial products, cell phones, or prescription drug plans. Sunstein and Thaler's book *Nudge* is full of similar policy ideas.

In a sense, choice architecture is simply using the insights of behaviorists and psychologists for public policy goals rather than to sell cigarettes, cars, or toothpaste. The choice architects are taking the suggestions like those in the previous section, aimed at individuals, and applying them more globally. In other words, they argue we should take advantage of humans' tendencies to conform their behavior to situational cues, to succumb to habit, and to make decisions based on irrationalities, and use these tendencies for good.

I'm a fan of Sunstein and Thaler's work, and I could get behind most of their very clever proposals. But I think we should nudge their views a little further.

The "nudgers" credit human decision making a great deal. They may call their suggestions libertarian paternalism, but it's still libertarian. As Sunstein and Thaler claim in their introduction, "Choices are not blocked, fenced off, or significantly burdened . . . If people want to smoke cigarettes, to eat a lot of candy, to choose an unsuitable health care plan, or to fail to save for retirement, libertarian paternalists will not force them to do otherwise—or even make things hard for them."[11]

Where I differ from them is that they imply that without nudges we operate in a world in which human autonomy and human choice flourishes. They feel they can "influence choices in a way that will make choosers better off, as judged by themselves,"[12] but they are defensive about nudges, especially those put into place by law or regulation. They consider a nudge a shift from a neutral position, one that has to be justified in order to merit the displacement of individual liberty.

If, on the other hand, the realm of human autonomy is small, then nudges will not always be enough. If without nudges our decision making faculties are already a battleground, then a nudge isn't a shift from neutrality. It is more like bringing a knife to a gun fight. Not enough.

Once we recognize the malleability of choice, and how we are already shoved in various ways by the market, authority, culture, and the like, we may need more than an occasional nudge to achieve important public policy results. To fight obesity, for example, we need to do more than put healthy food at the beginning of school lunch lines or disclose calorie counts. Perhaps we should engage in new and serious efforts to build public parks and maintain their safety. Perhaps we should ban fast food restaurants in new neighborhoods, as some cities and towns have done.[13] Perhaps we should ban trans fats or end the subsidies that make corn sweeteners artificially cheap. Perhaps we should tax supermarket companies that build in rich neighborhoods, and subsidize supermarket companies that build in poorer neighborhoods. Given the host of cultural, commercial, and biological forces brought to bear on people's food choices, an occasional nudge in favor of eating an apple will not come close to ending the obesity epidemic.

Moreover, once we realize the tenuousness of good decision making, we should be less sanguine about the power of disclosure. I do believe that the required disclosure of information can be helpful at times, especially when the information is about alternatives rather than merely costs. But disclosure is too often seen as an easily legislated panacea. Too much information can sometimes be worse than too little, since we are easily overwhelmed by details. Also, disclosure does little to alter the power relationships between the discloser and the disclosee, whether the disclosees are holders of credit cards, users of cell phones, or employees of coal mines.

Unlike the libertarian paternalists, I would not start with a presumption that whatever an individual has decided is necessarily correct. I would recognize that disclosure does not always do all that we want. I would be less skeptical of bans and mandates, especially with regard to choices that humans tend to make poorly, have high costs when made poorly, are difficult to learn from (for example, they do not repeat, or have effects that occur in the future), or are already subject to multiple malignant influences.

All in all, I think protecting a sphere where people can exercise their choice making powers is a laudable and important public policy goal, because protecting choice can be a good way to build it, and because sometimes even bad choices are better than none. But when we protect this sphere of human choice, we should not delude ourselves that we are preserving a natural space where autonomous individuals revel in their cognitive freedom. We should protect a sphere of human choice *despite* the fact it is a constructed, contested space where choices are sometimes manipulated and manufactured.

3.

We have come to the last and most difficult category of implications for the myth of choice. We've discussed what each of us can do individually to make ourselves better choice makers, and we've discussed how public policy can encourage better choices. We now need to talk about how public policy can be used to build the capacity to make better choices. How can we use external tools to get people to change their internal abilities? That is, how do we use nurture to change people's natures when it comes to choice making?

Answering this question may seem like a fool's errand. Why should we believe that public policy or legal tools can help people be better decision makers? The answer is that we already do it all the time, and sometimes it actually works. We require every child in the country to attend school, at least until age sixteen or so, in part because we want them to have the tools to make good choices in their lives. We require or encourage people who want to get a driver's license to take driver's education classes. We require people who want to be lawyers to go to law school, to develop not only the requisite knowledge but also some semblance of the judgment competent lawyers need.

So let me articulate three big, but general, ideas of how we might make it possible for more people, more of the time, to make good choices.

First, we should work to ensure that economic need is not a source of coercion. As we think about the range of bad choices people are forced into—to work for an employer who puts employees at risk, to sell sex for money, or to buy cheap, fatty food—many of the most problematic choices are brought about by simple economic need. Remember Henry Lamson from the first chapter, he of the ax-in-the-head case. He knew the risk of injury in his job but stayed anyway. Judge Oliver Wendell Holmes, Jr., said that Lamson should not be able to sue his employer, since he "stayed, and took the risk." The reason Lamson's decision does not sound like a real choice to modern readers is that we assume, I think reasonably, that he did not have a lot of other employment options and he had to provide for his family. A safety net for employees who lose their jobs not only would give those employees the choice to leave dangerous jobs but would incentivize employers to offer better jobs in the first place.

By similar reasoning, we could do much to alleviate the coercive aspects of the sex industry. As I mentioned early in the book, reasonable people across the political spectrum disagree about the nature of sex work and whether it can and should be a realm of choice and agency for women.

Some see it as inherently coercive; others argue that, given the right circumstances, it can be a legitimate line of work.

By my lights, there is nothing inherently different between selling one's sexual services (and being willing to suffer the risks of those activities) and selling one's expertise in mining coal, driving a cab, or butchering meat (and suffering the risks thereof). But most women involved in the sex industry around the world are doing it from coercion rather than by choice. The coercion in sex slavery and trafficking is easy to see.[14] A slightly less obvious coercion inheres in the fact that, as a matter of economics and culture, many women in the sex industry have few other ways to provide for themselves and their dependents. I would be more willing to entertain the notion that the sex industry should be more broadly destigmatized if there were more indicia of real choice among the women involved. One of the ways to build such choice is to make sure that no one is driven into the industry by economic coercion.

I recognize that it is extremely difficult to draw a clear line between choice and coercion when it comes to evaluating a decision to sell one's body for sex. But some things are certain. The less sex and gender equality in a culture, the less likely such a decision is a real choice. The fewer employment alternatives, the less likely such a decision is a real choice. The more such jobs are occupied by people at the lower rungs of the social, economic, and cultural power structures, the more we can presume the decision comes about as a result of powerlessness rather than autonomy. When these situations create the context of the decisions made, then we can have a great deal of certainty that efforts to expand economic, social, and cultural choice will be worth the effort.

A second way to build choice as a matter of public policy is to encourage political and cultural dissent and diversity. One of the things known to build capacity for choice is exposure to new ways of thinking and acting. Groups that contain a critical mass of dissenters—or at least those who question the prevailing wisdom—tend to make better decisions over time.[15] As noted in chapter eight, diverse, pluralistic groups are better than individuals or homogeneous groups at encouraging explanation, teasing out underlying assumptions, and identifying and defending animating values. When groups are too homogeneous, individuals in the group have a tendency to reinforce, rather than challenge, the cultural assumptions of others. Diversity is thus not just a feel-good word for liberals looking to broaden their electoral appeal. It actually improves decision making, whether in the political sphere, on university campuses, or in corporate boardrooms.

The need for diversity is a reason to continue affirmative action programs in government work, university admissions, and corporate hiring, even if invidious discrimination should someday cease to be a problem. In fact, the need for diversity would counsel expanding affirmative action for other classes of individuals who bring different perspectives to the table. A commitment to cultural and political diversity would also suggest that we should end the practice of gerrymandering congressional districts to make them safe Democratic or Republican strongholds. It might be better for all of us if we were forced to come out of our political enclaves every election year, to work with, fight with, and debate with those we oppose.

The need to encourage the habit of considering other perspectives would also suggest the importance of cross-cultural exposure. Educational exchange programs should be expanded, international and interstate cultural and artistic collaborations should be subsidized, and national service programs such as VISTA and the Peace Corps should be beefed up. English-only initiatives should be abandoned, along with the anti-immigrant xenophobia that motivates them.

Building the capacity for dissent in educational settings is also key. This is asking much of our educators, I admit, but teachers should insist less on socialization toward the broad middle and more on tolerance of difference and nurturing of the personal character necessary for dissent. This may mean less obsessing over saying the Pledge of Allegiance every day, and more protection of those who dress, think, or self-identify differently from the majority.

The third and final big idea I want to propose is that we should expand opportunities to make public commitments. People are sometimes able to protect themselves from the influences of situation through public or semi-public commitments. Two salient examples are the right to free speech and the institution of marriage. The constitutional right to free speech operates as a legal commitment to protect politically unpopular viewpoints even (or especially) in circumstances when a majority of the polity would not protect them. It's a commitment, entered into coolly and in a moment of detached reflection, that protects the polity from acting rashly in the heat of the moment. Marriage is also a commitment, solemnized before friends and family, that operates to protect individuals from the biological, economic, and cultural prods toward infidelity and shirking.

Such commitments, made enforceable in various ways, have a long tradition. The ancient Greek orator Demosthenes once shaved half his head to make sure he did not appear in public until it grew back. He spent the next three months working on his rhetoric.[16] Scholar Kwame Anthony Appiah has written about how the millennium-old practice of footbinding in China vanished in a generation in part because of public pledges made by families not to allow their daughters to be bound and not to allow their sons to marry daughters who were.[17] A more current example is the website StickK.com, created by three Yale academics. StickK allows people to "put a contract out on yourself!" by signing up to meet some kind of goal—quitting smoking, or writing a dissertation—and establishing penalties for failure. The penalties can be a donation to what the site calls an "anti-charity"—groups whose mission you oppose. These anti-charities include both the Clinton and Bush Presidential Libraries, the National Rifle Association, the National Abortion Rights Action League, and the fan club to the Manchester United soccer team. According to the site, enforceable commitment contracts can triple the probability of success in meeting the underlying goal.[18]

Not all pre-commitments appear to work. So-called chastity pledges, where teenagers commit to remain chaste until marriage, have a notoriously high failure rate, and some evidence suggests that those who break their pledges are more likely to engage in unsafe sex than teenagers who do not take a pledge.[19] Marriages, too, fail at a high rate, though I suspect they fail less often than relationships left unsolemnized.

I don't believe these commitments will cure all ills, but I'm convinced that they are underutilized as a public policy tool. Cities and towns could ask families to make public commitments to live "greener" by riding public transportation more, by recycling more, or by reducing energy use in homes. These commitments could be publicly memorialized in some way, perhaps by giving residents yard or window signs, to retard backsliding. Secondary schools with high dropout rates could begin fall semesters by asking for public commitments from students and families to meet definable goals during the year. Businesses could be asked to join coalitions of firms that publicly agree to set aside a percentage of profits for charitable donations. And the right to marry could be extended to same-sex couples in those states that do not yet allow it, in order to expand the benefit of marriage as pre-commitment.

As I write this final chapter, my newborn daughter is sleeping nearby. By the time this book is published, she will likely be toddling about the house under the watchful eyes of her parents and older brother. As she grows, what will I teach her about choices, about personal responsibility? Will I teach her that choice is a myth, and that she is merely an object on which her circumstances and situation will act?

Of course not. But I will not take her abilities to choose for granted. I will understand that her nature and character will have a huge impact on her destiny, so I will try my best to mold them while they are moldable. I will help her understand the influence of her environment and culture on her choices, and I will be mindful of which influences I should encourage and which I should protect her from. I will understand that her choice making powers are not innately strong, so I will seek out ways for her to strengthen them. I will understand that she will make mistakes, so I will seek to be empathetic and in doing so teach her to be empathetic of the mistakes of her father and others.

This is my pre-commitment to her, memorialized in print.

So in the end, I am not as bereft of hope as the title of this book might suggest. I do believe that most of us, most of the time, would do well to recognize how often real choice is a mirage and how frequently the rhetoric of choice is misleading. But it need not be so.

It would be a nice legacy if, little by little, choice became more real, not only for my daughter and my son, but for you and your family as well.

Acknowledgments

I OWE MANY PEOPLE A DEBT OF GRATITUDE for their assistance and encouragement while I wrote this book. Thanks go to those who read partial or complete drafts and offered helpful suggestions: Richard Albert, Victor Brudney, Nicolas Dunn, Janet Gilmore, Barbra Greenfield, Harold Greenfield, Cliff Guthrie, Owen Jones, Mike McCann, Sashank Prasad, Jed Purdy, and David Yosifon. Special thanks to my colleagues at Boston College Law School and the students there who sat through myriad discussions of these topics as my thoughts coalesced. I want to acknowledge the excellent research help of my librarian colleague Mary Ann Neary, as well as the wonderful help I have received from several years' worth of research assistants, most recently and notably Jason Burke, Colin Levy, and Meredith Regan. (I know it's trite to say, but I could not have done it without you!) The project benefited greatly from feedback received at faculty workshops at the University of British Columbia Faculty of Law, Husson University, the University of Indiana at Indianapolis, the University of Oregon School of Law, the University of Tulsa College of Law, Western New England College School of Law, and the University of Windsor Faculty of Law. Heartfelt thanks to Yale University Press's Jack Borrebach and Jaya Chatterjee, whose professionalism and intelligence enhanced the book greatly.

A few words about a handful of colleagues who especially helped with this project. Jon Hanson's scholarship and intellectual entrepreneurship around the power of situation was instrumental in my early interest in the topic of choice. Joe Singer and Larry Mitchell have both served as mentors to me not only in this project but in my career generally; I would not have enjoyed the professional success I have but for them. Dan Kanstroom has consistently offered friendship, collegiality, support, and a congenial laugh. My agent, Susan Schulman, recognized value in this project before almost anyone, and she generously saw me through to its completion at a time when, we both happily realize, the project has more currency than at any point in its development. My editor William Frucht's wise counsel and deft suggestions have improved the final product immensely. Frank Partnoy offered numerous helpful pieces of advice on writing and publishing, based on his extensive experience as a law professor writing (in his case, successfully) for a broader audience. Adam Winkler became my writing partner, challenging me with chapter deadlines and dutifully reading and commenting on each chapter as I produced them. I owe each of these friends a large debt of gratitude.

Of course the largest dollop of appreciation goes to my family. Ruby is my new joy. My son Liam, during our frequent hikes or trips to the library, offered encouragement and substantive comments the sophistication and insight of which would surprise only those who don't know him. This book is dedicated to my wife, Dana McSherry, who never flagged in her dedication to me or the project. She is the best choice I ever made.

Notes

CHAPTER I
Choices, Choices, Choices

1. JOHN COOK, THE BOOK OF POSITIVE QUOTATIONS 253 (2d ed. 1993) (Roosevelt); 406–07 (Camus); 416 (Bryan); 406 (Auden).
2. *Lamson v. American Axe & Tool Co.*, 177 Mass. 144, 58 N. E. 585 (1900).
3. *Costa v. Boston Red Sox Baseball Club*, 61 Mass.App.Ct. 299, 809 N.E.2d 1090 (2004).
4. See Kevin Baxter, *Foul Balls Are a Scary Part of Baseball*, LOS ANGELES TIMES, June 17, 2008.
5. For an excellent analysis of the role of individualism in American culture and how it can hide what is actually happening in social and economic terms, see generally LAWRENCE E. MITCHELL, STACKED DECK (1998).
6. For an excellent treatment of the nature of the choices made by the victims of Katrina, see generally Jon Hanson & Kathleen Hanson, *Blame Frames: Justifying Racial Oppression in America*, 41 HARV. CIV. RTS-CIV. LIB. L. REV. 413 (2006); for Brown, see *FEMA Chief: Victims Bear Some Responsibility*, CNN.com, Sept. 1, 2005; for Santorum, see Sean D. Hamill, *Santorum Retreats on Evacuation Penalty Remarks*, Post-Gazette.com, Sept. 7, 2005; *Editorial, Malfeasance of Citizenship*, WASH. TIMES, Sept. 9, 2005, at A22; Neal Boortz, Today's Nuze: Sept. 7, 2005, http://boortz.com.
7. See James Carney, *Living Too Much in the Bubble?*, TIME MAG., Sept. 11, 2005, at 42.
8. Wash. Post et al., *Survey of Hurricane Katrina Evacuees* 5 (2005), available at http://www.kff.org/newsmedia/7401.cfm.
9. *Study: People Found Unattractive If They Stand Next to Obese Friends*, USA TODAY, Oct. 15, 2003.
10. See *Pelman v. McDonald's Corp.*, 237 F.Supp.2d 512 (2003); Marc Santora, *Teenagers' Suit Says McDonald's Made Them Obese*, N.Y. TIMES, Nov. 21, 2002, at B1.

11. The best work in legal scholarship on the context of eating decisions is Adam Benforado, Jon Hanson & David Yosifon, *Broken Scales: Obesity and Justice in America*, 53 EMORY L. J. 311 (2004); for "It's the environment": Natasha Singer, *Fixing a World That Fosters Fat*, N.Y. TIMES, August 22, 2010.

12. In fact, in Michigan, adultery may be punishable by life in prison. See Mich. Comp. Laws § 750.520b(1)(c) (1979); Mich. Comp. Laws § 750.30 (1979); *People v. Waltonen*, 728 N.W.2d 881, 890 (2006).

13. *If Your Neighbor Poses as Your Husband, Is It Rape?*, National Public Radio, Day to Day (transcript), May 5, 2008, available at http://www.npr.org.

14. Steven G. Calabresi, *Lawrence, The Fourteenth Amendment, and the Supreme Court's Reliance on Foreign Constitutional Law: An Originalist Reappraisal*, 65 OHIO ST. L. J. 1097, 1123 (2004).

15. Noah Feldman, *Islam, Terror and the Second Nuclear Age*, N.Y. TIMES MAGAZINE, Oct. 29, 2006, at 50, 56.

16. Tatian's Address to the Greeks, in 3 ANTI-NICENE CHRISTIAN LIBRARY: TRANSLATIONS OF THE WRITINGS OF THE FATHERS DOWN TO A.D. 325 1, 11 (B.P. Pratten et al. eds., 1867); Saint Augustine, *Grace and Free Will* (De gratia et libero arbitrio), in 59 THE FATHERS OF THE CHURCH: A NEW TRANSLATION 243, 251 (Robert P. Russell trans., 1968); C. S. LEWIS, THE GREAT DIVORCE 75 (2001) (1946).

CHAPTER 2
In Love with Choice

Epigraphs: Matt Bai, *Democrat in Chief?*, N.Y. TIMES MAGAZINE, June 8, 2010. The Glenn Beck Program (radio), January 26, 2011 (see http://www.glennbeck.com).

1. Gregg Cebrzynski, *Burger King Revives "Your Way" Tag in New TV Campaign*, NATION'S RESTAURANT NEWS, Mar. 8, 2004; Michael McCarthy, *Burger King Tries Old Slogan Again*, USA TODAY, May 23, 2005.

2. See SHEENA IYENGAR, THE ART OF CHOOSING 187 (2010).

3. The Nielsen Company, Press Release, *Average U.S. Home Now Receives a Record 118.6 TV Channels, According to Nielsen*, June 6, 2008, available at http://en-us.nielsen.com.

4. Wendy's commercial entitled "Saloon," created by Saatchi & Saatchi, NY, 2007.

5. See Iyengar, *supra*, at 184–87; Sheena S. Iyengar & Mark R. Lepper, *Rethinking the Value of Choice: A Cultural Perspective on Intrinsic Motivation*, 76 J. OF PER-

SONALITY & SOC. PSYCHOL. 349 (1999); Sheena S. Iyengar & Mark R. Lepper, *When Choice is Demotivating: Can One Desire Too Much of a Good Thing?*, 79 J. OF PERSONALITY AND SOC. PSYCHOL. 995 (2000); *see also* BARRY SCHWARTZ, THE PARADOX OF CHOICE (2004).

6. "Death of freedom" was a comment of Tennessee Congresswoman Marsha Blackburn during the health care reform debate, as quoted in Ezra Klein, *Health Care and Freedom*, WASH. POST, Mar. 21, 2010; "growth of personal responsibility" and "movement to choice" were invoked by a newsletter published by the Center for Health Transformation, founded by former speaker of the House Newt Gingrich. Ronald Bachman, *ObamaCare, Megatrends, and Consumerism*, CONSUMERISM CORNER Vol.1, No. 1, available at http://www.healthtransformation.net.

7. For the statements of the Workforce Fairness Institute, see their "issues" page at http://www.workforcefairness.com; for the Facebook group, see The Employee Free Choice Act (EFCA) Is Bad for America, http://www.facebook.com/group.php?gid=35899106329; for the U.S. Chamber of Commerce page on the Employee Free Choice Act, see the "issues" tab for "labor" at http://www.uschamber.com.

8. Personal Responsibility in Food Consumption Act of 2005, H.R. 554, 109th Cong. (2005); for text and history, see http://www.govtrack.us.

9. Couric's interview of Palin is available at Katie Couric, *Palin Opens Up on Controversial Issues*, www.cbsnews.com, Sept. 30, 2008.

10. RICKIE SOLINGER, BEGGARS AND CHOOSERS: HOW THE POLITICS OF CHOICE SHAPED ADOPTION, ABORTION, AND WELFARE IN THE UNITED STATES 4–5 (2002).

11. *Odorizzi v. Bloomfield School District*, 54 Cal. Rptr. 533 (1966).

12. *Fain v. Commonwealth*, 78 Ky. 183 (1879).

13. See Deborah W. Denno, *Crime and Consciousness: Science and Voluntary Acts*, 87 MINN. L. REV. 269, 275 (2002) ("Doctrinally, all criminal liability depends on one 'fundamental predicate': A defendant's guilt must be based on conduct and that conduct must include a 'voluntary act' or omission to engage in a voluntary act that the defendant was capable of performing."); John A. Humbach, Free Will Ideology: Experiments, Evolution, and Virtue Ethics (Jan. 12, 2010) (working paper), available at http.//ssrn.org.

14. *United States v. Drayton*, 536 U.S. 194 (2002).

15. *West Virginia State Bd. Of Education v. Barnette*, 319 U.S. 624 (1943).

16. David Byers et al., *Gang Rape Releases Cause Aboriginal Fury*, THE TIMES, Dec. 10, 2007, available at http://www.timesonline.co.uk; Padraic Murphy, Natasha

Robinson & Tony Koch, *Gang-Rape Judge in New Child Sex Furore*, THE AUS-TRALIAN, Feb. 15, 2008, at 1.

17. "Rape is not committed" in *People v. Carey*, 119 N.E. 83 (N.Y. 1918); "outward manifestation of nonconsent" in Roger B. Dworkin, Note, *The Resistance Standard in Rape Legislation*, 18 STAN. L. REV. 680, 689 (1966).

18. *State in Interest of M.T.S.*, 609 A.2d 1266 (N.J. 1992).

19. Michelle J. Anderson, *Negotiating Sex*, 78 S. CAL. L. REV. 1401 (2005).

20. See "Decriminalize Prostitution!" Meetup group, San Francisco, available at http://www.meetup.com/decriminalize.

CHAPTER 3
Our Choices, Our Brains

Epigraphs: "Don't Look at Me That Way" (from "Paris"), words and music by Cole Porter, copyright © 1928 (renewed) Warner Bros. Inc. All rights reserved; used by permission. GREGORY MAGUIRE, WICKED: THE LIFE AND TIMES OF THE WICKED WITCH OF THE WEST 231 (1996, 1st paperback ed.).

1. AMBROSE BIERCE, CYNIC'S WORD BOOK 39 (1906).

2. Gene Weingarten, *Fatal Distraction*, WASH. POST MAG., Mar. 8, 2009, at 14.

3. You can hear the 911 call at *Mom Acquitted but Tortured by Son's Death*, ABC News, Jan. 28, 2008, http://abcnews.go.com. For an award-winning, in-depth look at the problems of "forgotten baby syndrome" see Weingarten, *supra*, at 8.

4. Weingarten, *supra*, at 12–14.

5. *Mom Acquitted but Tortured by Son's Death*, *supra*; Weingarten, *supra*, at 25–26.

6. Weingarten, *supra*, at 12–14. An accessible treatment of the nature of how our brains evolved is GARY MARCUS, KLUGE: THE HAPHAZARD EVOLUTION OF THE HUMAN MIND (2008).

7. JONAH LEHRER, HOW WE DECIDE 151–52 (2009). See also Sandra Aamodt & Sam Wang, *Tighten Your Belt, Strengthen Your Mind*, N.Y. TIMES, Apr. 2, 2008 (discussing the brain's "limited capacity for self-regulation" and how it can be over-taxed by exertion of willpower). The leading scholar in this area of brain science is Roy Baumeister. See, for example, Roy Baumeister, Ellen Bratslavsky, Mark Muraven & Diane Tice, *Ego Depletion: Is the Active Self a Limited Resource?*, 74 J. OF PERSONALITY & SOC. PSYCHOL. 1252 (1998) (test subjects who ate radishes instead of chocolates quit attempts to solve a puzzle sooner); Diane Tice, Roy Baumeister, Dikla Shmueli & Mark Muraven, *Restoring the Self: Positive Affect Helps Improve Self-Regulation Following Ego Depletion*, 43 J. OF EXP. SOC. PSY-

CHOL. 379 (2007) (discussing ways to "recharge" willpower by using comedy or an unexpected gift).

8. Weingarten, *supra*, at 12–14; Marcus, *supra*, at 52

9. See generally, Model Penal Code § 210.2, cmt. at 16 (1980); SAMUEL H. PILLS-BURY, JUDGING EVIL: RETHINKING THE LAW OF MURDER AND MANSLAUGHTER, 79–186 (1998); for a discussion of the law surrounding the heat of passion, see generally Stephen P. Garvey, *Passion's Puzzle*, 90 IOWA L. REV. 1677 (2005); for a classic case of recklessness and manslaughter, see *Commonwealth v. Welanksy*, 316 Mass. 383, 55 N.E.2d 902 (1944) (holding a nightclub owner liable for reckless disregard for violating occupancy levels and fire codes).

10. In New York, for example, a defendant can only be charged with first-degree murder "in a variety of special circumstances, such as when the victim is a police officer or an employee of a state or local correctional institution, or when the crime is committed while a defendant is either in custody under a life sentence or is at large after having escaped from such custody." See NY PENAL § 125.27. In Pennsylvania murder is divided into three degrees. See 18 Pa.C.S.A. § 2502.

11. For the influence of brain science on punishment, see generally O. Carter Snead, *Neuroimaging and the Complexity of Capital Punishment*, 82 N.Y.U. L. REV. 1265 (2007) and Tenielle Brown & Emily Murphy, *Through a Scanner Darkly: Functional Neuroimaging as Evidence of a Criminal Defendant's Past Mental States*, 62 STAN. L. REV. 1119 (2009–2010). For less technical analyses of the possible implications of brain science on criminal law, see: Jeffrey Rosen, *The Brain on the Stand*, N.Y. TIMES MAG., Mar. 11, 2007; Robert Lee Hotz, *The Brain, Your Honor, Will Take The Stand*, WALL ST. J., January 15, 2009.

12. SILENCE OF THE LAMBS (Orion Pictures Corp. 1991).

13. Benedict Carey, *Brain Injury Said to Affect Moral Choices*, N.Y. TIMES, Mar. 22, 2007.

14. J.J. Thompson, *The Trolley Problem*, 94 YALE L. J. 1395 (1985). Another accessible treatment of the trolley car problem is in MICHAEL SANDEL, JUSTICE: WHAT'S THE RIGHT THING TO DO? (2009).

15. Carey, *supra*. See also Nikhil Swaminathan, *Kill One to Save Many? Brain Damage Makes Decision Easier*, SCIENTIFIC AMERICAN, Mar. 21, 2007.

16. For a host of resources on the Whitman killings, see the Whitman Archives of the *Austin Statesman*, available at http://www.statesman.com.

17. Rosen, *supra*.

18. Robin Nixon, *The Bikini Effect Makes Men Impulsive*, LiveScience.com, June 10, 2008; Bram Van Den Bergh, Siegfried Dewitte & Luk Warlop, *Bikinis Instigate*

Generalized Impatience in Intertemporal Choice, 35 J. OF CONSUMER RESEARCH 85, 85–97 (2008).

19. Marcus, *supra*, at 75–77.

20. See Brian Knutson et al., *Neural Predictors of Purchases*, 53 NEURON, Jan. 4, 2007, 147–56. For a description of the results, see John Tierney, *The Voices in My Head Say "Buy It!" Why Argue?*, N.Y. TIMES, Jan. 16, 2007. See also Scott Rick, Cynthia Cryder & George F. Loewenstein, *Tightwads and Spendthrifts* (June 28, 2007), available at http://ssrn.com; Alain Dagher, *Shopping Centers in the Brain*, NEURON (Previews) 7–8, Jan. 4, 2007.

21. Tierney, *supra*.

22. See Knutson, *supra* ("Together, these findings suggest that activation of distinct brain regions related to anticipation of gain and loss precedes and can be used to predict purchasing decisions.")

23. Marcus, *supra*, at 8. Original study is M. G. Haselton & D. M. Buss, *Error Management Theory: A New Perspective on Biases in Cross-Sex Mind Reading*, 78 J. OF PERSONALITY AND SOC. PSYCHOL. 81 (2000).

24. Stephanie Saul, *Gimme an Rx! Cheerleaders Pep Up Drug Sales*, N.Y. TIMES, Nov. 28, 2005.

25. Marcus, *supra*, at 49–50.

26. Raymond S. Nickerson, *Confirmation Bias: A Ubiquitous Phenomenon in Many Guises*, REV. OF GEN. PSYCHOL. 175 (1998).

27. Murray Webster, Jr. & James E. Driskell, Jr., *Beauty as Status*, 89 AMER. J. OF SOCIOLOGY, 140–65 (Jul., 1983). See also Carl Senior & Michael J. R. Butler et al., *Interviewing Strategies in the Face of Beauty: A Psychophysiological Investigation into the Job Negotiation Process*, 1118 ANNALS OF THE N.Y. ACAD. OF SCIENCES, 142–62 (Nov. 2007) (finding that the attractiveness of interviewees can significantly bias outcome in hiring practices, showing a clear distinction between the attractive and average-looking interviewees in terms of high- and low-status job packages offered); NANCY ETCOFF, SURVIVAL OF THE PRETTIEST: THE SCIENCE OF BEAUTY (1999); Carey, *supra*, at 42; for more on the halo effect, see Richard E. Nisbett & Timothy DeCamp Wilson, *The Halo Effect: Evidence for Unconscious Alteration of Judgments*, 35 J. OF PERSONALITY AND SOC. PSYCHOL. 250, 250–56 (1977); Daniel S. Hamermesh & Jeff E. Biddle, *Beauty and the Labor Market*, 84 AMER. ECON. REV. 1174, 1174–94 (Dec. 1994); Jessica Bennett, *The Beauty Advantage*, NEWSWEEK, July 19, 2010 ("Asked to rank employee attributes in order of importance . . . [hiring] managers placed looks above education: of nine character traits, it came in third, below experience (No. 1) and confidence

(No. 2) but above 'where a candidate went to school' (No. 4)."); Stephen Ceci & Justin Gunnell, *When Emotionality Trumps Reason*, forthcoming in BEHAVIORAL SCIENCES AND THE LAW, summary available at http://www.news.cornell.edu/ stories/May10/AttractivenessStudy.html (finding that unattractive defendants tend to get hit with longer, harsher sentences—on average twenty-two months longer in prison); Harold Sigall & Nancy Ostrove, *Beautiful but Dangerous: Effects of Offender Attractiveness and Nature of the Crime on Juridic Judgment*, 31 J. OF PERSONALITY AND SOC. PSYCHOL. 410, 410–414 (1975).

28. Marcus, *supra*, at 44.

29. Amos Tversky & Daniel Kahneman, *Judgment under Uncertainty: Heuristics and Biases*, 185 SCIENCE 1124 (1981).

30. See Jon Hanson & David Yosifon, *The Situational Character: A Critical Realist Perspective on the Human Animal*, 93 GEO. L.J. 1, 61–62 (2004).

31. See Online News Hour, *Bush Defends "RATS" Ad*, September 12, 2000, available at http://www.pbs.org/newshour. The ad is readily available on YouTube by searching for "bush rats ad." "RATS" appears approximately twenty-five seconds into the ad.

32. DREW WESTEN, THE POLITICAL BRAIN 58–59 (2007); see also DANIEL GILBERT, STUMBLING ON HAPPINESS 173 (2006) (explaining a study that showed that volunteers who watched a computer screen on which words such as "hostile," "elderly," and "stupid" appear for only a few milliseconds are unaware of the words but affected by them).

33. See BARRY SCHWARTZ, THE PARADOX OF CHOICE (2004) 61–62.

34. *Id.* at 62.

35. See Gilbert, *supra*, at 78, 202–05; Schwartz, *supra*, at 49; Daniel Kahneman, *Objective Happiness*, in WELL-BEING: FOUNDATIONS OF HEDONIC PSYCHOLOGY 3–25 (Daniel Kahnemen, Ed Diener & Norbery Schwartz, eds., 1999).

36. MEMENTO (Newmarket 2000).

37. Schwartz, *supra*, at 50; Donald A. Redelmeier & Daniel Kahneman, *Patients' Memories of Painful Medical Treatments: Real-Time and Retrospective Evaluations of Two Minimally Invasive Procedures*, 66 PAIN 3, 3–8 (1996).

38. Gilbert, *supra*, at 203.

39. Gilbert, *supra*, at 238.

40. Schwartz, *supra*, at 51; Daniel Read & George Lowenstein, *Diversification Bias: Explaining the Discrepancy in Variety Seeking between Combined and Separated Choices*, J. OF EXP. PSYCH.: APPLIED 1, 34–49 (1995).

41. DAN ARIELY, PREDICTABLY IRRATIONAL (rev. ed., 2009).

CHAPTER 4
Choice and Culture

Epigraphs: LES BACK, THE ART OF LISTENING 15 (2007). TOM PERROTTA, LITTLE CHILDREN 9 (2004).

1. See Mohamed Osman & Sarah el Deeb, *Lubna Hussein Trial: Police Beat Women Opposing Sudan Dress Code*, Associated Press, Aug. 4, 2009; see also *"Tight Pants" Woman Jailed for Not Paying Fine*, CNN.com, Sept. 7, 2009.

2. JOHN R. BOWEN, WHY THE FRENCH DON'T LIKE HEADSCARVES 1–4 (2007); T. Jeremy Gunn, *Under God but Not the Scarf: The Founding Myths of Religious Freedom in the United States and Laïcité in France*, 46 J. CHURCH & ST. 7, 18 (2004).

3. *Sarkozy Says Burqas Are "Not Welcome" in France*, Associated Press, June 22, 2009; David Gauthier-Villars & Charles Forelle, *French Parliament Passes Law Banning Burqas*, WALL ST. J., Sept. 15, 2010.

4. Jan Hoffman, *Can a Boy Wear a Skirt to School? When Gender Bends the Dress Code, High Schools Struggle to Respond*, N.Y. TIMES, Nov. 8, 2009, at ST1, 10.

5. *Id.* at 10.

6. I Corinthians 11:3–10.

7. Maureen Dowd, *The Nuns' Story*, N.Y. TIMES, Oct. 25, 2009.

8. CAROLYN P. BLACKWOOD, THE PASTOR'S WIFE (1951) at 15, 51, 52.

9. *Id.* at 44.

10. See *Williams v. Saxby*, 433 F. Supp. 654 (D. D.C. 1976), rev'd in part on other grounds, vacated in part 587 F.2d 1240 (2d Cir. 1978); see also Wendy Pollack, *Sexual Harassment: Women's Experience v. Legal Definitions*, 13 HARV. WOMEN'S L.J. 35, 41–50 (1990); see generally Michelle J. Anderson, *Marital Immunity, Intimate Relationships, and Improper Inferences: A New Law on Sexual Offenses by Intimates*, 54 HASTINGS L.J. 1465 (2003).

11. See *Reed v. Reed*, 404 U.S. 71 (1971).

12. The case is *Commonwealth v. Berkowitz*, 609 A.2d 1338 (Pa. Super. 1992), *aff'd in part and rev'd in part*, 641 A.2d 1161 (Pa. 1994). The discussion in the text owes much to Dan Kahan, *Culture, Cognition, and Consent: Who Perceives What, and Why, in "Acquaintance Rape" Cases*, 158 U. PA. L. REV. 729 (2010).

13. 609 A.2d at 1340.

14. 641 A.2d at 1164.

15. Dale Russakoff, *Where Women Can't Just Say "No,"* WASH. POST, June 3, 1994, at A1 ("worst setbacks") (quoting Cassandra Thomas, president of the National Coalition Against Sexual Assault); Editorial, *When "No" Means Nothing*, ST. LOUIS POST-DISPATCH, June 6, 1994, at 6B ("most unambiguous word")

(quoting Deborah Zubow of the Women's International League for Peace and Freedom); see Rosemary J. Scalo, *What Does "No" Mean in Pennsylvania? The Pennsylvania Supreme Court's Interpretation of Rape and the Effectiveness of the Legislature's Response*, 40 VILL. L. REV. 193, 216–19 (1995); for Pennsylvania's current laws on sexual crimes, see 18 Pa. Cons. Stat. Ann. §§ 1321–28; see also Mustafa K. Kasubbai, *Destabilizing Power in Rape: Why Consent Theory in Rape Law Is Turned on Its Head*, 11 WIS. WOMEN'S L.J. 37, 63 (1996).

16. Kahan, *supra*, at 733, 734.

17. See, e.g., Dan Kahan & Donald Braman, *Cultural Cognition and Public Policy*, 24 YALE L. & POL. REV. 147 (2006); see generally the work of Kahan's Cultural Cognition Project at Yale Law School, http://www.culturalcognition.net.

18. Kahan borrows these classifications from the work of Mary Douglas. See MARY DOUGLAS, NATURAL SYMBOLS 54–68 (1970); MARY DOUGLAS & AARON WILDAVSKY, RISK AND CULTURE (1982). See also Kahan & Braman, *supra*, at 150–51.

19. See MALCOLM GLADWELL, THE TIPPING POINT (2000); Sushil Bikhchandani, David Hirshleifer & Ivo Welch, *A Theory of Fads, Fashion, Custom, and Cultural Change as Informational Cascades*, 100 J. POL. ECON. 992 (1992); Sushil Bikhchandani, David Hirshleifer & Ivo Welch, *Learning from the Behavior of Others: Conformity, Fads, and Informational Cascades*, 12 J. ECON. PERSP. 151 (1998).

20. An account of the mugging appeared in the *Boston Globe*. See John R. Ellement & John M. Guilfoil, *Bystanders Help Stop Attack, Parking Valet and Victim Strike Back*, BOSTON GLOBE, Nov. 4, 2009.

21. ELIZABETH LOFTUS & KATHERINE KETCHAM, WITNESS FOR THE DEFENSE: THE ACCUSED, THE EYEWITNESS, AND THE EXPERT WHO PUTS MEMORY ON TRIAL 11–12 (1991).

22. See Devah Pager et al., *Discrimination in a Low-Wage Labor Market*, 74 AM. SOC. REV. 777, 777 (2009) (study showing that "black applicants were half as likely as equally qualified whites to receive a callback or job offer. In fact, black and Latino applicants with clean backgrounds fared no better than white applicants just released from prison").

23. See *Lynch v. Donnelly*, 465 U.S. 668, 673 (1984) ("The concept of a 'wall' of separation is a useful figure of speech probably deriving from views of Thomas Jefferson . . . but the metaphor itself is not a wholly accurate description of the practical aspects of the relationship that in fact exists between church and state.").

24. The case is *Salazar v. Buono*, 559 U.S. ___ (2010). The best web resource for Supreme Court opinions is Cornell University Law School's Legal Information Institute website: see http://www.law.cornell.edu/supct/index.html.

25. Transcript of Oral Argument in *Salazar v. Buono*, available at http://www .supremecourtus.gov/oral_arguments/argument_transcripts/08–472.pdf.

26. Adam Liptak, *So, Guy Walks Up to a Bar, and Scalia Says . . .* , N.Y. Times, Dec. 31, 2005.

27. 559 U.S. ___ (2010) (opinion of Kennedy, J.).

28. See Don Braman, "Scalia and the Cross," a blog entry on the website of the Cultural Cognition Project, available at http://www.culturalcognition.net/blog (quoting Penn Law Professor Stephen Burbank: "Because they are not generally aware of their own disposition to form factual beliefs that cohere with their cultural commitments [judges] manifest little uncertainty . . . But much worse, because they can see full well the influence that cultural predispositions have on those who disagree with them, participants in policy debates often adopt a dismissive and even contemptuous posture towards their opponents' beliefs. . . . ").

29. *Id.*

30. See David Koon, *A Boy and His Flag: Why Will Won't Pledge*, Arkansas Times, Nov. 5, 2009.

31. President Bush quoted in James Gerstenzang, *Response to Terror: Bush Works to Get a Point Across: Time for Life to Return to Normal*, L.A. Times, Sept. 29, 2001, at 3; Giuliani quoted in Lisa Anderson & Dan Mihalopoulos, *A Grim Search in a Shattered City*, Chi. Trib., Sept. 13, 2001, at 1; Governor Bush quoted in David Lazarus, *This Way, Consumers All, To the Cash Register*, S.F. Chron., Nov. 25, 2005, at C1.

32. Juliet Schor, *The New Politics of Consumption: Why Americans Want So Much More Than They Need*, The Boston Review, Summer 1999, available at http:// bostonreview.net.

33. *Id.*

34. Richard Dawkins, The God Delusion (2006); Christopher Hitchins, God is Not Great: How Religion Poisons Everything (2007); Religulous (Thousand Words 2008); Jeffrey M. Jones, *Some Americans Reluctant to Vote for Mormon, 72-Year-Old Presidential Candidates*, Gallup News Service, Feb. 20, 2007, available at http://www.gallup.com (reporting that 53 percent of Americans would not vote for an atheist); Penny Edgell et al., *Atheists as "Other": Moral Boundaries and Cultural Membership in American Society*, 71 Am. Soc. Rev. 211, 216, 218 (2006).

35. See The Pew Forum on Religion and Public Life, *Faith in Flux, Changes in Religious Affiliation in the U.S.*, Apr. 2009, available at http://pewforum.org/Faith-in-Flux.aspx (full report available at http://pewforum.org) (showing that 56 percent of Americans have the same religion as their childhood religion and that

15 percent have switched from one Protestant religion to another); see also Barna Group, *Survey Finds Lots of Spiritual Dialogue but Not Much Change*, Sept. 27, 2010, available at http://www.barna.org.

36. See Barna Group, *Do Americans Change Faiths?*, Aug. 16, 2010, available at http://www.barna.org.

37. ARIEL LEVY, FEMALE CHAUVINIST PIGS: WOMEN AND THE RISE OF RAUNCH CULTURE 185, 195 (2005).

38. *Id.* at 197.

39. Judith Warner, *The Choice Myth*, N.Y. TIMES, Oct. 8, 2009, available at http://opinionator.blogs.nytimes.com.

CHAPTER 5
Choice and Power

Epigraphs: MARIO PUZO, THE GODFATHER 39 (1969). ANTHONY BURGESS, A CLOCKWORK ORANGE 83 (1962).

1. This is a close paraphrase of the statements in the actual experiment. This description of the experiment borrows from STANLEY MILGRAM, OBEDIENCE TO AUTHORITY (Perennial Classics ed., 2004). For pictures of the experiment, see *A Famous Experiment*, N.Y. TIMES, JULY 1, 2008, http://www.nytimes.com/slideshow/2008/06/30/science/070108-MIND_index.html.

2. Milgram at 13–26.

3. *Id.* at 27–31.

4. *Id.* at 35.

5. *Id.* at 35, 60.

6. *Id.* at 113–22.

7. *Id.* at 47, 83, 54.

8. Jerome S. Bruner, *Foreword*, in MILGRAM, OBEDIENCE TO AUTHORITY, at xiii.

9. See Benedict Carey, *Decades Later, Still Asking: Would I Pull That Switch?*, N.Y. TIMES, July 1, 2008; Jerry M. Burger, *Replicating Milgram: Would People Still Obey Today?*, 64 AMER. PSYCHOLOGIST 1, 1–11 (2009) (finding obedience rates in a 2006 replication were only slightly lower than those Milgram found forty-five years earlier).

10. The British show was a reality television special called *The Heist*, starring Derren Brown, discoverable on YouTube. For an account of the French show, see Eleanor Beardsley, *Fake TV Show "Tortures" Man, Shocks France*, National Public Radio, All Things Considered, Mar. 18, 2010, available at http://www.npr.org.

11. Police report of arrest, available at The Smoking Gun, http://www.thesmoking gun.com/archive/years/2009/0723092gates1.html.

12. Michael Joseph Gross, *James Ray Defends Himself*, NEW YORK MAG., Jan. 24, 2010, available at http://nymag.com.

13. John Dougherty, *For Some Seeking Rebirth, Sweat Lodge Was End*, N.Y. TIMES, Oct. 22, 2009.

14. J. J. Hensley & Glen Creno, *Differing Accounts of Ray's Behavior in Sweat-Lodge Deaths*, THE ARIZONA REPUBLIC, Dec. 29, 2009; Ryan Smith, *Sweat Lodge Guru James Arthur Ray Ignored Broken Bones, More, Leading Up To 3 Deaths, Say Court Docs*, CBSNews.com, Dec. 29, 2009.

15. Dougherty, *supra*; Smith, *supra*.

16. Smith, *supra*; Paul Harris, *Police Report Gives First Details of Arizona Sweat Lodge Deaths*, THE OBSERVER, Jan. 3, 2010.

17. Milgram, at 51.

18. *Id*. at 51–52.

CHAPTER 6
Choice and the Free Market

Epigraphs: WILLIAM SHAKESPEARE, THE TAMING OF THE SHREW, Act I, Scene 1, lines 138–39 (George Lyman Kittredge, ed., The Complete Works of Shakespeare, 1936). James Baldwin, *The Black Boy Looks at the White Boy*, ESQUIRE (May 1961).

1. For the figure of 45,000 grocery store items, see SHEENA IYENGAR, THE ART OF CHOOSING 187 (2010); for Coca-Cola products (in all, more than three thousand around the world), see company website, http://www.thecoca-colacompany .com/brands/product_list_c.html.

2. See http://www.pet-super-store.com/pet-supplies/orthopedic-dog-beds (dog beds); http://www.blavish.com/treadmill-just-for-the-kids (treadmill for children); http://www.skymall.com/shopping/detail.htm?pid=102727481&c=10441 (compass).

3. The average earnings for the top twenty-five hedge fund managers in 2008 was $464 million. See David Walker, *$2.5 Billion in Pay Makes Simons Hedge Fund World's Top Earner*, available at http://blogs.wsj.com/deals/2009/03/25/ the-hedge-fund-worlds-top-2008-earner-james-simons/tab/print. Compared to hedge fund managers, quarterbacks in the National Football League do not earn so much. In 2009, the quarterback with the highest base salary in the NFL was Peyton Manning, who earned $14 million. With bonuses, the highest-paid

quarterback in the NFL was actually Jay Cutler of the Bears, who earned a total compensation of over $22 million. See *USA Today* Salaries Database, available at http://content.usatoday.com/sports/football/nfl/salaries/playersbyposition .aspx?pos=144. In the summer of 2010, Tom Brady of the New England Patriots signed a new contract that promised him $72 million over four years, making him the highest-paid player in the NFL. See *Tom Brady Signs Extension*, ESPN.com, available at http://sports.espn.go.com/boston/nfl/news/story?id=5552561.

4. One of the leading critics of the conventional wisdom about markets, particularly securities markets, is Lawrence Mitchell. See, for example, Lawrence E. Mitchell, *Who Needs the Stock Market?*, 1 ACCOUNTING, ECONOMICS AND LAW—A CON-VIVIUM (2010); Lawrence E. Mitchell, *The Morals of the Marketplace*, 20 STAN. L. & POL. REV. 171 (2009); Lawrence E. Mitchell, *Fairness and Efficiency (of What?)*, 2 BERKELEY BUS. L. J. 153 (2005); LAWRENCE E. MITCHELL, CORPORATE IRRE-SPONSIBILITY: AMERICA'S NEWEST EXPORT (2001); LAWRENCE E. MITCHELL, STACKED DECK (1998).

5. "Sixteen Tons," words and music by Merle Travis, copyright © 1947 (renewed) Merle's Girls Music, all rights administered by Warner-Tamerlane Publishing Corp. All rights reserved; used by permission. For more history of the song, see ACE COLLINS, THE STORIES BEHIND COUNTRY MUSIC'S ALL-TIME GREATEST: 100 SONGS 91–93 (1996).

6. See generally 29 C.F.R. § 531.34 and AMJUR LABOR § 3093 Scrip.

7. JON JETER, FLAT BROKE IN THE FREE MARKET: HOW GLOBALIZATION FLEECED WORKING PEOPLE (2009).

8. See Edward Luce, *The Crisis of Middle-Class America*, FINANCIAL TIMES, July 30, 2010, available at http://www.ft.com ("Dubbed 'median wage stagnation' by economists, the annual incomes of the bottom 90 per cent of US families have been essentially flat since 1973—having risen by only 10 per cent in real terms over the past 37 years. That means most Americans have been treading water for more than a generation. Over the same period the incomes of the top 1 per cent have tripled. In 1973, chief executives were on average paid 26 times the median income. Now the multiple is above 300."). A wonderful resource of economic data is the Economic Policy Institute, http://www.epi.org, particu-larly its running series entitled "The State of Working America," available at http://www.stateofworkingamerica.org. For data on inequality, see http://www.stateofworkingamerica.org/features/view/1. For data on rate of change in income, see Lawrence Mishel, *Where Has All the Income Gone? Look Up*, Mar. 3, 2010, available at http://www.epi.org. For stagnant incomes, see "When Income Grows, Who Gains?", an interactive chart available at http://www

.stateofworkingamerica.org/pages/interactive#/?start=1917&end=1918, us-ing as its source Emmanuel Saez & Thomas Piketty, *Income Inequality in the United States, 1913–1998*, Q. J. Econ. 118(1) (2003), tables available at http://www.econ.berkeley.edu/~saez/TabFig2008.xls; also Lawrence Mishel, *Another Day, One Less Dollar*, June 3, 2010, available at http://www.epi.org. For increase in working hours, see Jared Bernstein, *The Rise in Family Work Hours Leads Many Americans to Struggle to Balance Work and Family*, July 7, 2004, available at epi.org. For data on debt, see *Household Debt Soars in Past Two Decades*, avail-able at http://www.stateofworkingamerica.org/charts/view/214. For data on poverty, see Elise Gould & Heidi Shierholz, *A Lost Decade: Poverty and Income Trends Paint a Bleak Picture for Working Families*, Sept. 16, 2010, available at http://www.epi.org.

9. See Jonah Lehrer, How We Decide 59–61 (2009).

10. Now we understand this phenomenon scientifically. Remember the study dis-cussed in chapter three revealing that the part of the brain that anticipates pain lights up when you see the price of a product. If the pain of paying can be re-duced—by the use of chips, for example—then you are more likely to spend, or bet, more.

11. Richard Posner, Economic Analysis of Law 15 (3d ed., 1986).

12. See generally, Philip J. Hilts, Smoke Screen: The Truth Behind the To-bacco Industry Cover-Up (1996).

13. See Lester P. Silverman & Nancy L. Spruill, *Urban Crime and the Price of Heroin*, 4 J. of Urban Econ. 80, 80–103 (Jan. 1977) (estimating that a 50 percent in-crease in the price of heroin would result in a 13 percent decrease in the quantity of heroin consumed); Don Weatherburn & Browyn Lind, *The Impact of Law Enforcement Activity on a Heroin Market*, 92 Addiction, 557, 557–569 (May 1997) (finding that two-thirds of those who sought entry to methadone programs in Australia indicated the price as a reason for stopping using heroin).

14. See, e.g., Jon Hanson & Douglas Kysar, *Taking Behavioralism Seriously: The Problem of Market Manipulation*, 74 N.Y.U. L. Rev. 632 (1999); Adam Benforado & Jon Hanson, *The Great Attributional Divide: How Divergent Views of Human Behavior Are Shaping Legal Policy*, 57 Emory L.J. (2008).

15. Iyengar, *supra*, at 185–87.

16. This account is based on reporting by CNN. See Nic Robertson, *Man Must Choose Between Selling Kidney or Child*, CNN.com, July 16, 2009.

17. Larry Rohter, *The Organ Trade: A Global Black Market; Tracking the Sale of a Kidney on a Path of Poverty and Hope*, N.Y. Times, May 23, 2004; Jeneen In-terlandi, *Not Just Urban Legend*, Newsweek, Jan. 19, 2009, available at http://

www.newsweek.com; David Porter & Carla K. Johnson, *1st Case of U.S. Organ Trafficking? NYC Man Accused of Buying Kidneys Abroad, Selling at Hefty Profit*, The Associated Press, July 24, 2009

18. Interlandi, *supra*.

19. See *Baby-Selling by Organised Syndicates Is Big Business in Malaysia*, AsiaNews. it, Sept. 28, 2005.

20. UNICEF, Child Protection from Violence, Exploitation and Abuse, http://www.unicef.org/protection/index_exploitation.html (last updated Sept. 11, 2010). Andrew Bushell, *Sale of Children Thrives in Pakistan*, THE WASHINGTON TIMES, Jan. 21, 2002. More recently, there is evidence that children are being sold to the Taliban for use as suicide bombers. Prices for children, as young as eleven, are between $6,000 and $12,000. Nic Robertson, *Pakistan: Taliban Buying Children for Suicide Attacks*, CNN, July 7, 2009, available at http://edition.cnn.com/2009/WORLD/asiapcf/07/07/pakistan.child.bombers/index.html. The European Union Times, *Thai Couple Regrets Selling Their 13 yr. Daughter for $114, They Wish They'd Got $228*, Mar. 22, 2010, available at http://www.eutimes.net.

21. Associated Press, *Parents Accused of Selling Sex with Teen Daughter to Pay Off Minivan*, Mar. 3, 2010, available at http://www.komonews.com/news/national/86256247.html.

22. See (actually, don't): TAKEN (Twentieth Century Fox 2008).

23. For wombs, see Sam Dolnick, *Pregnancy Becomes Latest Job Outsourced to India*, Associated Press, Dec. 30, 2007; Yoo Jin Jung, *Outsourcing Pregnancy?*, ILLINOIS BUS. LAW JOURNAL., Feb. 6, 2008. For votes, see Ryan Hagen, *Is It Smarter to Sell Your Vote or to Cast It?*, N.Y. TIMES, Nov. 16, 2007, available at http://freakonomics.blogs.nytimes.com (66 percent of respondents said they would trade their voting rights for a free four-year ride at N.Y.U.; 20 percent would give up the vote for an iPod Touch worth $299). For sex, see Chris Matyszczyk, *Teen Reveals Aftermath of Selling Her Virginity Online*, CNET News, May 20, 2009, available at http://news.cnet.com/8301-17852_3-10246204-71.html.

CHAPTER 7
The Problem with Personal Responsibility

Epigraphs: Melvin B. Tolson, "An Ex-Judge at the Bar," in RENDEZVOUS WITH AMERICA 19 (1944), used by permission of Dr. Melvin B. Tolson, Jr. MIGUEL DE CERVANTES SAAVEDRA, DON QUIXOTE 271 (John Rutherford trans., Penguin Books USA 10th ed., 2003) (1605).

1. Joshua Rhett Miller, *Some Parents Choose Not to Allow Their Kids to Hear Obama's National Address*, FOXNews.com, Sept. 3, 2009; Michael Alison Chandler & Michael D. Shear, *Some Schools Will Block or Delay Obama's Pep Talk for Students*, WASH. POST, Sept. 4, 2009; *September 8, 2009: National Keep Your Child at Home Day*, AmericanElephant, Sept. 1, 2009, available at http://americanelephant .com .

2. The White House, Office of the Press Secretary, Sept. 8, 2009, *Remarks by the President in a National Address to America's Schoolchildren*, Wakefield High School, Arlington, Virginia.

3. See transcript of press conference, Nov. 7, 2008, available at http://articles.cnn .com.

4. Adam Liptak, *A Rare Rebuke, in Front of a Nation*, N.Y. TIMES, Jan. 29, 2010, at A12 (Justice Samuel Alito); Carl Hulse, *In Lawmaker's Outburst, a Rare Breach of Protocol*, N.Y. TIMES, Sept. 10, 2009, at A26 (Rep. Joe Wilson).

5. See Mark Lilla, *The Tea Party Jacobins*, N.Y. REV. OF BOOKS, May 27, 2010, available at http://www.nybooks.com (noting that modern-day libertarians favor "individual opinion, individual autonomy and individual choice, all in the service of neutralizing, not using, political power").

6. John Tate, *Government Regulation of Salt Would Violate the Constitution*, U.S. NEWS & WORLD REPORT, May 25, 2010, available at http://www.usnews.com.

7. See Karl Rove, *ObamaCare Isn't Inevitable*, WALL ST. J., June 25, 2009 ("Americans are increasingly concerned about the cost—in money and personal freedom—of Mr. Obama's nanny-state initiatives."); Ronald Bachman, *ObamaCare, Megatrends, and Consumerism*, CONSUMERISM CORNER Vol.1, No. 1, available at http://www.healthtransformation.net/cs/ConsumerismCorner041310 ("The health mandates violate the growth of personal responsibility and self-reliance. Government required plan designs violate the cultural movement to choice."); Bill O'Reilly, *Great Divide: Control Versus Freedom*, S. FLA, SUN-SENTINEL, Mar. 27, 2010, at 15A; Bob Unruh, *U.S. House Plan Overturning Obamacare Halfway There*, WorldNetDaily, July 7, 2010, available at http://www.wnd. com (quoting Congressman Steve King, R-Iowa, as saying, "Republicans are the proponents of limited government, personal responsibility and constitutional liberties, principles which 'Obamacare' violates"). See also Mike Cosgrove, *Restoring Once-Vibrant Economy Hinges On Repeal Of ObamaCare*, INVESTOR'S BUS. DAILY, Aug. 30, 2010, at A11 ("The size of the federal deficit and costs of Obama-Care appear to make a value-added tax the default case. That means to avoid the value-added tax ObamaCare must be repealed. It may seem like a long shot, but to restore the pillars of the American economy—wealth creation, economic

growth and personal responsibility—it has to go. The equity market will boom once the pillars of ObamaCare start to crumble.").

8. I am thankful to my friend and colleague Joe Singer, who helped me develop this insight.

9. Cass R. Sunstein, *Legal Interference with Private Preferences*, 53 U. Chi. L. Rev. 1129, 1140 (1986) ("Laws may, in short, reflect the majority's 'preference about preferences,' or second-order preferences, at the expense of first-order preferences. This phenomenon—voluntary foreclosure of consumption choices—is the political analogue of the story of Ulysses and the Sirens.").

10. For smartphone software, see http://www.textecution.com; for lessons from Ulysses, Jon Elster, Ulysses and the Sirens: Studies in Rationality and Irrationality (1979).

11. See Cass Sunstein & Richard Thaler, Nudge: Improving Decisions About Health, Wealth, and Happiness (2008).

12. See Perry A. Zirkel, *Confident about Confidences?*, 73 The Phi Delta Kappan 732 (May 1992). The case is *Eisel v. Bd. of Educ. of Montgomery Co.*, 597 A.2d 447 (Md. 1991).

13. *Eisel*, 597 A.2d at 454; for additional context for the case in a discussion of liberalism and feminism, see Ann Scales, Legal Feminism: Activism, Lawyering & Legal Theory, 66–68 (2006).

14. *Eisel*, 597 A.2d at 456.

15. See *Pelman v. McDonald's Corp.*, 237 F.Supp.2d 512 (2003); Marc Santora, *Teenagers' Suit Says McDonald's Made Them Obese*, N.Y. Times, Nov. 21, 2002, at B1.

16. Personal Responsibility in Food Consumption Act of 2005, H.R. 554, 109th Cong. (2005); for text and history, see http://www.govtrack.us.

17. David Yosifon, *The Consumer Interest in Corporate Law*, 43 U.C. Davis L. Rev. 253, 277 (2009); David Burnett, *Fast-Food Lawsuits and the Cheeseburger Bill: Critiquing Congress's Response to the Obesity Epidemic*, 14 Va. J. Soc. Pol'y & L. 357, 365 (2007).

18. Katherine M. Flegal, et al., *Prevalence and Trends in Obesity Among US Adults, 1999–2008*, 303 J. Am. Med. Ass'n 235 (2010), available at http://jama.ama-assn.org; see also Centers for Disease Control and Prevention, Overweight and Obesity, http://www.cdc.gov/obesity/data/index.html; Cynthia Ogden & Margaret Carroll, *Prevalence of Obesity Among Children and Adolescents: United States, Trends 1963–1965 Through 2007–2008*, available at http://www.cdc .gov (table 1 showing obesity for children ages 6–11 going from 4.0 percent in the early 1970s to 19.6 percent in 2007–08, and obesity for children ages 12–19

going from 6.1 percent to 18.1 percent in the same timeframe); J. A. Skelton, S. R. Cook, P. Auinger, J. D. Klein & S. E. Barlow, *Prevalence and Trends of Severe Obesity Among U.S. Children and Adolescents*, 9 ACAD. PEDIATRICS 322 (2009); Greg Keller, *Number of Fat People in U.S. to Grow, Report Says*, Associated Press, Sept. 23, 2010, available at http://abcnews.go.com. For an excellent treatment of the problems of obesity for legal and regulatory theory and practice, see Adam Benforado, Jon Hanson & David Yosifon, *Broken Scales: Obesity and Justice in America*, 53 EMORY L. J. 311 (2004).

19. Seth Doane, *Battling Obesity in America*, CBS Reports, Jan. 7, 2010, available at http://www.cbsnews.com.

20. Megan Woolhouse, *As City Census Starts, Homeless Man Dies*, BOSTON GLOBE, Dec. 19, 2007, at B1.

21. JOSEPH WILLIAM SINGER, THE EDGES OF THE FIELD 38–39 (2000).

CHAPTER 8
Umpires, Judges, and Bad Choices

Epigraphs: Charles M. Schulz, *Peanuts*, appearing in newspapers on Dec. 30, 1991. TERRY TEMPEST WILLIAMS, PIECES OF WHITE SHELL, 134–35 (1987).

1. See Baseball-Reference.com, *No-hitter*, http://www.baseball-reference.com/bullpen/No-hitter.

2. See NASA, *Apollo*, http://www.nasa.gov/mission_pages/apollo/index.html; see also Baseball Almanac, *Perfect Games by Pitcher*, http://www.baseball-almanac.com/pitching/piperf.shtml.

3. *Joyce Tops Survey; Players Nix Replay*, ESPN.com, June 13, 2010.

4. Details of the game can be found at *Cleveland Indians v. Detroit Tigers—Recap—June 2, 2010*, ESPN.com, http://scores.espn.go.com.

5. Brian Dickerson, *Umpire Made All the Right Calls after His Big Mistake*, DETROIT FREE PRESS, June 4, 2010 ("Unless he figures out how to plug the oil leak in the Gulf of Mexico, Jim Joyce has likely written the first paragraph of his obituary.").

6. This quote is from the Associated Press recap of the game, available at *Cleveland Indians v. Detroit Tigers—Recap*, *supra*.

7. Paul White & Seth Livingstone, *Missed Call Leaves Detroit's Armando Galarraga One Out Shy of Perfect Game*, USA TODAY, June 6, 2010.

8. *Kurkjian on Joyce's Disputed Call*, ESPN, June 2, 2010, available at http://espn.go.com; *Jim Joyce Moving On After Tough Week*, ESPN, June 6, 2010, available at http://espn.go.com.

9. James Joyce, Ulysses 125 (Digireads.com Publishing 2009) (1922).

10. Malcolm Gladwell, Blink: The Power of Thinking Without Thinking 6 (2005).

11. Jonah Lehrer, How We Decide 1 (2009).

12. Scott Brown, Commencement Lecture, Boston College Law School, May 28, 2010, available at http://www.bc.edu/bc_org/rvp/pubaf/10/Brown_speech_2010.pdf.

13. James Surowiecki, The Wisdom of Crowds: Why the Many Are Smarter Than the Few and How Collective Wisdom Shapes Business, Economies, Societies and Nations (2004).

14. See S. E. Asch, *Effects of Group Pressure upon the Modification and Distortion of Judgment*, in Groups, Leadership and Men (H. Guetzkow, ed., 1951) (describing a study in which participants were seated together in a room and asked a series of questions about a series of lines; when a set of control individuals gave incorrect answers, the non-control participants' answers conformed).

15. For an example of the dangers of groupthink, see Marleen O'Connor, *The Enron Board: The Perils of Groupthink*, 71 U. Cinn. L. Rev. 1233 (2003).

16. See *United States v. Booker*, 543 U.S. 220, 247 (2005). See also *Porter v. McCollum*, 558 U.S. ____ (2009) (in capital case, war trauma of defendant should be available for jury to consider in deciding whether to impose sentence of execution).

17. *Roberts: "My Job Is to Call Balls and Strikes and Not to Pitch or Bat,"* CNN, Sept. 12, 2005, http://www.cnn.com.

18. Jake Tapper & Sunlen Miller, *POTUS Interrupts Press Briefing to Announce Souter's Retirement, Announce Qualifications for Next Supreme*, May 1, 2009, available at http://blogs.abcnews.com.

19. Steven G. Calabresi, *Obama's "Redistribution" Constitution*, available at http://online.wsj.com.

20. See Walter R. Fisher, Human Communication as Narration: Toward a Philosophy of Reason, Value, and Action (1989) (arguing that all human communication is a form of storytelling).

21. See, for example, Cass Sunstein, *The Law of Group Polarization*, 10 J. Pol. Phil. 175 (2002).

22. *Kyles v. Whitley*, 514 U.S. 419 (1995).

23. For an account of the case, see Jed Horne, Desire Street: A True Story of Death and Deliverance in New Orleans (2005).

24. *United States v. Drayton*, 536 U.S. 194 (2002).

25. See Daniel T. Drubin, Letting Go of Your Bananas: How to Become More Successful by Getting Rid of Everything Rotten in Your Life 35

(2006) ("Every excuse I ever heard made perfect sense to the person with the excuse.").

26. See, for example, Jon D. Hanson & David Yosifon, *The Situation: An Introduction to the Situational Character, Critical Realism, Power Economics, and Deep Capture*, 152 PA. L. REV. 129 (2003); see also Adam Benforado & Jon D. Hanson, *The Great Attributional Divide: How Divergent Views of Human Behavior are Shaping Legal Policy*, 57 EMORY L. J. 311 (2008). See also Edward E. Jones & Victor Harris, *The Attribution of Attitudes*, J. OF EXPER. SOC. PSYCH., 3, 1–2 (1967).

27. *Briefing: Rough Justice in America; Too Many Laws, Too Many Prisoners*, THE ECONOMIST, July 24, 2010, at 26.

CHAPTER 9
Building Choice in a World of Limits

Epigraphs: Leo Tolstoy, *Some Social Remedies* 29, in PAMPHLETS. Translated from the Russian (1900); available at Google books. "Free Bird," words and music by Allen Collins and Ronnie Van Zant, copyright © 1973, 1975 Songs of Universal, Inc., copyrights renewed. All rights reserved. Reprinted by permission of Hal Leonard Corporation.

1. THE CRYING GAME (Miramax Films 1992).

2. See *Woman Accused of Church Theft Blames Satan*, Mar. 22, 2009, available at http://weirdnewsfiles.com/weirdnews/woman-accused-of-church-theft-blames-satan.

3. SHEENA IYENGAR, THE ART OF CHOOSING 9 (2010).

4. Iyengar, *supra*, at 7.

5. Some studies in fact show that willpower can grow over time with use. In effect, willpower acts like a muscle, growing stronger as it is exercised more. For an accessible description, see Sandra Aamodt & Sam Wang, *Tighten Your Belt, Strengthen Your Mind*, N.Y. TIMES, Apr. 2, 2008 ("Consistently doing any activity that requires self-control seems to increase willpower—and the ability to resist impulses and delay gratification is highly associated with success in life."). See also Mark Muraven & Roy F. Baumeister, *Self-Regulation and Depletion of Limited Resources: Does Self-Control Resemble a Muscle?*, PSYCHOLOGICAL BULLETIN, 126, 247 (2000).

6. HENRY MILLER, THE WISDOM OF THE HEART 2 (1951).

7. JOHN SEYMOUR & JOSEPH O'CONNOR, INTRODUCING NEURO-LINGUISTIC PROGRAMMING: THE NEW PSYCHOLOGY OF PERSONAL EXCELLENCE (1993).

8. J. M. Darley & C. D. Batson, *From Jerusalem to Jericho: A Study of Situational and Dispositional Variables in Helping Behavior*, 27 J. PERSONALITY & SOC. PSYCHOL. 100–108 (1973). For the parable, see Luke 10:30–37.

9. See Better Business Bureau, *United States Lemon Laws*, available at http://www.bbb.org; Legal Information Institute, Marriage Laws, available at http://topics.law.cornell.edu/wex/table_marriage.

10. CASS SUNSTEIN & RICHARD THALER, NUDGE: IMPROVING DECISIONS ABOUT HEALTH, WEALTH, AND HAPPINESS 6 (2008).

11. *Id.* at 5.

12. *Id.* at 5.

13. See *LA's Fast Food Ban Draws Skepticism*, Reuters News Service, Sept. 3, 2008, available at http://www.reuters.com/article/idUSN0343855220080903.

14. See U.S. Department of Health and Human Services, The Campaign to Rescue and Restore Victims of Human Trafficking, *About Human Trafficking*, available at http://www.acf.hhs.gov/trafficking/about/index.html.

15. See, for example, Kent Greenfield, *Proposition: Saving the World with Corporate Law*, 57 EMORY L.J. 947, 981–83 (2008).

16. Christopher Shea, "Scholar, Flog Thyself," in *Brainiac: Highlights from the Ideas Blog*, BOSTON GLOBE, Mar. 29, 2009.

17. Kwame Anthony Appiah, *The Art of Social Change*, N.Y. TIMES MAGAZINE, Oct. 22, 2010; see also KWAME ANTHONY APPIAH, THE HONOR CODE: HOW MORAL REVOLUTIONS HAPPEN (2010).

18. See StickK, *FAQ*, http://www.stickk.com/faq.php.

19. Rob Stein, *Premarital Abstinence Pledges Ineffective, Study Finds*, WASH. POST, Dec. 29, 2008.

Credits

ILLUSTRATIONS

p. 11: Oliver Wendell Holmes, Jr. Photo from Wikimedia Commons, originally from *The World's Work*, Vol IV. (1902).

p. 17: Mt. Hood. Copyright James R. Hearn, 2011. Used under license from Shutterstock.com.

p. 34: Lesbian Judy Wagner wears a shirt reading "Gay by Nature, Proud by Choice" as she looks at Christians. David McNew / Getty Images News / Getty Images.

p. 40: The Pledge of Allegiance, 1943. Photographed by Marjory Collins. Farm Security Administration—Office of War Information Photograph Collection, Library of Congress. Reproduction number: LC-USW3–017675-E (b&w film nitrate neg.); LC-USZ62–131506 (b&w film copy neg. from print).

p. 57: Charles Whitman. Photo from Wikimedia Commons, originally from the 1963 *Cactus*, the student yearbook of the University of Texas.

p. 60: A fourth-century mosaic in the Villa del Casale, Sicily. Photo from Wikimedia Commons.

p. 65: The Republican National Committee's infamous "RATS" ad from the 2000 presidential campaign. Screenshot from The Vigilant Citizen, http://vigilantcitizen.com.

p. 73: The burqa. Photo by Steve Evans, 2005, from Wikimedia Commons. Reproduced under the Creative Commons Attribution 2.0 Generic License.

p. 75: A young woman wearing the nun's white habit and praying. Photographed by Fitz W. Guerin, no date. Prints and Photographs Division, Library of Congress. Reproduction number: LC-USZ62–74347.

p. 79: *New Yorker* cartoon, July 9, 2001. Copyright Peter Steiner / The New Yorker Collection / www.cartoonbank.com.

p. 90: Justice Antonin Scalia. Collection of the Supreme Court of the United States. Photographer: Steve Petteway.

pp. 100, 105: The Milgram experiment. From the film *Obedience*, copyright 1968 by Stanley Migram, renewed 1993 by Alexandra Milgram, and distributed by Penn State Media Sales. Reproduced courtesy of Alexandra Milgram.

p. 152: "Hard Hearted Hannah." Photo from Wikimedia Commons; originally published 1924 by Ager, Yellen & Bornstein, Inc.

p. 156: *Ulysses and the Sirens* by Herbert James Draper. Image from Wikimedia Commons.

p. 161: *New Yorker* cartoon, July 19, 1999. Copyright Michael Maslin / The New Yorker Collection / www.cartoonbank.com.

p. 174: Chief Justice John Roberts. Collection of the Supreme Court of the United States. Photographer: Steve Petteway.

p. 178: Justice David H. Souter. AP Photo / Jim Cole.

p. 195: *New Yorker* cartoon, November 20, 2000. Copyright J. C. Duffy / The New Yorker Collection / www.cartoonbank.com.

POETRY AND SONG LYRICS

p. 47 (epigraph): "Don't Look at Me That Way" (from "Paris"), words and music by Cole Porter, copyright © 1928 (renewed) Warner Bros. Inc. All rights reserved; used by permission.

p. 124: "Sixteen Tons," words and music by Merle Travis, copyright © 1947 (renewed) Merle's Girls Music, all rights administered by Warner-Tamerlane Publishing Corp. All rights reserved; used by permission.

p. 143 (epigraph): Melvin B. Tolson, "An Ex-Judge at the Bar," in RENDEZVOUS WITH AMERICA 19 (1944), used by permission of Dr. Melvin B. Tolson, Jr.

p. 185 (epigraph): "Free Bird," words and music by Allen Collins and Ronnie Van Zant, copyright © 1973, 1975 Songs of Universal, Inc., copyrights renewed. All rights reserved. Reprinted by permission of Hal Leonard Corporation.

Index

brain damage: in the case of Charles
Whitman, 56–58; and concepts of
good and evil, 56–59; cost-benefit
analysis, 55, 56; criminal behavior, 55, 56–57; impact on decision
making, 56–58; impaired judgment,
56–58
brain processes: appetite system in, 59;
bias towards attractive people, 63;
bikini effect, 59–60, 62, 128, 132; in
the case of Raelyn Balfour, 47–49,
51, 52, 183, 212n3; memory, 66–67,
191–92; pleasure, 59, 61, 62, 128;
prefrontal cortex, 49–51, 53, 54, 56;
priming, 63, 64; purchasing decisions, 61; satisfying cravings, 59; and
self-regulation, 50, 212n7; structure
of, 49–50; subconscious word-
associations, 64–65, 215n32; subliminal associations, 64–65, 215n31
Braman, Don, 91, 218n28
Brown, Kirby, 112
Brown, Michael, 14
Brown, Scott, 167–68
Bruner, Jerome, 106
Bryan, William Jennings, 8
building the ability to choose, 188–89,
196–97
Burbank, Stephen, 218n28
Burger King, 26, 28
burqa, 2, 73–74
Bush, George W., 64

Calabresi, Steven, 22, 175
Camus, Albert, 7–8
capacity to make better choices, 187,
200–201
Carbrera, Miguel, 165
card check bill, 32

casinos, 128–29, 222n10
causal chains, 157–60, 161–62
Chamber of Commerce, 32
chastity pledges, 205
Cheeseburger Bill (Personal Responsibility in Food Consumption Act),
33, 159
children and youth: agency in making
choices, 9, 205–6; age of consent in
law of sex, 41–42; capacity to resist
bad influences, 189–90; child care,
77, 95; forgotten baby syndrome,
47–49, 51, 212n3; obedience of, 8–9,
107–8; President Barack Obama's
speech to, 143–45, 147; public school
attendance, 39; suicide pacts, 157–58;
teenagers on dating, 63; trafficking
in, 138, 223n20
Children by Choice, 34
child trafficking, 138, 223n20
chips for gambling, 129, 222n10
choice: acknowledgment of limitations
and irrational tendencies, 190–92;
architecture of, 197–98; and assessment of danger, 12–14; bad choices,
16–19, 29–30, 169–70, 182; building the ability to choose, 188–89,
196–97; compulsion, 58, 82, 130–32,
133–34, 155; dissent and diversity
encouraged for, 116–18, 168, 176,
202–3; expertise in making choices,
29–30, 132–33, 167–68, 173;
government interventions in, 2,
136, 151–53, 197–98; information as
basis for, 15–16; as meaningless, 28;
memory, 50, 66–67, 190–92; mental
contamination, 63–64; personal
responsibility as, 146–53, 154–56,
157–58; power of situation and cir-

cumstance, 106–7, 180–81, 189–90, 194, 228n5; rhetoric of, 24–25, 31–35, 36–37; risk of regret, 29–30; sexuality as, 33–34; slogans, 1, 26–28, 32; strength of, 206. *See also* authority; brain damage; brain processes; coercion; culturally-mediated perceptions; decision making; free market; Milgram experiment; obedience; personal responsibility

Christianity, 23, 75, 89–90

cigarette companies, 130–31

Civil Rights Act (1964), 77

clergy wives, 76–77

Cleveland Indians, 163–64, 165

coercion, 32, 37–38; by authority figure, 101; in casinos, 129; choice, 35–36, 77–79; conditional funding of universities, 40–41; control of free speech, 39–41; economic need as source of, 10–12, 39, 125, 137–38, 201, 223n20; employment as source of, 10–11, 39, 201; influence, 111–13, 115; in Milgram experiment, 101; rape, 20–21, 43, 82–83, 172; scrip payments, 123–25; in sex work, 43–44, 201–2; threat of funding cutoff as, 40–41; in union organizing, 32

collective action problem, 135–36

colonoscopies, pain after, 67

commitments, 204–6

commodification of sex, 59–60, 62, 132, 138

Commonwealth v. Berkowitz, 80–82

company stores, 123–24

compulsion, 58, 82, 130–32, 133–34, 155

confirmation bias, 63, 176

congressional districts, gerrymandering of, 203

consensual searches, 38–39, 116, 179

consent: democratic consent, 30; for police searches, 38–39, 116, 177–79; in sexual relations, 20–21, 41–44, 77, 82–83, 172

consumer decisions: advertisements, 26, 27, 64–65, 93, 215n31; bikini effect, 59–60, 62, 132; brain in studies on, 61; in the collective action problem, 135–36; compulsive spending, 131–32; expert assistance in making choices, 29–30, 132–33, 167, 168; fast-food companies, 18, 26, 28–29, 33, 131, 159, 160; food options, 18, 27–28, 68, 159–60; gambling, 128–29, 131, 222n10; habits affecting, 59–62, 94, 132, 192–94; on health care, 31–32, 224n5, 224–25n7; impact on hometown businesses, 135–36; jam sampling experiment, 29, 133; memory, 50, 66–67, 190–92; in the presence of overwhelming choice, 29–30, 120–21; purchasing decisions, 61, 65–66, 121–22, 131–32; responsibility for obesity, 17–18, 159–60, 181, 199, 210n11; shopping in American culture, 92–93, 121; shortcuts in, 132–33, 134, 192–93; television, 27, 28, 30, 94–95

contracts and contract law, 20, 21–22, 30, 35–36

Costa, Jane, 12–13, 17, 19, 20

Costa v. Boston Red Sox, 12–13, 17, 19, 20

cost-benefit analysis in decision making, 55–56

credit cards, 123

criminal law, 37–38, 52–53, 171, 213n9
criminal liability, 211n13
Crying Game, 185–86
cult figures, 111–15, 183
culturally-mediated perceptions: of
    Aboriginal culture, 42; awareness
    of, 193–95; in the case of Lubna
    Hussein, 71–72, 85; confirmation
    bias, 63, 176; constraints on choice,
    78–79, 97; cultural differences,
    70–72, 194–95, 202–3; in eyewitness
    accounts, 86; gender roles, 71–77,
    94–95; in jury selection, 83–85;
    the meaning of "no," 82–83, 172,
    216–17n15; patriotism, 39, 40, 91–93,
    92, 203–4; personal perceptions of,
    85–86; recognition of, 91, 218n28; of
    religious symbols, 89–91; of sexual
    behavior, 80–85, 95–96, 172; stereo-
    types, 77, 86, 87, 96, 111, 217n22;
    traditional views, 42, 71–75, 82–83,
    94–95; women's dress, 71–75, 77. *See
    also* authority; Milgram experiment;
    obedience; religion

Dawkins, Richard, 93
death of freedom, 32, 211n6
debt, 123–25, 128, 138, 221n8
decision making: brain processes'
    influence on, 56–58, 61; building the
    ability to choose, 188–89, 196–97;
    in casinos, 129; choice architecture,
    197–98; cognitive shortcuts to,
    132–33, 134, 192; detachment for,
    194; disclosure of information, 122,
    123, 197, 199–200; emotional aspects
    of, 54–55; encouraging people to
    make better decisions, 196–97;
    flawed decisions, 165–66, 173, 184;

government intervention, 2, 136,
    151–53, 197–98; in groups, 116–17,
    168, 176–77, 202–3; immorality in,
    137–39; incentives for good deci-
    sions, 197–98; influence of authority
    on, 101–2, 103–5, 109–11, 113–16;
    influence of power on, 98–116;
    listening to stories in, 173, 174–75,
    177, 180, 182, 184; long-range
    impact of, 135–36; multiple purchas-
    ing decisions making a change,
    135; persistence of error, 169–70;
    predictions of, 61; preferences about
    preferences, 154–55, 225n9; price
    of, 121–22, 135–36; role of authority
    in, 101, 103–6; self-control, 189–90,
    228n5; snap judgments, 167–68;
    texting while driving, 154–55
Declaration of Independence, 31
deficiencies in the ability to remember,
    66–69
democratic consent, 30
dependency, 127
Detroit Tigers. *See* Galarraga,
    Armando
Diamond, David, 51
disclosure of information, 122, 123,
    197, 199–200
discrimination, 40–41, 78, 87, 97, 111,
    203; cultural context of, 78–79
displays of religious symbols on public
    property, 88–91
dispositionalists, 180–81
dissent, 8–9, 116–18, 176, 202–3
diversity: affirmative action, 203;
    cultural differences, 70–72, 194–95,
    202–3; group decision making, 168,
    176–77, 202–3
Donald, Jason, 165

free market (*continued*)
    everything, 3, 137–40, 138, 201–2,
    223n20; price mechanism, 121–22;
    product placement, 65–66, 131; pub-
    lic policy, 199; rational actors theory,
    55–56, 129–30; scarcity created by,
    127–28, 221–22n8; valorization of
    products, 120, 121; wages in the, 121,
    126–28, 220–21n3, 221–22n8
free speech, 39–41, 204; women's
    clothing in cases of, 71–77
future predictions, 67–68

Galarraga, Armando, 163–66, 167, 169,
    173, 183, 184
Gallup Poll, 93
gambling, 128–29, 131, 222n10
Gates, Henry Louis, 110
gay rights, 2, 20, 22, 33, 36, 40–41, 91
gender norms: in the case of Lubna
    Hussein, 71–72, 85; child care, 77,
    95; clothing, 71–77; domesticity,
    76–77; sexual freedom, 95–96; shop-
    ping habits, 59–62, 132; women's
    behavior, 76–77. *See also* rape;
    women
Gilbert, Daniel, 67
Gladwell, Malcolm, 167
Good Samaritan parable, 195–96
government interventions, 2, 40–41,
    136, 151–53, 197–98
groups and group processes: dissent in,
    116–18, 176, 202–3; diversity, 168,
    202–3; empathy, 176–77; groupthink,
    169; herd instinct, 176, 177; homoge-
    neity, 176–77; peer pressure, 104–5,
    168, 176; wisdom of crowds, 168
guilt: based on conduct, 37–38, 211n31;
    cultural norms influencing

presumptions of, 82–83; evidence
    of brain damage, 57–58; physical
    appearance in presumptions of, 63,
    214n27

habitability, 170
habits, 59–62, 94, 132, 192–94
Hannibal Lecter (*The Silence of the
    Lambs*), 53–54
Hanson, Jon, 180–81
happiness, memories of, 66–67
"Hatchet in the head case." See *Lamson
    v. American Axe and Tool Co.*
"Have It Your Way" (Burger King
    slogan), 26, 28
head coverings for women, 72, 75
health care reform, 31–32, 153–54,
    224n5, 224–25n7
heat of passion, 52, 213n9
helmet-wearing, 146, 147–48, 149,
    150–51
herd instinct, 176, 177
heroin addiction, 131, 222n13
hidden evidence, 177, 178
hijabs, 72–73
hippocampus, 49, 51
Hitchens, Christopher, 93
Holmes, Oliver Wendell, Jr., Justice,
    10–11, 39, 201
homelessness, 160–62
homosexuality, 2, 33, 36
How We Decide (Lehrer), 167
human trafficking, 137–38, 201–2
Hurricane Katrina, 14–16, 169, 181
Hussein, Lubna, 71–72, 85

incentives for commitment, 204–5
insula (pain, disgust), 61
intellectual empathy, 177, 180, 182–83

children's, 107–8; consequences of irresponsibility, 146–47; and the constraints of human character, 185–88; for criminal activity, 37, 211n31; defining, 146, 147–48; deliberate intentional acts, 51–53, 158, 159, 213n9; for eating habits, 17–18, 33, 158, 198, 210n11; for education, 39, 143–45; for habits, 192–93; for health care, 31, 152–54; for homelessness, 160–61; hurricane victims, 14–16; motorcycle helmets, 146, 147–48, 149, 150, 151; of Mount Hood climbers, 16–17, 183; President Obama's address on, 143–45, 147; for shortcuts to decision making, 132–33, 134, 192–93; suicide, 157 58. *See also* brain damage; brain processes

personal-responsibility-as-choice: consequences, 146–52; imposed cost on society, 151; legal consequences of, 151–53, 155–56, 157–58; medical attention as a result of not being responsible, 151; as pure choice, 146–49; suicide, 157–58

Personal Responsibility in Food Consumption Act (Cheeseburger Bill), 33, 159

Phillips, Will, 91–92

physical appearance: biases in decision making, 63, 214–15n27; bikini effect, 59–60, 62, 128, 132; judging people by, 17–18, 191, 210n11; presumptions of guilt, 63, 214n27

pleasure centers of the brain, 59

Pledge of Allegiance, 39, 40, 91–92, 203–4

police: consensual searches, 38–39, 116, 170, 177–79; hidden evidence,

177, 178; obedience to, 109–11, 116; search and seizure, 38–39, 116, 179

political advertisements, 64–65, 215n31

Posner, Richard, 130

poverty, 15, 127, 160–62

pre-commitments, 204–5

preferences: created by the market, 134, 176; cultural context of, 78–79; in decision making, 154–55, 225n9; prediction of, 66–69; prices influencing, 63–64, 65, 121–22; used by rational actors, 129–30

prefrontal cortex, 49–51, 53, 54, 56

priming, 63–64

property law, 170

public policy: capacity to make better choices, 200–201; commitments as public policy tool, 204–6; encouraging dissent and diversity, 202–3; good decisions encouraged by, 197–98; personal-responsibility-as-choice, 146–49

public school attendance as choice, 39

punishment: cultural insistence on individuality as basis for, 182; influence of brain science on, 52–53; influence of physical appearance on, 215n27; intent as basis of, 51–53, 213n9; and remedies, 171; scientific research on, 98–102

racial stereotypes, 87, 111

rape: in the case of Robert Berkowitz, 80–82; coercion, 43, 172; defining, 80–81, 82; domestic, 42, 77; force as defining, 82; the meaning of "no," 82–83, 172, 216–17n15; physical force used in, 42, 43, 82–83; as sex without consent, 20–21, 41–44, 77,

voluntary searches, 38–39, 116, 179
voting to restrict behaviors/choice,
    154–56

wages, 121, 126–28, 220–21n3,
    221–22n8
wall of separation, 88, 217n23
Walmart, 135
Warner, Judith, 97
Wendy's commercial, 28–29
West Virginia State Bd. of Education v.
    Barnette, 39
"wheel of fortune" experiment (Kahne-
    man and Tversky), 63–64
Whitman, Charles, 56–58

willpower, 50, 189, 212n7, 228n5
wisdom of crowds, 168
women: brain chemistry's impact on,
    61; case of Lubna Hussein, 71–72,
    85; as clergy wives, 76–77; cultural
    norms on dress, 71–75, 77; domestic
    roles of, 76–77; employment options
    for, 78, 97; gender roles, 94–96; on
    the meaning of "no," 82–83, 172,
    216–17n15; mothers' autonomy, 97;
    sexual freedom, 96
work, 1–2, 32, 78, 97, 126–27
Workforce Fairness Institute, 32
Workforce Freedom Initiative, 32, 211n7
workplace safety, 10–12, 39, 125, 201